BASEBALL RESEARCH JOURNAL

T0385434

Volume 53, Number 1
Spring 2024

Published by the Society for American Baseball Research

BASEBALL RESEARCH JOURNAL, Volume 53, Number 1

Editor: Cecilia M. Tan
Interior design and production: Lisa Hochstein
Assistant editors: King Kaufman and Davy Andrews
Proofreaders: King Kaufman and Keith R.A. DeCandido
Fact checker: Clifford Blau

Front cover art by Gary Cieradkowski / Studio Gary C

Published by:
Society for American Baseball Research, Inc.
Cronkite School at ASU
555 N. Central Ave. #406C
Phoenix, AZ 85004

Phone: (602) 496–1460
Web: www.sabr.org
Twitter: @sabr
Facebook: Society for American Baseball Research

Copyright © 2024 by The Society for American Baseball Research, Inc.
Printed in the United States of America
Distributed by the University of Nebraska Press

Paper: ISBN 978-1-960819-07-9
E-book: ISBN 978-1-960819-06-2

All rights reserved.
Reproduction in whole or part without permission is prohibited.

Contents

From the Editor   Cecilia M. Tan   4

LEGACIES EXAMINED

Rickwood Field Adds to its Legacy as the Major Leagues
     Return to Alabama   John Shorey and Kevin Warneke   5

Jimmie Foxx
     Baseball's "Forgotten" Super Slugger   Thomas Ferraro   10

Mary Dobkin
     Baltimore's Grand Dame of Baseball   David Krell   18

Major and Minor League Occupancy at Cleveland's League Park, 1914–15   Alan Cohen   23

WHAT MIGHT HAVE BEEN

The Ill-Fated Dodgers and Indians World Baseball Tour of 1952   Matthew Jacob   30

"Death to Flying Things"
     The Life and Times of a Spurious Nickname   Richard Hershberger   34

Shining Light on the Smiling Stan Hack Mirror
     A Bill Veeck Gamesmanship Ploy—Was It Real or Mythical?   Herm Krabbenhoft   38

NINETEENTH CENTURY

Teenage Umpires of the Nineteenth Century   Larry DeFillipo   44

The International Association of 1877–80
     The Third Professional Baseball Organization   Woody Eckard   54

The Union Association War of 1884   Richard Hershberger   64

ANALYZING DATA

An Infield Hit Model from the MLB 2023 Season
     "Hit 'Em Where They Ain't"   Donald Slavik   75

Plummeting Batting Averages Are Due to Far More than Infield Shifting
     Part One: Fielding and Batting Strategy   Charlie Pavitt   86

Going Beyond the Baseball Adage "One Game at a Time"
     A Geek's Peek at Streaks   Ed Denta   94

Jews and Baseball
     Part One: History and Demographics   Peter Dreier   115

CHADWICK AWARDS

Sarah Langs   Karl Ravech   124

Larry Gerlach   Steve Gietschier   125

Leslie Heaphy   Roberta Newman   126

Contributors   128

From the Editor

We live in the best of times and the worst of times for information. The best of times: I now have vast libraries and thousands of newspapers accessible from home. From my sickbed last year, I read not only COVID-19 treatments, I downloaded archived newspaper accounts of the 2004 Red Sox trophy tour for an essay I wrote in *Sox Bid Curse Farewell*.

But, the worst of times: misinformation is proliferating endlessly. Some is political disinformation: leaders and candidates spout falsehoods with impunity these days. But some is from another source: generative AI. ChatGPT launched the AI hype in 2022, but news outlets have already been using so-called "AI" to generate articles for more than 10 years—and sports coverage in particular. Does your local newspaper website have coverage for every high school and college football game in your area? How can they, with fewer writers than ever before? They've been using a tool like Wordsmith (from a company called Automated Insights—AI, get it?) Wordsmith produced 300 million pieces of content in 2013, and by 2014—ten years ago!—that amount had already jumped to a billion.[1] The Associated Press bought into Automated Insights in 2014.[2] And AI-generated "news" content keeps growing exponentially.[3]

If you're not horrified by this, you should be. What use is access to the world's newspapers from my home if all I find is robot-written articles all sourced from the same data feed? A researcher like Herm Krabbenhoft can look at 12 different newspaper accounts from a baseball game in Detroit and determine that Hank Greenberg had an RBI that day—even though the official American League records erred and did not record it. But if a stringer noting game stats today makes a typo, it'll be reproduced in every story as if it's the truth—it will *become* the truth. These are not the droids you're looking for.

It gets worse. One problem with Large Language Models is that once they ingest too much *content generated by AI*, their output degrades and their reliability plummets.[4] Since the bots themselves can no longer read the Internet, companies like OpenAI have been—unscrupulously and perhaps illegally—training their models on the text of hundreds of thousands of published books.[5] (And fanfiction![6])

Which brings us to the downfall of *Sports Illustrated*. The former pinnacle of both quality in sports journalism and the pay scale, *Sports Illustrated* is now functionally dead, with a mass layoff of the writers and staff in January 2024.[7] The venerable brand name was caught filling their site with AI-written junk—junk so bad that readers caught on immediately that no sane human would have written it.[8] Caught with their hand in the cookie jar, they decided to smash the jar entirely. Not only does this not make sense as journalism, it doesn't even make sense as capitalism. AGM/Arena Group just bought *Sports Illustrated* in 2019 for $110 million. Now, they've made it worthless.

Turning the Internet into a money machine has meant that any inherent human value in words has been entirely discarded in favor of their dollar value. But information, facts, and knowledge have a value to humans other than a dollar amount! Every word you see written here in the *BRJ* and on the SABR website, has been lovingly, painstakingly, researched, written, edited, fact-checked, and proofed by an actual human being who felt that the work was worth doing.

If you see the value in that, there are multiple ways to aid in the effort. One is to donate, of course—SABR is a non-profit! The other, though, is to join the effort, and donate your energy or time. Become a researcher, write for the BioProject or the Games Project, or elbow your way up to the table where the editors, proofreaders, and fact-checkers are pushing our pencils. The words we publish add value to our lives and I feel better and better about that with each passing day.

— Cecilia M. Tan
April 2024

1. Lance Ulanoff, "Need to Write 5 Million Stories a Week? Robot Reporters to the Rescue," Mashable, July 1, 2014, https://mashable.com/archive/robot-reporters-add-data-to-the-five-ws.
2. Jason Abbruzzese, "The Associated Press Turns to Computer Automation," Mashable, June 30, 2014, https://mashable.com/archive/the-associated-press-turns-to-computer-automation-for-corporate-earnings-stories.
3. Andreas Graefe, "Guide to Automated Journalism," *Columbia Journalism Review*, January 7, 2016, https://www.cjr.org/tow_center_reports/guide_to_automated_journalism.php.
4. Ben Lutkevich, "Model Collapse Explained: How Synthetic Training Data Breaks AI," TechTarget, July 7, 2023, https://www.techtarget.com/whatis/feature/Model-collapse-explained-How-synthetic-training-data-breaks-AI.
5. Blake Brittain, "Pulitzer-winning authors join OpenAI, Microsoft copyright lawsuit," Reuters, December 20, 2023, https://www.reuters.com/legal/pulitzer-winning-authors-join-openai-microsoft-copyright-lawsuit-2023-12-20/.
6. Rose Eveleth, "The Fanfic Sex Trope That Caught a Plundering AI Redhanded," *Wired*, May 15, 2023, https://www.wired.com/story/fanfiction-omegaverse-sex-trope-artificial-intelligence-knotting/.
7. Nicole Kraft, "Mass Layoff Appears to be the End of Sports Illustrated," *Forbes*, January 21, 2024, https://www.forbes.com/sites/nicolekraft/2024/01/21/mass-layoff-appears-to-be-the-end-of-sports-illustrated/?sh=50c2176075e5.
8. Maggie Harrison Dupre, "Sports Illustrated Published Articles by Fake, AI-Generated Writers," *Futurism*, November 27, 2023, https://futurism.com/sports-illustrated-ai-generated-writers.

Rickwood Field Adds to Its Legacy as the Major Leagues Return to Alabama

John Shorey and Kevin Warneke

The oldest professional baseball park in the United States—Rickwood Field in Birmingham, Alabama—adds another chapter to its rich history this summer when it hosts the San Francisco Giants and St. Louis Cardinals in a regular-season game.[1] The specialty game will coincide with Juneteenth celebrations and honor Hall of Famer Willie Mays, who played for the Birmingham Black Barons at Rickwood Field in 1948.[2]

The Giants-Cardinals contest will be the first American or National League game held at Rickwood Field as well as the first in Alabama.[3]

MLB RECOGNIZES THE NEGRO LEAGUES

In December 2020, Commissioner Rob Manfred announced that Major League Baseball was correcting "a longtime oversight" in the game's history by officially recognizing that the Negro Leagues were deserving of the designation "major"—joining the Federal League, American Association, and several other defunct leagues that share that status.[4] The announcement said that MLB was proud to showcase the contributions of those who played in seven distinct leagues from 1920 through 1948. "With this action, MLB seeks to ensure that future generations will remember the approximately 3,400 players of the Negro Leagues during this time period as Major League–caliber

ballplayers. Accordingly, the statistics and records of these players will become a part of Major League Baseball's history."[5]

"I've always recognized Negro League players as major-league quality," Larry Lester, a co-founder of the Negro Leagues Baseball Museum in Kansas City, said. "I didn't need an official governing body to tell me that. I'm happy they did. They finally recognized that Black men played the game also."[6]

IMPACT ON OTHER STATES

Alabama is one of four states that had their connection to the major leagues altered with MLB's announcement. In the past decade, MLB has scheduled regular-season games in North Carolina, Nebraska, and Iowa—all of which had hosted regular-season Negro League games:

NORTH CAROLINA – Called the "Fort Bragg Game," the July 3, 2016, contest between the Atlanta Braves and the Miami Marlins was the first regular-season event of any professional sport played on an active military base.[7] The game was also labeled a major-league first for the state of North Carolina—and held that distinction until MLB's announcement recognizing the Negro Leagues.[8] Now, a May 25, 1948, game between the Homestead Grays and the Philadelphia Stars at Talbert Park in Rocky Mount holds the distinction of being the

The exterior of Rickwood Field, as seen in 2010, the park's 100th season.

THE GEORGE F. LANDEGGER COLLECTION OF ALABAMA PHOTOGRAPHS IN CAROL M. HIGHSMITH'S AMERICA, LIBRARY OF CONGRESS, PRINTS AND PHOTOGRAPHS DIVISION

first standings-relevant major-league game played in the state. Lefty Bell went nine innings for the Grays in Homestead's 9–3 victory over the Stars, both members of the Negro National League. Wilmer Fields collected four runs batted in for the winners.[9]

NEBRASKA – The Kansas City Royals' 7–3 victory over the Detroit Tigers in June 2019 before a sellout crowd of 25,454 at Omaha's TD Ameritrade Park was called Nebraska's first major-league game. Eighteen months later, after MLB's announcement, that distinction changed to a Kansas City Monarchs-Chicago American Giants game at Landis Field in Lincoln on July 27, 1939. Nearly 1,000 fans saw the Monarchs win, 3–2, by scoring two runs on a bad-hop, bases-loaded single in the bottom of the ninth.[10]

IOWA – Manfred's announcement that MLB was recognizing the Negro Leagues as major leagues came between the announcement of a regular-season game on the site where *Field of Dreams* had been filmed and that game's first pitch.[11] The August 12, 2021, matchup pitted the New York Yankees against the Chicago White Sox, two historic franchises, with the White Sox featured in the film. John Thorn, MLB's official historian, pointed out that Iowa had a rich major-league history long before the Yankees and White Sox came to town.[12] Although no teams recognized as major league by MLB had franchises in Iowa, barnstorming was a major component of Negro League operations. At least 30 games between Negro League teams that counted in the standings were played in the Iowa communities of Charles City, Council Bluffs, Davenport, Des Moines, and Sioux City from 1937 to 1948. The first was apparently in Des Moines on May 27, 1937—following three previous attempts that were rained out—between the Cincinnati Tigers and the Birmingham Black Barons. Birmingham used a five-run outburst in the top of the fifth to go ahead in its 8–4 win.[13]

FIRST MAJOR LEAGUE GAME AT RICKWOOD FIELD
The specialty game this summer will not only celebrate the Negro Leagues and Willie Mays, it will commemorate the 100th anniversary of the debut of major-league baseball at Rickwood Field. Black Barons pitcher Bill Powell said playing at Rickwood was special: "I don't know what it is, but when I was playing at Rickwood Field, I was always itching to get to the ballpark. We played all over the United States, and when we got here, you just loved coming here to play in this park. There was just something about the baseball in that park."[14]

The change in status for the Negro Leagues means that a game played 100 years ago at Rickwood between the Black Barons and the Cuban Stars has moved to the front of the line as the first major-league game played at the historic ballpark—and in the state of Alabama.

While North Carolina, Nebraska, and Iowa never had Negro League franchises that called their states home, Alabama had two Negro League franchises that are now recognized as major league: the Birmingham Black Barons and the Montgomery Grey Sox.[15] The Black Barons benefitted by playing their home games at Rickwood, the crown jewel of southern baseball. Built in 1910 for the Barons, a Class A Southern Association team comprising white players, by their owner, A.H. "Rick" Woodward, the venue also hosted Negro League contests.[16] The ballpark name, combining the nickname and part of the last name of the owner, was suggested by a fan in a newspaper contest.[17]

With the growing popularity of Black baseball in Birmingham, Woodward saw an economic opportunity and rented out his ballpark to Black teams for a percentage of the gross ticket sales.[18] A 1919 Labor Day doubleheader at Rickwood between Black teams from Birmingham and Montgomery drew 15,000 spectators. The *Birmingham Age-Herald* reported that the doubleheader saw "the largest crowd of Negroes that ever attended a ball game in the United States and next to the largest, irrespective of color, that ever jammed into Rickwood."[19]

The same year that Rube Foster organized the Negro National League in 1920 (the earliest Negro League to be recognized as major league), the Birmingham Black Barons were formed. The team's original nickname, Stars, was quickly changed to Black Barons, a reference to the white team in Birmingham. The Black Barons were a founding member of the Negro Southern League. In 1923, Birmingham hotel owner Joe Rush purchased the team and joined the Negro National League as an associate member, meaning the Black Barons were affiliated with the league but their games didn't count in the standings.[20] The transition to the new league came in July after the Black Barons dominated the Negro Southern League with a 24–8 record in the first half of the 1923 season.[21]

The move by the Black Barons to the Negro National League was touted by the *Birmingham News* as the first baseball team from Birmingham to have membership in a major-league association.[22] A large interracial crowd attended the first home game in the new league on July 19, 1923, against the Milwaukee Bears.[23] The Bears jumped out to an early 2–0 lead and had the locals wondering whether the Black Barons were out of their class. The Black Barons battled back and pulled ahead, 4–3, with two tallies in the bottom of the eighth inning. Milwaukee pushed across a run in the top of the ninth to knot the score at 4–4. After a scoreless 10th inning, the contest was halted due to darkness.[24]

Birmingham ended the 1923 season as an associate member of the Negro National League with a record of 15–23.[25] When the Chicago American Giants, the premier team of the Negro National League, traveled to Birmingham later in the season to take on the Black Barons, the *Chicago Defender* commented: "For the first time in the history of the Negro National League the American Giants of Chicago will leave home during the middle of the season and make a trip South, playing in Birmingham on Aug. 20, 21 and 22. These three days will be gala days in the Southern metropolis and many people are expected to come out and witness the new Southern entry into the Negro National League play Rube Foster's club, thrice winners of the league pennant."[26]

The first official major-league baseball game in the state of Alabama took place the following year on April 28, 1924, at Rickwood Field after the Birmingham Black Barons became full members of the Negro National League. A crowd of 10,600, the second largest to ever see a Negro League game at Rickwood Field at that time, poured into the ballpark to witness the successful debut of the Black Barons. The Cuban Stars pushed across a pair of runs in the top of the third on three singles and a throwing error to take a short-lived lead. The Black Barons answered back immediately in the bottom of the frame with a five-run outburst on five singles and a dropped fly ball. Both teams scored an additional run to make the final 6–3, Black Barons.[27]

NOTABLE BIRMINGHAM BLACK BARONS PLAYERS

The Birmingham Black Barons fielded a team on and off in various Negro Leagues for 33 seasons. They won five Negro American League titles in the 1940s and 1950s.[28] During their seasons that are now recognized as major league, the Black Barons' rosters included four Hall of Famers.

Midway through the 1927 season, the Black Barons purchased a young, hard-throwing pitcher from the Chattanooga Black Lookouts named Leroy "Satchel" Paige.[29] Paige won his first major-league game while posting a 7–2 record for the Black Barons in his rookie season.[30] His first big game with his new team in late June was notable for a hit-and-run, but not the sort common to baseball lingo. When a Paige heater smacked St. Louis Stars catcher Mitchell Murray on the hand, Murray charged the mound waving his bat. Paige outran Murray to the dugout, but not the bat. The bat struck Paige above the hip. A near riot ensued, with players massing from both benches along with knife- and rock-wielding fans. After police restored order, the umpire tried to resume play after ejecting Paige and Murray. The Black Barons refused to take the field without their pitcher, thus forfeiting the game.[31]

In 1929, his third season with the Black Barons, Paige struck out a record 17 Detroit Stars batters in a 5–1 win on July 29.[32] He ended his tenure with the Black Barons when he was sold to the Nashville Elite Giants in 1931.[33]

Another Hall of Famer who made his major-league debut with the Black Barons was George "Mule" Suttles. Early in his career, the power-hitting first baseman's home run total was hampered by the dimensions of his home park at Rickwood: 411 feet to the left-field fence and 485 feet to the center-field wall.[34] (The outfield dimensions at Rickwood Field have periodically changed over the years.) The long distances to left and center fields were inspired by Shibe Park, home of Connie Mack's Philadelphia A's. After meeting Woodward shortly after the opening of Shibe Park in 1909, Mack agreed to come to Birmingham to help design the new ballpark.[35]

After two major league seasons with the Black Barons, Suttles blossomed into a star with the St. Louis Stars during the 1926 season. In just 89 games that season, Suttles produced 32 home runs, 28 doubles, 19 triples, 15 stolen bases, and 130 RBIs. He ended the season with a .425 batting average.[36]

Rube Foster's brother Bill, who was inducted into the National Baseball Hall of Fame in 1996, appeared in just one game for the Black Barons in 1925, pitching a one-hit complete game shutout before returning to his original team, the Chicago American Giants.[37] Foster was a hard-throwing lefty with pinpoint control and a great changeup. On the last day of the 1926 season, he won both ends of a crucial doubleheader to clinch the pennant for the American Giants.[38]

In the final year that the Black Barons are recognized as major-league caliber, 1948, a 17-year-old center fielder collected two hits in the second game of a doubleheader.[39] Those were the first two of 3,293 hits for Willie Mays during his Hall of Fame career.[40] His two hits came off of Cleveland Buckeyes' hurler Chet Brewer, who had broken into the league with the Kansas City Monarchs in 1925, six years before Mays was born.[41]

The Black Barons featured other notable players besides their four Hall of Famers. Ted "Double Duty"

THE GEORGE F. LANDEGGER COLLECTION OF ALABAMA PHOTOGRAPHS IN CAROL M. HIGHSMITH'S AMERICA, LIBRARY OF CONGRESS, PRINTS AND PHOTOGRAPHS DIVISION

Players in the annual Rickwood Classic in front of the iconic Rickwood Field scoreboard, photographed in 2010.

Radcliffe played for the Black Barons in the mid-1940s as a catcher and a pitcher, hence the moniker "Double Duty." During a 1932 Negro World Series doubleheader early in Radcliffe's career, he caught Paige in the first game and then pitched a shutout in the second game.[42]

Reece "Goose" Tatum played two seasons for the Black Barons in the early 1940s, earning his first major-league hit in the summer of 1941. While Tatum's major-league baseball career was short-lived, he went on to become the main attraction of the Harlem Globetrotters basketball team.[43] Tatum's connection between baseball and basketball was facilitated by a new part owner of the Birmingham Black Barons, Abe Saperstein, who founded the Globetrotters.[44]

RICKWOOD FIELD

Rick Woodward was determined to enhance his jewel of Southern baseball, which had been built in 1910 at a cost of $75,000.[45] Starting in 1924, he extended the grandstand roofs in phases down the right- and left-field bleachers to protect the fans from the brutal Alabama summer sun. A 40-foot-high scoreboard was erected in left-center, and the iconic Spanish mission–style façade with twin parapets was added to Rickwood's front gate in 1928.[46] The unique steel-frame light towers, which reach out past the grandstand roof, were added in 1936.[47]

Rickwood Field also became the home ballpark of an affiliated minor-league team in the 1930s as the Birmingham Barons became the farm team of various major-league teams—the Cubs, Reds, Pirates, A's, Red Sox, Yankees, Tigers, and, since 1986, the White Sox.[48]

The Black Barons joined the Negro American League in 1937. They enjoyed their greatest success in the 1940s, winning three Negro American League championships.[49]

The integration of major league baseball by Jackie Robinson in 1947 signaled the gradual decline of the Negro Leagues. Toward the end of their existence, the Black Barons became more of a traveling team and finally folded after the 1962 season.[50]

Rickwood Field continued to be the home park for a Double A affiliate of major-league teams through the 1987 season. The White Sox moved the Birmingham Barons to a new ballpark in Hoover, Alabama, a suburb of Birmingham, in 1988.[51]

In order to preserve the legendary ballpark, a group of Birmingham fans, businesses, and civic leaders formed the "Friends of Rickwood" in 1992. Over the next decade more than $2 million was spent maintaining and restoring Rickwood Field.[52] The following year, the National Parks Service's Historic American Building Survey officially recognized Rickwood Field as the oldest professional baseball park in the United States.[53]

Due to the preservation efforts over the past several decades, Rickwood Field has continued to thrive. The Rickwood Classic is an annual event in which the Birmingham Barons play one regular-season game at the old ballpark while wearing throwback Negro League uniforms. A full slate of high school games and wood-bat tournaments are held there each year.[54] It is also the home field for Miles College, a historically black college in suburban Fairfield, and has served as a location for baseball films such as *Cobb* (1994), *Soul of the Game* (1996), and *42* (2013).[55] ■

Notes

1. "Rickwood Field to host MLB, MiLB games in 2024," MiLB.com, June 20, 2023, https://www.milb.com/news/rickwood-field-to-host-mlb-milb-games, accessed November 19, 2023.
2. "Rickwood Field to host MLB."

3. Bob Nightengale, "MLB to play 2024 regular season game at Birmingham's historic Rickwood Field," *USA Today*, June 20, 2023, https://www.usatoday.com/story/sports/mlb/2023/06/20/birminghams-historic-rickwood-field-to-host-mlb-game-in-june-2024/70336931007/, accessed November 19, 2023; Patrick Andres, "Giants, Cardinals to Play 2024 Game at Birmingham's Historic Rickwood Field," *Sports Illustrated*, June 20, 2023, https://www.si.com/mlb/2023/06/20/giants-cardinals-to-play-in-birmingham-2024-rickwood-field-willie-mays-juneteenth, accessed November 19, 2023.

4. A note on the confusing capitalization: Major League Baseball, when capitalized, identifies the current corporate entity that is made up of the 30 teams in the American and National Leagues. The major leagues, lowercase, is a descriptor of baseball's top level of play, which Major League Baseball announced in 2020 included the Negro Leagues. Note also that MLB, in its press releases, capitalizes major league in all uses.

5. "MLB officially designates the Negro Leagues as 'Major League,'" MLB.com, December 16, 2020, https://www.mlb.com/press-release/press-release-mlb-officially-designates-the-negro-leagues-as-major-league.

6. Kevin Warneke and John Shorey, "This small Nebraska town hosted Negro League clubs and possibly a Major League game," *Flatwater Free Press*, March 31, 2023, https://flatwaterfreepress.org/this-small-nebraska-town-hosted-negro-league-clubs-and-possibly-an-official-major-league-baseball-game/.

7. John Schlegel, "Stars and Spikes: July 3 game at Fort Bragg!" March 8, 2016, MLB.com, https://www.mlb.com/news/braves-marlins-play-fort-bragg-game-on-july-3-c166636990, accessed October 30, 2023.

8. Arthur Weinstein, "Braves, Marlins make history in game at Fort Bragg military base," *Sporting News*, July 3, 2016, https://www.sportingnews.com/us/mlb/news/braves-marlins-fort-bragg-field-mlb/d9yjuy7bczvq1wkgxli0a615g, accessed November 19, 2023.

9. "Homestead Grays (HOM) 9 Philadelphia Stars (PH5) 3," Retrosheet, https://www.retrosheet.org/NegroLeagues/boxesetc/1948/B05250HOM1948.htm, accessed February 6, 2024.

10. Warneke and Shorey, *Flatwater Free Press*.

11. John Shorey and Kevin Warneke, "Major League Baseball in Iowa," *The National Pastime* 51 (2023), 63.

12. John Thorn tweet, August 21, 2021, https://twitter.com/thorn_john/status/1425441694481330179.

13. Shorey and Warneke, 64.

14. Allen Barra, *Rickwood Field: A Century in America's Oldest Ballpark* (New York: Norton, 2010), ix.

15. The Montgomery Grey Sox achieved major-league status for one season when MLB designated the Negro Southern League as major-league caliber for the 1932 season.

16. Barra, 21–22.

17. Barra, 24.

18. Barra, 58.

19. Barra, 58.

20. Larry Powell, *Black Barons of Birmingham* (Jefferson, NC: McFarland, 2009), 10.

21. "Negro Southern League (1920–1951)," Center for Negro League Baseball Research, https://www.cnlbr.org/Portals/0/Standings/Negro%20Southern%20League%20(1920–1951)-2020.pdf, accessed November 20, 2023.

22. "Black Barons Play First Game As Big Leaguers Thursday," *Birmingham News*, July 17, 1923, 26.

23. The *Birmingham News* story incorrectly identified the Milwaukee team as the Giants. The correct moniker for Milwaukee in 1923 was the Bears.

24. "Black Barons Tie First Big League Game," *Birmingham News*, July 20, 1923, 18.

25. "Negro National League Standings (1920-1948)," Center for Negro League Baseball Research, https://www.cnlbr.org/Portals/0/Standings/Negro%20National%20League%20(1920-1948)%202016-08.pdf, accessed November 20, 2023.

26. "Black Barons Face Hard Week's Work," *Birmingham News*, July 29, 1923, 34.

27. "Record Crowd Sees Rushmen Annex Opener," *Birmingham News*, April 29, 1924, 16.

28. "Birmingham Black Barons," the Negro Leagues, https://www.mlb.com/history/negro-leagues/teams/birmingham-black-barons, accessed November 20, 2023.

29. Powell, *Black Barons of Birmingham*, 19.

30. "Satchel Paige," Baseball Reference, https://www.baseball-reference.com/players/p/paigesa01.shtml, accessed November 20, 2023.

31. Larry Tye, *Satchel: The Life and Times of an American Legend* (New York: Random House, 2009), 43.

32. Powell, 20.

33. Robert Peterson, *Only the Ball Was White* (Oxford, UK: Oxford University Press, 1992), 133.

34. Powell, 29.

35. Barra, *Rickwood Field*, 2–4.

36. "Mule Suttles," Baseball Reference, https://www.baseball-reference.com/players/s/suttlmu99.shtml, accessed November 20, 2023.

37. "Bill Foster," Baseball Reference, https://www.baseball-reference.com/players/f/fostebi99.shtml, accessed November 20, 2023.

38. National Baseball Hall of Fame and Museum, *National Baseball Hall of Fame and Museum 2022 Yearbook* (Lynn, MA: H.O. Zimman, 2022), 75.

39. James S. Hirsch, *Willie Mays: The Life, The Legend* (New York: Simon & Schuster, 2010), 43.

40. "Willie Mays," Baseball Reference, https://www.baseball-reference.com/players/m/mayswi01.shtml, accessed November 20, 2023.

41. Hirsch, 42–43.

42. Powell, 48.

43. Powell, 50.

44. Mark Ribowsky, *A Complete History of the Negro Leagues, 1884 to 1955* (New York: Carol Publishing Group, 1995), 248.

45. Hirsch, 41.

46. Barra, 75–79.

47. Barra, 117.

48. "Birmingham Barons," Baseball Reference, https://www.baseball-reference.com/bullpen/Birmingham_Barons, accessed December 18, 2023.

49. "Negro American League Standings (1937–1962)," Center for Negro League Baseball Research, https://www.cnlbr.org/Portals/0/Standings/Negro%20American%20League%20(1937-1962)%202016-08.pdf, accessed December 18, 2023.

50. "Negro American League Standings (1937–1962)."

51. Barra, 201.

52. Barra, 205.

53. Barra, 211.

54. Bruce Markusen, "Rickwood Field features baseball's past and present," National Baseball Hall of Fame, https://baseballhall.org/discover/rickwood-field-features-baseballs-past-and-present, accessed December 18, 2023.

55. "Field of Dreams Game 2024," FieldOfDreamsGameTickets, https://www.fieldofdreamsgametickets.com, accessed December 18, 2023.

Jimmie Foxx

Baseball's "Forgotten" Super Slugger

Thomas Ferraro

Long before Aaron Judge broke the single-season American League home-run records formerly held by fellow New York Yankees Babe Ruth and Roger Maris, a young man from a small farm on the Maryland Eastern Shore was on pace to hit more dingers than any of them.[1] His name was Jimmie Foxx, nicknamed "the Beast" for superhuman strength and monstrous homers, many of them among the longest in the history of the game, reportedly soaring upwards of 450 and even 500 feet, high over outfield walls, grandstands, and out of sight.[2]

On April 12, 1932, Opening Day, Foxx, first baseman for the Philadelphia Athletics, blasted a solo shot to begin a six-month assault on what eventually became one of the most coveted records in sports: Ruth's 60 homers hit five years earlier. By late July, Foxx was on track to club 64, more than enough to top Ruth's mark, and a record that would have survived Maris's 61 in 1961 and Judge's 62 in 2022.

If Foxx had kept hammering round-trippers at that clip, he would have been crowned the new home-run king and likely still reign as one of America's most famous athletes. Instead, he slowed down in August, supposedly lost two homers to rainouts at some point in the season, and finished strong in September, with five homers in the last five games to end up with 58 that counted.[3] Following a bittersweet 20-year career that did put him in the Baseball Hall of Fame, this gentle Beast quietly faded away as arguably the game's least-remembered phenom.

"If you asked the average American baseball fan if they ever heard of him, you'd get a lot more noes than yeses," said John Bennett, a SABR member who has researched and written extensively about Foxx.[4]

"He was one of the all-time greats," said John Odell, curator of history and research at the National Baseball Hall of Fame and Museum. "You would think more people would know him. People just don't."[5]

"Foxx is the forgotten man among baseball's all-time super sluggers. 'Double X' was poison to pitchers, the first man to challenge Ruth as the home run king," John Thorn, Major League Baseball's official historian

since 2011, wrote in his 1998 book *Treasures of the Baseball Hall of Fame*.[6]

Though forgotten, Foxx remains a historical trailblazer—the first three-time winner of the Most Valuable Player award, the first to hit 30 or more homers in 12 straight seasons, and the first after Ruth to hit 500 career homers. Along the way, Foxx banged out a lifetime batting average of .325, with the seventh-highest slugging average, .609, and the 10th-most runs batted in, 1,922.

THE BABE'S SHADOW

When it came to winning public admiration, however, particularly in the long term, Foxx repeatedly struck out—a victim of bad timing, a less-than-ideal location, and his low-key personality. Foxx also had the misfortune of playing in the smothering shadow of the highly charismatic Ruth, "the Great Bambino." Ruth performed on center stage in New York City, the media capital of the world, which helped make him an international icon and still the biggest name in the game. With a talented supporting cast, Ruth showcased himself in seven World Series with the Yankees, drawing even more national and global acclaim.[7]

Foxx starred off-Broadway, in Philadelphia and later in Boston with the Red Sox. He played in three World Series, all with the A's.[8] In both cities, Foxx drew cheers. But he didn't get the national recognition bestowed on Ruth and other legendary Yankees, particularly Lou Gehrig. In the inaugural All-Star game in 1933, Gehrig played the entire game at first base while Foxx, who would win the Triple Crown and his second straight MVP award at the end of that season, remained on the bench.[9]

Foxx's best years were during the Great Depression, in the 1930s, when attendance and salaries were down, and fans were more interested in finding a job than attending a game. Foxx retired in 1945, not long before baseball began being televised regularly, which helped make many of Foxx's successors become well-paid household names while he quietly filed for bankruptcy.[10] If he had played two more seasons, he would have qualified for baseball's new player pension program.

"You made only one mistake, Jimmie," Joe DiMaggio told Foxx. "You were born 25 years too soon." Said Foxx, "I guess, I was born to be broke."[11]

Foxx was born in Sudlersville, Maryland, on October 22, 1907. Ruth, 12 years older than Foxx, was born and raised in Baltimore, across Chesapeake Bay from the Eastern Shore, where the Beast grew up and worked on his parents' farm. Swinging from opposite sides of the plate, the Beast and the Sultan of Swat hit many of the game's longest homers, prompting sportswriters to call Foxx "the right-handed Babe Ruth"

He was 16 when he signed his first pro baseball contract, with the Easton (Maryland) Farmers of the Class D Eastern Shore League, where he impressed fellow players with his big bat.[12] After a year in the minors, Foxx took that big bat to the big leagues as a member of Connie Mack's Philadelphia Athletics. On May 1, 1925, he debuted with a pinch-hit single.[13] Foxx was then 17 years, six months, and nine days old, easily placing him among the youngest 1% of the 20,000-plus players in major-league history at the time of their respective debuts.[14]

In 1932, at just 24, Foxx won the first of his two consecutive MVP awards. Yet *The Sporting News*, the weekly "Bible of Baseball," gave him relatively scant notice, particularly compared to Ruth. According to the publication's online reporting system, Foxx had six mentions by name in the magazine during the 1932 season; Ruth got 91. During the 1933 season, Foxx, en route to another MVP, was mentioned by name a few dozen times; Ruth's name appeared more than 250 times.[15]

"When you study the man's factual record and know what he did, it is actually hard for me to wrap my arms around the disproportionately low amount of recognition that he gets," said baseball historian and author Bill Jenkinson. "He, to me, is clearly baseball's most underrated player ever."[16]

While the average baseball fan today may have never heard of Foxx, those who have studied the game place him near the top of just about any list of all-time greats. In 1998, *The Sporting News* ranked Foxx as the 15th greatest player ever, with Gehrig No. 6 and Ruth No. 1.[17] A generation later, in 2022, Foxx's stock had slipped a bit, at least at ESPN. In its Top 100 all-time players, the global sports station put Foxx at No. 40. Fourteen players whose careers had been over by 1998 and who had been behind Foxx in *The Sporting News* list—and whose profiles were boosted by TV—leapfrogged over the Beast on ESPN's ranking. They included Mickey Mantle, Roberto Clemente, Pete Rose, Yogi Berra, and Jackie Robinson. Ruth and Gehrig remained No. 1 and No. 6.[18]

In terms of wins above replacement, or WAR, which measures a player's value in all aspects of the game, Foxx ranks at number 41 in career WAR among the more than 20,000 players in major-league history. He is ahead of a long line of far more famous players who profited from TV exposure, including Ken Griffey Jr. (58), Pete Rose (67), Joe DiMaggio (69), Derek Jeter (95), and Johnny Bench (83).

On January 26, 1951, it was announced that Foxx got the required 75 percent vote of the Baseball Writers Association of America to win admittance into the Hall of Fame. Mel Ott also received the required votes. Foxx had more lifetime homers and RBIs, and a higher lifetime batting average than Ott. Yet Ott, like Ruth a beneficiary of the New York stage, drew 87.2 percent of the vote compared to 79.2 percent for Foxx. Foxx made it into the Hall in his sixth year of eligibility. Ott made it in his fourth.[19]

Days after being elected to the Hall, Foxx downplayed his success. "All the years I played, all the great players I saw, played against, read about and watched—I never expected this honor," Foxx told the Associated Press. "I'll never forget it."[20]

THE "LOST" HOME RUNS

In that AP interview, Foxx said he actually hit 60 homers in 1932, but two got erased in rainouts, preventing him from tying Ruth's record. Widespread reports of those washed-out dingers persist online and in books and other publications. Yet a review of the record in researching this paper on Foxx found no confirmed word on when or where he supposedly clubbed those four-baggers, raising the question of whether they ever happened. "It's become one of those baseball legends," Cassidy Lent, library director at the Hall of Fame, said when asked about the lack of evidence. "I guess it persists the way all legends persist. ...It makes for a good story."[21]

In addition to the rained-out homers, Foxx's "good story" includes reports that he hit upwards of a dozen or so long drives in 1932 that would have been homers but bounced off, rather than cleared, newly raised outfield barriers in St. Louis, Philadelphia, and Cleveland.[22]

"That story of Foxx's 'missing' home runs may never sustain a fact check," MLB historian Thorn wrote in a 2022 email exchange.[23] There may never be a definitive fact-check. Neither the Hall of Fame, MLB, nor Baseball Reference maintains records of players' performance in rained-out games or how high the balls they hit bounced off outfield walls.[24]

Newspapers routinely report rained-out contests. But there's no guarantee that they always did. And even if newspapers reported a rainout, they may not have always provided much, if any, detail. Furthermore, even if a newspaper included details—like any homers hit that day—there is no certainty that the newspaper could now be found on some bookshelf, online, or on microfilm, said David Smith, a baseball historian and researcher. "You can't prove it didn't happen."[25]

In his 1951 AP interview, Foxx said he hit five long balls in 1932 that should have been homers—the two that got erased by rainouts, and three others stopped by an outfield design change, namely the placing of strands of wire atop a right field fence to prevent kids from sneaking in. "I hit three drives in 1932 that struck the wires and bounced back," he is quoted as saying. "When the Babe hit his 60, those drives would have gone over. But they called the ball in play when I hit 'em and I was cheated out of three homers. That would have made 61." The AP story didn't identify which park this took place in, but Foxx was likely referring to Philadelphia's Shibe Park where such wire had been placed.[26]

Researcher Robert Schaefer reviewed Foxx's 1932 play-by-play record in St. Louis's Sportsman Park, where sportswriters said he lost a dozen home runs in 1932 to a new outfield screen. In the spring 2013 issue of the *Baseball Research Journal*, Schaefer wrote that he found just one instance, on June 15, when a ball struck by Foxx hit the screen.[27]

Jenkinson had also examined this decades earlier, and said he had also shown that a batted ball by Foxx hit the screen in St. Louis that day. In addition, Jenkinson found that Foxx belted a ball on July 1 of that year that bounced off the wire contraption atop the fence in Shibe Park for a triple.[28] The next day's *Philadelphia Inquirer* wrote: "The triple just missed clearing the wall. It hit the very top, but bounded the wrong way after hanging momentarily."[29]

Jenkinson also reviewed Foxx's 1932 game-by-game record as part of his decades-long examination of the careers of Foxx and other players. He checked records primarily by visiting libraries, including the Library of Congress in Washington, where he searched through microfilm of old newspapers, reading game stories and box scores. Jenkinson said he found 10 of Foxx's games rained out in 1932, most before the first pitch: "My research found that he didn't hit a homer in any of them."

Jenkinson is confident that the Beast, who had a reputation for being modest, didn't deliberately fabricate the rained-out homers: "What I think is that after he retired, somebody told him he had two homers rained out in 1932, and by the 1950s, he believed it."[34]

Schaefer offered another possibility: "Some old players, in talking about the old days, simply misremember some things."[30]

At the Hall of Fame, curator Odell cited "an old story that Foxx kept a newspaper clipping in his wallet that he would pull out to show he had two homers rained out in 1932." He continued, "Baseball is full of these second-hand and third-hand stories that somebody told somebody something."[31] One of these is in Ted Taylor's 2010 book *The Ultimate Philadelphia Athletic Reference Book, 1901–1954*: "According to [Foxx's] daughter, Nanci Foxx Canaday, he carried a newspaper clipping with him in his wallet until the day he died that told of additional home runs lost to rainouts that season."[32]

In a 2023 telephone interview, Canaday said she didn't recall saying such a thing. She also said her father wouldn't have made up two rained-out homers as an excuse for failing to tie Ruth's record. "No way," Canaday said. "He didn't even care about records. When Willie Mays broke Daddy's home run record, Daddy sent him a telegram of congratulations." Mays topped Foxx's record for most home runs by a right-handed hitter when he hit his 535th career homer on August 17, 1966.[33]

WHAT MIGHT HAVE BEEN

Ruth was impressed regardless of how many more homers Foxx may have had in 1932. After the season, Ruth, then 37 and near the end of his career, said, "Foxx is the greatest batsman in major league baseball today. There's no question about that. He's a swell fellow—well-liked by the players and the fans. In fact, he's such a nice kid, I was kind of sorry for him when he came so close to the record and missed."[34]

An equally respectful Foxx said, "If I had broken Ruth's record, it wouldn't have made any difference. Oh, it might have put a few more dollars in my pocket, but there was only one Ruth."[35]

While there will always be only one Ruth, a few more homers by the Beast would have forever changed the narrative. "If Foxx had busted Ruth's record in '32, his career and place in history would be a whole other story," Schaefer said. "Foxx would have owned the new home-run gold standard for decades, one that future sluggers would have all chased."[36]

After the 1932 season, the *Brooklyn Daily Eagle* asked players and managers: Who hit the ball harder, Foxx or Ruth? With strong arguments on behalf of each slugger, Cleveland Indians Manager Roger Peckinpaugh asked, "Why make a choice between the two? Just give the crown of the left-handed hitters to Ruth and concede

SABR/THE RUCKER ARCHIVE

Earl Averill (L) and Jimmie Foxx (R).

that Foxx hits the ball harder than any other right-handed batsman."[37] While Foxx led the major leagues in homers in 1932, Ruth was a distant second with 41.

Ruth remained center stage in his final years. Yet Foxx, his apparent successor, began winning more ink and plaudits, as he did on August 15, 1933, after the 25-year-old slugger had a day like none other. "Foxx, New Ruler of Swat, Far Shy of Ruth in Personality, But a Greater Terror at Bat," read the headline atop a story in the *Washington Evening Star*. The story, by the AP's Edward J. Neil reads: "There's a new brilliant shining today in the bonnet of pink-cheeked Jimmie Foxx, a new American League record of nine runs batted in in one game added to the walloping achievements of the new king of baseball's sluggers. As the old dynasty of Babe Ruth fades slowly…the wonder of Foxx, the easy-going farmer boy from Maryland's somnolent Eastern Sho' steadily rises." Neil added that while the younger "barrel-chested horsehide buster" lacked the "flair" and "booming personality" of Ruth, "never in all of the Babe's 20 years of big-league play has he loosed more devastation at the plate than Foxx unleashed yesterday as the Athletics slaughtered Walter Johnson's Cleveland Indians, 11 to 5."[38]

On September 24, 1940, Foxx, 32, then with the Red Sox, hit his 500th career homer, putting him on pace to top the Babe's record of 714. "What a man," teammate Ted Williams was quoted in the next day's *Philadelphia Evening Bulletin*. "And I'll bet he does it, too."[39]

But Foxx, battling alcohol and other health issues, including a nagging sinus problem apparently stemming from getting hit in the head with a pitched ball six years earlier, was soon reduced to a part-time player.[40] He hit only 34 more home runs before retiring in 1945—after bouncing from the Red Sox to the Chicago Cubs to the Philadelphia Phillies. Historian

Jenkinson quoted Williams as telling him in a 1986 interview, "Jimmie felt obligated to emulate the Bambino in every way. And that was not good. Ruth liked to party, but not as much as Foxx seemed to think."[41]

Jenkinson, in his 2010 book, *Baseball's Ultimate Power: Ranking the All-Time Greatest Distance Home Run Hitters*, put Ruth and Foxx first and second among the "Top 100 Tape-Measure Sluggers." Jenkinson used his own ranking formula: a player's longest homer, 10 longest homers, and career home-run total. Jenkinson's findings included that in 1932 alone, 24 of Foxx's homers went 450 feet or more, including a 500-footer over the left-center field bleachers in St. Louis. "It was," Jenkinson wrote, "a season for the ages."[42]

"THE TEAM THAT HISTORY FORGOT"

The stock market crashed in 1929, a few months after Foxx appeared on the July 29 cover of *TIME* magazine as the young face of the powerhouse A's, then headed to the first of three straight World Series. They won the first two. "I worked on a farm and I'm glad of it," Foxx told *TIME*. "Farmer boys are stronger than city boys….Never realized then it was helping me train for the Big Leagues."[43]

Foxx was considered the best player on perhaps the most overlooked great team, the 1929–31 Athletics, who, including Foxx, had four future Hall of Famers. "The Team that History Forgot," read the headline on the cover of *Sports Illustrated* on August 19, 1996. The A's, like Foxx, were overshadowed by Ruth and the Yankees, particularly the 1927 World Series champions, widely considered the greatest baseball team of all time. "Those A's never got the credit they deserved," *SI* quoted the *Washington Post*'s Shirley Povich as saying. "The A's were victims of the Yankee mystique. Perhaps the 1927 Yankees were the greatest team of all time. But if there was a close second, perhaps an equal, it was those A's."[44]

The Babe's 60 homers were a big part of the 1927 Yankees' mystique. His record was long seen as unbreakable by anyone other than the 6-foot-2, 215-pound Ruth himself, since he alone hit more home runs that year than most teams. But five years later, the 6-foot, 195-pound Foxx—with a sculpted body likened to that of a Greek god and sleeves cut to expose bulging biceps—rose to the challenge. He slugged four homers in the first five games of the 1932 season. After a nine-game lull, he hit 25 dingers in May and June combined, and then walloped another 12 in July.[45]

"I think I had about 41 homers by the first week in August," Foxx said in September 1961 as Maris closed in on Ruth's record. "Then I hurt my wrist sliding into second base to break up a double play. I stayed in the lineup but later learned I had a chipped bone. I was able to get base hits, but for three weeks, I didn't have the power to hit for distance."[46]

Once Foxx regained his power, he went on another long-ball rampage. He smacked 10 homers in September, five in the last five games of the season, including one on the final day, September 25. He ended up two homers short of Ruth's 60.[47] "Well, I gave her a ride to the finish boys," Foxx's nephew, Dell Foxx, quoted him as telling reporters after the game. Dell Foxx said, "He was disappointed but not depressed."[48]

It's difficult to compare players from different eras, given that—thanks to better diet and improved exercise—they, along with the rest of humanity, have gotten bigger and stronger. Yet Foxx appears to have been among the best of the best. "I never saw a player with more natural ability than Double X," said Hall of Fame shortstop Joe Cronin, who spent nearly a half-century in the big leagues as a player, manager, general manager, and president of the American League. "He had everything you could ask for in a player."[49]

"A LEAGUE OF THEIR OWN"

Foxx left high school to play baseball and after retiring, had a series of short-term jobs, including stints in public relations and as a paint salesman, a restaurant greeter, a sports announcer, a college coach, and as manager of the 1952 Fort Wayne Daisies of the All-American Girls Professional Baseball League, immortalized in the 1992 movie, *A League of Their Own*.[50]

Tom Hanks played Jimmy Dugan, portrayed as a former baseball player turned loud, profane, and falling down–drunk manager. The character was said to be based largely on Foxx, but former Daisies disputed the movie's depiction of him. They said Foxx drank, but was no Jimmy Dugan. "He was always a gentleman," said Katie Horstman. She said Foxx shared with her the key to his powerful swing after he learned that she grew up on a farm, milking cows, just as he had, and he saw her belt a towering home run. "I knew you could hit," Horstman said Foxx told her. "That's how I got my strong wrist action, too, from years of milking cows."[51]

Several years later, on January 23, 1958, United Press quoted Foxx as saying. "I earned about $270,000 in my 20 years in the Major Leagues," equivalent to several million dollars today. "I don't have anything now."[52]

In 1962, Foxx worked as a sporting goods salesman in a Cleveland department store, after having filed for bankruptcy. "I didn't want to do it, but a food company I had been associated with collapsed, and all of a sudden I got a big bill that wasn't mine. I had no choice," he told The Associated Press. In the article, dated January 20, 1962, he was described as unable

At the 1934 All-Star Game, Foxx (far right) is photographed with three other slugging greats, Al Simmons, Lou Gehrig, and Babe Ruth. All four batters, plus Joe Cronin, would be struck out in a row by National League starting pitcher Carl Hubbell, setting the record for consecutive strikeouts in an All-Star Game at five.

SABR/RUCKER ARCHIVE

to afford a telephone but in good spirits. Asked why he was smiling, Foxx said, "Why not? I'm alive."[53]

Sudlersville cheered Foxx when he played the game, but after he retired and did not move back to town, it began to see him as a divorced, broken-down has-been with a drinking problem and difficulty holding a job. "Sudlersville had pretty much disowned Daddy," said his stepdaughter, Nanci Foxx Canaday. "I really don't know why. But I knew Daddy could handle it. Daddy taught us if someone is mean to us, kill them with kindness. That's what Daddy always did."[54]

Baltimore native Gil Dunn moved to the Eastern Shore in 1953 and opened a pharmacy. He was surprised and saddened to see the lack of local interest in Foxx, a boyhood idol. Dunn erected a Foxx museum in his store in the 1960s and wrote the Beast, asking if he had anything he would like to contribute. Not long after, Foxx, unannounced, drove to the pharmacy with a donation: a trunk full of memorabilia. "You might as well have this all," Dunn quoted Foxx. "No one else seems to want it."[55]

REMEMBERING "UNCLE JIM"

Years after Foxx died in 1967 at 59—he choked on food while having dinner with his younger brother, Sam—his nephew Dell delivered a speech about "Uncle Jim" to the Sudlersville Lions Club. Dell Foxx does not recall the date of his speech, but he kept a copy of it. "This man never attracted the attention or the salary of Babe Ruth," he wrote. "He was an amazing hitter, but he was no showman on or off the field. When others complained that he didn't receive his share of attention, he would smile and say, 'It's all right. It's a lot of fun anyway.'"[56]

"But it's sad, really," Dell Foxx added, "because of all the super sluggers in baseball, Jimmie Foxx is still the least known and remembered. There have been no books written about him, and many fans who still marvel at Babe Ruth have never heard of old 'Double X.'"[57]

Since then, a half dozen books have been written about Foxx, but none made him anything near a household name. By comparison, dozens of biographies of Hall of Famers such as Ruth, Gehrig, and Mays have burnished their already robust legends.[58]

In 1981, following Dunn's lead, Sudlersville reembraced Jimmie Foxx posthumously. It dedicated a small park in his honor and posted a sign reading, "Welcome to Sudlersville, Birthplace of Jimmy Foxx." (Foxx changed the spelling of his first name from Jimmy to Jimmie after he entered the big leagues, but town folks still remember him as Jimmy.) On October

24, 1987, the Sudlersville Community Betterment Club dedicated a stone memorial in Foxx's honor in the park at the corner of Church and Main Streets. Hundreds of people attended, including family, friends, elected officials, sportswriters, and former players.[59]

"It was overdue," said Betterment Club member Loretta Walls. "He deserved it."[60]

Unable to attend, Ted Williams mailed a handwritten tribute: "I'll never forget my old teammate and how nicely he treated me as a young brash rookie and what an impression he made on me when I first saw him hit. I really don't believe anyone ever made the impact of the ball and bat sound like it did when he really got a hold of it... Born in farm country, I really don't think he ever left it. He was as down to earth as anyone I ever met."[61]

Over the years, relatives, sportswriters, and fans have suggested Foxx may have been an even better player and better remembered if he'd been more aggressive, more of a showman, and more selfish. At the memorial dedication, Hurtt Deringer of the nearby *Kent County News* rejected such talk. "I think he was best as he was," Deringer said, "a man genuinely liked by everyone in baseball. His niceness just shone through."[62]

In 1992, Chestertown, another Eastern Shore town, dedicated a statue to its hometown baseball hero, Bill "Swish" Nicholson. Nicholson, like Foxx, was a former farm boy. He led the Cubs in homers in eight straight seasons and also led the National League in homers and RBIs in 1943 and 1944. But he was no Hall of Famer.[63] "If Chestertown had a statue for Swish, Sudlersville should have one for its Hall of Famer, Jimmie Foxx," said Walls. She helped rally community support to build one.[64]

On October 25, 1997, a life-size bronze statue of the Beast was dedicated in Sudlersville, near his memorial. At the dedication, former Maryland Governor Harry Hughes said, "We recall Jimmie Foxx as an example for all youth who would play the game."[65] A natural athlete, Foxx had been a state sprint champ in high school.[66] In the majors, he was primarily a first baseman but early on he'd been a standout catcher. Foxx ended up playing every position except second base and center field in the big leagues. Late in his career, he pitched 23⅔ innings over 10 games. He had a 1–0 record with an earned run average of 1.52.

Nephew Dell Foxx looked much like his uncle and was a model for the statue. Now a retired banker, he recalls playing high school baseball on the Maryland Eastern Shore in the 1950s, where fans in the stands compared him unfavorably to the Beast. Speaking from his home in North East, Maryland, a 45-minute car ride from Sudlersville, Foxx said: "I'd be at bat while a bunch of old men sat behind the screen, mumbling, 'He sure doesn't hit like his uncle.'" With a chuckle, Foxx added: "I remember thinking, 'Not many people hit like my Uncle Jim.'"[67]

On October 20, 2007, baseball historian Jenkinson helped Sudlersville celebrate the 100th anniversary of Foxx's birth. In doing so, he advised the town how to treat the memory of "The Gentle Beast." Said Jenkinson, "History has not been fair to Jimmie. As the years pass, his legacy and memory continue to diminish in the minds of most Americans. Despite his imperfections, he was an amazing man who should endure as one of the nation's true athletic icons."

"So, what do we do?" Jenkinson remarked "Tell the truth…. Foxx was a marvel."[68]

The Sudlersville Community Betterment Club helped spread the word. It printed a pamphlet, *Jimmy Foxx: Honoring Our Hometown Hero*. The club quoted what Double X had said decades earlier when asked to name his "greatest day in baseball." Foxx picked Game 5 of the 1930 World Series, on October 6, when he squared off in the ninth inning of a scoreless contest against fellow future Hall of Famer Burleigh Grimes of the St. Louis Cardinals. "I was nervous. But Grimes was cool as ice," Foxx said. "He was deliberately slow in getting ready to pitch, so I stepped out of the box. I got some dirt in my hands and stepped in again. He raised his hand to his mouth in his spitter motion. Then he threw the first pitch. I knew in a flash second it wasn't a spitter. For it was coming in close. It was a curve, and I swung."[69]

He went on: "Well, that was it—the big thrill. I heard the Athletic bench yell all at once, and there it went. Some fan reached up and pulled it down when it hit the left field bleachers for a home run" that won the game and successfully positioned the A's, two days later, to capture their second consecutive World Series championship, four games to two.[70]

According to the next day's *Philadelphia Inquirer*, Foxx called the winning shot, telling teammates as he picked up his big bat and headed to the plate, "I'll just bust up this ball game right now."[71]

In 1997, the Eastern Shore Baseball Hall of Fame Museum opened at the Arthur W. Perdue Stadium in Salisbury, home of the Class A Delmarva Shorebirds. With old bats, balls, uniforms, photos, and displays, the shrine honors hundreds of pro and amateur players from the Eastern Shore, including a former farm boy unknown to most of America. However, says Newt Weaver, a member of the museum's board of directors,

that former farm boy, Jimmie Foxx, "is our biggest draw—him and his 534 home runs," including the 58 in 1932.[72] ∎

Source

All stats are from Baseball Reference except as noted.

Notes

1. "Jimmie Foxx 1932 Game by Game Batting Logs," Baseball Almanac, https://www.baseball-almanac.com/players/hittinglogs.php?p=foxxji01&y=1932. Foxx hit 40th homer on July 23, 1932, the 96th game of the season, to put him on pace to finish with 64.
2. Bill Jenkinson, *Baseball's Ultimate Power: Ranking the All-Time Greatest Distance Home Run Hitters* (Guilford, CT: Lyons Press), 237.
3. "Jimmie Foxx 1932 Game by Game Batting Logs."
4. John Bennett, telephone interview, January 2023.
5. John Odell, telephone interview, March 14, 2022.
6. John Thorn, *Treasures of the Baseball Hall of Fame* (New York: Random House, 1980), 61.
7. "Babe Ruth World Series Stats," Baseball Almanac, https://www.baseball-almanac.com/players/playerpost.php?p=ruthba01&ps=ws.
8. "Jimmie Foxx World Series Stats," Baseball Almanac, https://www.baseball-almanac.com/players/playerpost.php?p=foxxji01&ps=ws.
9. "1933 All-Star Game Box Score, July 6," Baseball Reference, https://www.baseball-reference.com/allstar/1933-allstar-game.shtml.
10. Curt Smith, "TV brought baseball to fans who had never seen a game," National Baseball Hall of Fame, https://baseballhall.org/discover/television-brought-baseball-to-millions; Andrew Martin, "MLB Legend Jimmie Foxx Had To Become A Working Man Years After HOF Induction," Medium, May 14, 2022, https://historianandrew.medium.com/mlb-legend-jimmie-foxx-had-to-become-a-working-man-years-after-hof-induction-d9223bd64326.
11. Bob Broeg, *Super Stars of Baseball* (St. Louis: The Sporting News, 1971), 85–86.
12. Franklin Snyder, interview in Annapolis, Maryland, July 26, 2023. Snyder, a retired Maryland homebuilder, remembers Jimmie Foxx. "He and my father [Frank] played together," Snyder said, pointing at an old black-and-white photo of their team, the Easton Farmers. "That's my father, in front of Jimmie Foxx. My father was the catcher. Jimmie Foxx played first base. My father told me Jimmie Foxx was a heck of a player. Big bat"; "About Jimmie Foxx," National Baseball Hall of Fame, https://baseballhall.org/hall-of-famers/foxx-jimmie.
13. "Jimmie Foxx," Baseball Reference BR Bullpen, https://www.baseball-reference.com/bullpen/Jimmie_Foxx.
14. "Jimmie Foxx Debuts May 1, 1925," Baseball Sisco Kid Style, May 1, 2015, https://baseballsiscokidstyle.blogspot.com/2015/05/jimmie-foxx-debuts-may-1-1925.html; "Player Batting Season & Career Stats Finder," Stathead Baseball, https://stathead.com/tiny/biDjg. Note that there are duplicate entries in those results because of players such as Roy Campanella debuting in different major leagues; Red Bradley, who was 18 at his debut, appears in error.
15. Online search of *The Sporting News* Archives.
16. Bill Jenkinson interview, March 2023.
17. "Baseball's 100 Greatest Players by The Sporting News (1998)," Baseball Almanac, https://www.baseball-almanac.com/legendary/lisn100.shtml.
18. "Top 100 MLB players of all time," ESPN.com, February 1, 2022, https://www.espn.com/mlb/story/_/id/33145121/top-100-mlb-players-all. Players whose career was over in 1998 who had leapfrogged Foxx were, in ascending order: Yogi Berra, Jackie Robinson, Joe Morgan, Tris Speaker, Josh Gibson, Pete Rose, Bob Gibson, Sandy Koufax, Johnny Bench, Roberto Clemente, Tom Seaver, Frank Robinson, Mike Schmidt and Mickey Mantle. One player who had been ahead of Foxx in 1998 fell behind him on the 2022 list: Pete Alexander.

19. "Foxx, Ott enter Hall of Fame together," National Baseball Hall of Fame, https://baseballhall.org/discover/inside-pitch/ott-foxx-enter-hall-of-fame-together.

20. Associated Press, "Foxx Figures Breaking of Ruth Record Would Help," *Hagerstown* (Maryland) *Morning Herald*, January 29, 1951.

21. Cassidy Lent, telephone interview and follow up email exchange, 2023.

22. Broeg, *Super Stars of Baseball*, 84. Robert H. Schaefer, "Double X and His Lost Dingers," *Baseball Research Journal*: Spring Vol. 42, No. 1, 2013 (Phoenix: Society for American Baseball Research, 2013), https://sabr.org/journal/article/double-x-and-his-lost-dingers/; Norman Macht, *The Grand Old Man of Baseball, Connie Mack* (University of Nebraska Press, 2015), 16.

23. John Thorn, email exchanges, 2023 and 2024.

24. David Smith, telephone interviews, 2022 and 2023.

25. Smith.

26. Associated Press, "Old Double X Says New Home Run Champ Needed," *Springfield* (Missouri) *News-Leader*, January 29, 1951. Foxx told the AP: "Sure. I would have liked to break the Babe's record. I think it would be a good thing if someone broke it now." Details about Shibe Park from Macht, *The Grand Old Man of Baseball*.

27. Robert Schaefer, email exchange, 2022. See also Schaefer, "Double X and His Lost Dingers."

28. Jenkinson, telephone interview.

29. James C. Isaminger, "Mackian," *Philadelphia Inquirer*, July, 2, 1932, 12.

30. Jenkinson.

31. John Odell, telephone interview, March 14, 2022.

32. Ted Taylor, *The Ultimate Philadelphia Athletic Reference Book, 1901–1954* (Bloomington, IN: Xlibris, 2010), 126.

33. Nanci Foxx Canaday, telephone interview, 2023.

34. Jack Cuddy, "Babe Ruth Thinks His Home Run Record Is Safe," *Paterson* (New Jersey) *Morning Call*, December 20, 1932, 25.

35. Joseph J. Veccihione, *New York Times Book of Sports Legends* (New York: Simon & Schuster, 1991).

36. Schaefer, telephone interview, 2023.

37. Henry P. Edwards, "Hard to Tell Which Hits a Ball Harder, Babe Ruth or Foxx," *Brooklyn Daily Eagle*, February 5, 1933, 44.

38. Edward J. Neil, "Foxx, New Ruler of Swat, Far Shy of Ruth in Personality, but Greater Terror at Bat," *Washington Evening Star*, August 15, 1933, 29.

39. "Boston Red Sox slugger Jimmie Foxx hits his 500th home run," This Day in Baseball, https://thisdayinbaseball.com/boston-red-sox-slugger-jimmie-foxx-hits-his-500th-home-run/.

40. Bill Jenkinson, "The Real Jimmie Foxx," *The National Pastime: From Swampoodle to South Philly* (Phoenix: SABR, 2013), https://sabr.org/journal/article/the-real-jimmie-foxx/.

41. Jenkinson, telephone interview, 2023.

42. Jenkinson, *Baseball's Ultimate Power*, 184, 237

43. "Philadelphia's Foxx," *TIME*, July 29, 1929.

44. William Nack, "Lost in History," *Sports Illustrated*, August 19, 1996.

45. "Jimmie Foxx 1932 Game by Game Batting Logs."

46. Mark Millikin, *Jimmie Foxx, The Pride of Sudlersville* (Lanham, MD: Scarecrow Press, 1998), 255–56.

47. "Jimmie Foxx 1932 Game by Game Batting Logs."

48. Dell Foxx, personal copy of his speech to the Sudlersville Lions Club, date unknown.

49. Stephen Stilianos, "Jimmie Foxx," Pennsylvania Center for the Book, Spring 2008, https://pabook.libraries.psu.edu/literary-cultural-heritage-map-pa/bios/Foxx__James.

50. John Bennett, "James E. Foxx," All-American Girls Professional Baseball League, https://www.aagpbl.org/profiles/james-e-foxx-jimmie-and-double-x-and-beast/689.

51. Katie Hortsman, telephone interview, July 2023.

52 . United Press, "Bosox Name Jimmy Foxx Minneapolis Farm Coach," *Hartford Courant*, January 24, 1958, 21

53. Associated Press, "Jimmie Foxx Handling Bats Again," *The Kansas City Star*, January 21, 1962, 31.

54. Nancy Canaday Foxx, telephone interview, 2023.

55. Gil Dunn, "#1 Fan Remembers the Great Jimmie Foxx," *Sudlersville's Celebration of the Anniversary of Jimmie' Foxx's Birth 1907–2007* (pamphlet), October 20, 2007.

56. Dell Foxx speech.

57. Dell Foxx speech.

58. A Google search finds dozens of biographies of popular Hall of Famers, many of whom played in New York, including Mickey Mantle, Willie Mays, Yogi Berra, Jackie Robinson, Babe Ruth, and Lou Gehrig.

59. Dunn, "#1 Fan Remembers."

60. Loretta Walls, telephone interview, 2023.

61. Ted Williams, hand-written remarks read at Foxx's tribute, October 25, 1997.

62. Mark Millikin, *Jimmie Foxx*, 264.

63. Gary Livacari, "Another Edition of Baseball's Forgotten Stars! Bill 'Swish' Nicholson!" Baseball History Comes Alive, https://www.baseballhistorycomesalive.com/another-edition-of-baseballs-forgotten-stars-bill-swish-nicholson/.

64. Loretta Walls, telephone interview, March 24, 2023.

65. "Jimmie Foxx - Player," Eastern Shore Baseball Hall of Fame Museum, http://www.esbhalloffame.org/index.cfm?ref=30200&ref2=149.

66. Bill Jenkinson, "The Real Jimmie Foxx," *The National Pastime: From Swampoodle to South Philadelphia*, 2013, https://sabr.org/journal/article/the-real-jimmie-foxx/.

67. Dell Foxx, telephone interview, October 10, 2023.

68. Jenkinson, spoken remarks at Sudlersville's 100th anniversary celebration of Jimmie Foxx's birth, October 20, 2007.

69. John Carmichael, *My Greatest Day in Baseball as Told to John Carmichael and Other Noted Sportswriters* (New York: Grosset & Dunlap, 1951). Foxx's day as told to Lyall Smith.

70. Carmichael, *My Greatest Day*.

71. "Foxx Predicted He Would Win Game with Homer," *Philadelphia Inquirer*, October 7, 1930, 22.

72. Newt Weaver, telephone interview, June 12, 2023.

Mary Dobkin

Baltimore's Grande Dame of Baseball

David Krell

Nineteen-seventy-nine was quite a year for Baltimore. The Orioles returned to the World Series for the first time in eight years and one of the city's most impactful residents got well-deserved national recognition. Her name was Mary Dobkin. Aunt Mary. Nearing 80 years of age with spryness belying her declining physical condition—which included prosthetics because of the amputation of both feet and half of a leg—Dobkin stood in the box of Commissioner Bowie Kuhn at Memorial Stadium under a nighttime sky in mid-October. Baseball's decision makers had bestowed upon her the honor of throwing out the ceremonial first pitch for Game Six of the World Series against the Pittsburgh Pirates.[1]

Doug DeCinces, the home team's third baseman, was her battery mate. Though not a nationally known VIP, Dobkin was baseball royalty in Chesapeake Bay's environs; she created teams for kids who wanted to play baseball but otherwise wouldn't have had the opportunity.

Dobkin's story is heartbreaking, which makes her resilience even more inspiring. When she and her parents came from Russia to America, her mother left the family and her father died. An aunt and uncle, already with five kids, took Mary in and they moved to Baltimore. The family either never went looking for her or gave up too soon when 6-year-old Mary

Mary Dobkin at age 77, while speaking to the press about the TV movie Aunt Mary.

wandered the streets during a cold night, suffering frostbite and a loss of consciousness.

A Good Samaritan took Mary to the hospital. Speaking only Russian, and with severe physical challenges, which eventually led to her amputations, Mary was never reclaimed by her aunt and uncle. She became a ward of the city and lived at the Johns Hopkins Hospital until she was in her late 30s. But her spirit would not be quashed by her lifelong problems, which the frostbite had triggered. "By all known rules, I should have died," she said. "If God was good enough to let me live, I made up my mind that I would work with children for the rest of my life."[2]

Mary learned English through radio broadcasts and newspapers, which is a familiar tale for twentieth-century immigrants. Baseball was both an outlet and a salve. "Then one summer she got to attend therapy camp," reads a 1979 *Los Angeles Times* profile. "From her wheelchair, she was taught to catch and hit a baseball. It was magic. Quiet, reclusive Mary Dobkin returned to the hospital a new person, ignited by direct experience with baseball."[3]

She combined her dedication to kids and love of baseball in the early 1940s.[4]

Baltimore's leading newspaper, the *Sun*, reported on Dobkin being more than an organizer when one of her teams got selected to play at Memorial Stadium in 1954. It was part of an Interfaith Night sponsored by B'nai B'rith, Knights of Columbus, and the Boumi Temple Shrine. She was a coach. "Miss Mary goes out to the ball field and directs some of the teams some nights, either from her wheelchair or on her crutches or from the aluminum beach chair her boys bought her," the *Sun* reported.[5]

Dobkin learned the fundamentals of baseball from TV broadcasts of Orioles games and often hosted kids at her apartment to join her in this endeavor. Neither her sex nor her infirmity, marked by 110 operations, were an issue in gaining their confidence. "The boys themselves wanted me to manage their team and never once have they made reference to the fact that I'm a woman doing what normally is a man's job," she said.[6]

Her efforts impressed local merchants and the business community, who launched the Dobkin Children's Fund. Donations included "many thousands of dollars' worth of sports equipment and facilities." The number of boys in Dobkin's operation was estimated to be "about 200" in 1958.[7]

That year, Dobkin was honored by the TV show *End of the Rainbow*, described on IMDb as a show that ran in 1957–58, with co-hosts Bob Barker and Art Baker going across America and surprising "the less-fortunate who helped others when they could barely help themselves." Dobkin's bounty included uniforms and equipment for her teams in baseball, basketball, and football along with a television and $1,000 for the Mary Dobkin Children's Fund.

The program had an emotional wallop for the woman who represented toughness, perseverance, and encouragement for Baltimore's kids. She shared a promise that she'd made during her own childhood: "If God is good enough to let me live to be a grown-up, I'll devote my whole life to helping children."[8]

But Dobkin's appearance did not happen solely because of the production staff. The board members of the children's fund had written letters advocating for Dobkin to be a guest on *This Is Your Life*, a 30-minute show that usually focused on the lives of celebrities. Ralph Edwards produced both shows. The board never heard back about *This Is Your Life* but did hear from *End of the Rainbow*.[9]

No less an authority than the Baltimore Police Department certified Dobkin's impact on the community. Captain Millard B. Horton said, "We all recognize that there is a juvenile problem in these underprivileged areas, but Miss Dobkin is one of the few people who really went out and did something about solving it."[10]

Don Gamber was one of the kids who played for Dobkin. "Mary was friends with the crossing guard, Miss Helen, and she used to ask her to take us to the Fifth Regiment Armory to see the Ringling Brothers Circus every year," recalls Gamber, a pitcher and outfielder on Dobkin's teams. "One time, she called my mom and said, 'Pat, can I take your boys for a surprise?' She brought me, my brother John, my cousin Danny, and some other neighborhood kids to Memorial Stadium to throw a surprise birthday party for Bubba Smith after a Colts practice.

"Mary was selfless and she loved the kids. She didn't take any crap. Other managers didn't like her. She argued with umps. There were certain kids that she got close with. I was one. She knew that I had a lot of talent with baseball and football and introduced me to Bob Davidson, owner of a Ford dealership on York Road. He got me involved in Ford Punt Pass and Kick competitions. Mary got me tryouts with the Orioles, Pirates, and Reds."[11]

At the beginning of 1960, a front-page story appeared in the *Evening Sun* describing the questionable future of the fund. Even with donations, Dobkin didn't have the means to pay rent for the clubhouse at 1323 Harford Avenue.[12]

Moved by Dobkin's efforts, some people paid for newspaper ads asking for contributions. In March, Samuel Stofberg and Stanley Stofberg sponsored an announcement revealing that the donations had allowed the fund to pay for part of the clubhouse but more would be needed to pay each month; the fund didn't own it outright.[13]

Through donations inspired in part by personal newspaper advertisements, Dobkin got enough to start another clubhouse in the Armistead Gardens neighborhood. It was sorely needed. Dobkin's efforts gave kids an outlet that protected them from submitting to self-destructive activities. When an adult saw some kids wearing her team's uniforms and asked her whether they had a game, Dobkin said, "Those kids are wearing my uniforms because they don't have anything else to wear to school."[14]

The consistent goodwill toward Dobkin and the kids she supervised did not go unnoticed. In January 1964, she wrote a letter to the editor of the *Evening Sun* highlighting the generosity of the holiday season reflected in parties held by the Baltimore Polytechnic Institute's junior class and faculty members; Toys for Tots donations from the US Marine Corps First Engineer Battalion; and the American Sokol-Club and St. Francis Xavier Church giving space for parties. "We hope members of our community will continue to help us with our year-round program for underprivileged children as long as the need exists," she wrote.[15]

In March, the *Evening Sun* ran a feature story that allowed her to dispel a misperception about the donations, which included a block of 500 tickets to a Baltimore Bullets basketball game. "Whenever I get publicity, it seems that people get the notion that we're rich and have all we need," said Dobkin. "That just isn't the case. In September we were broke."[16]

Dobkin also ran a softball team for girls called Dobkin's Dolls.[17]

In 1966, a banquet honoring her 25 years of generosity drew luminaries including Rocky Marciano, Johnny Unitas, Brooks Robinson, Dave McNally, Jim

PUBLIC DOMAIN

Jean Stapleton played Dobkin in Aunt Mary, *which aired on CBS in 1979.*

Palmer, Steve Barber, and announcer Chuck Thompson, who served as the toastmaster. Robinson said what the people in Chesapeake Bay's environs had known since the early 1940s: "Mary Dobkin can't be repaid in full for the wonderful work she has done in Baltimore." Unitas noted her impact as well: "The work Mary has done has cut down juvenile delinquency and I hope there will be many more Mary Dobkins."[18]

In 1973, Dobkin was part of a group of two dozen Baltimore citizens honored during the City Fair for being "Special Baltimoreans." They were selected by a committee from "among several hundred nominations…for outstanding contributions to the quality of city life."[19]

Dobkin's life became the basis for *Aunt Mary*, a 1979 *Hallmark Hall of Fame* movie starring Jean Stapleton. It aired on CBS on December 5, about seven weeks after Dobkin's moment in the World Series spotlight. Harold Gould and Martin Balsam had supporting roles. According to the *Baltimore News-American*, watching *Aunt Mary* was part of a homework assignment for "thousands of Baltimore school children," along with reading a copy of the script.[20]

Jay Mazzone, a former Dobkin player who was a batboy during the Orioles' 1966–71 heyday, perhaps best represented Aunt Mary's determination because of a similar situation—doctors amputated his hands after his snowsuit caught fire when he was 2 years old. In *Aunt Mary*, Tim Gemelli plays an amputee whom Dobkin recruits; Gemelli didn't have a right hand at birth.[21]

At the time that the TV movie was in production, Dobkin had endured 155 operations.[22]

She recalled that her involvement with underprivileged kids began when she realized they didn't have equipment that other kids had. East Baltimore wasn't Pikesville or Reisterstown, after all. So she organized

a raffle for a radio. Once the kids had an outlet for their restlessness, the streets were quieter. The merchants calmer. Amos Jones owned a food joint called the Dog House and praised Dobkin because there were no more break-ins, so he decided to buy uniforms for Dobkin's Dynamites.[23]

Jones's tale was one of several represented in the movie. Dobkin provided color commentary during the broadcast for *Sun* writer Michael Wentzel, who watched it in her East Baltimore apartment along with some of her friends. The events portrayed were steeped in fact. "That is for real," Dobkin would say. "She would say it often during the film," Wentzel wrote. A rock crashing through the glass in Dobkin's living-room window. Dobkin blowing a whistle into the phone when she gets obscene phone calls. The tough kid named Nicholas.[24]

Many of the players kept in touch with their guidepost through adulthood, including Nicholas. "The real one stopped in earlier to say hello," Dobkin said on the night of the broadcast. "He's an engineer now."[25]

Aunt Mary condenses the real story into a 1954–55 setting and emphasizes the pioneering aspect of her coaching. A key scene involves Dobkin subtly threatening a racist sporting goods store owner to provide a uniform for a Black player on her team, lest Tommy the Torch, a neighborhood arsonist, use his skills. Racial integration on Dobkin's teams happened in 1955. *Aunt Mary* ends with her bringing a girl on the team; she actually busted the gender line in 1960.[26]

New York Times TV critic John J. O'Connor praised Stapleton's portrayal as "an effective blend of compassion and toughness."[27] O'Connor's counterpart at the *Boston Globe*, Robert A. McLean, was equally positive: "The best part is that Aunt Mary is for real, and it's her life story that Stapleton portrays with depth and dignity and a fine flair for humor in the face of adversity."[28]

The *Sun*'s Michael Hill also endorsed this story of Baltimore's grande dame of baseball. After praising Stapleton's performance, he wrote: "Indeed, the strength of 'Aunt Mary' is its near-perfect casting. Martin Balsam is his usual fine self as the across-the-hall neighbor, Dolph Sweet is perfect as the impresario of A.J.'s Dog House, the team's sponsor, and even the kids, normally stumbling blocks in films like this, are quite believable."[29]

Sun TV critic Bill Carter concurred: "[Stapleton] is an actress of intelligence; she knows how to cut through the schmaltz to the basics," he wrote.[30]

Stapleton recalled meeting Dobkin early in the shooting of the movie in Los Angeles, though the Baltimore icon didn't stay around to see the entire production. "She had a great PR talent," Stapleton said.

JEAN STAPLETON: HOW EDITH BUNKER BECAME AUNT MARY

When Jean Stapleton took on the role of Mary Dobkin for the TV movie *Aunt Mary*, she didn't set out to do an impersonation.

"I'm not trying to imitate her but to catch her spirit," said Stapleton, the winner of four Emmy Awards and two Golden Globe Awards during the glorious nine-year run of *All in the Family*. "I'm trying to perceive her thinking; I'm watching her pace. I'm searching for her motivations because that's where you have to start."[1]

Aunt Mary had initially been a project for Hallmark and NBC, but it fell through. Ellis Cohen, an alumnus of Dobkin's teams who provided the story for *Aunt Mary* said, "So she's been boycotting Hallmark for the past year and a half."[2] *Hallmark Hall of Fame* moved from NBC to CBS in 1979.

Burt Prelutsky wrote the script and Peter Werner directed.

"I'm a businessman, so to a certain extent you're drawn because you think you can sell it," producer Michael Jaffe said. "But once we had it sold and I had a chance to talk with Aunt Mary herself and meet some of the people associated with her and get the movie cast, then it became interesting. Peter did a great job in capturing the humor. This was his second movie. Jean was wonderful, gracious, cooperative, hard-working, and sweet. A perfect human being. Dolph Sweet was one of the great character actors of all time. The story was funny where it needed to be funny and serious where it needed to be serious."[3]

Aunt Mary was Stapleton's first TV production after *All in the Family*, which ended in 1979, and her appearances in five episodes of its spinoff, *Archie Bunker's Place*, which began airing that fall. Lucille Ball had expressed an interest in playing Dobkin. Show business columnist Cecil Smith mentioned it as part of a 1977 *Los Angeles Times* feature about the iconic comedian: "There are other roles Lucille Ball itches to play—a legless legend of a woman who has been a patron saint of the ghetto kids of Baltimore, for one."[4]

Werner, the director, doesn't seem to have been bothered that that didn't work out. "From the moment I met Jean," he said, "she was interested in my ideas and wanted to rehearse. I loved that kind of preparation. We continued to have a personal friendship."

Of course, the movie also featured what Werner called "a bunch of young actors."

"The most challenging part was directing the 'cute' out of them," he said. "I studied the Bowery Boys movies, which had street type kids."[5]

Robbie Rist was one of those young actors. Best known for his six-episode stint as Cousin Oliver in the last season of *The Brady Bunch*, Rist recalled, "Peter made an effort for us to be a team, a unit. Mary came to the set a couple of times. I think aside from it being a very sweet movie, we need more Mary Dobkins in the world. We need more people who care. We need more people who have souls. All of us kids were aware of the fact, somehow, of what she brought to the world.

"I think it was an acting choice on Jean Stapleton's part that she took on the same maternal role off camera. She was super cool and close with everybody. A true character actor."[6]

Anthony Cafiso and his brother Steven played brothers Nicholas and Tony in *Aunt Mary*. "Mary Dobkin came to the set in a wheelchair," Anthony said. "She was very quiet, very humble. She had a face of awe, almost in shock that said, 'This is all about me.' Later on, I could only imagine what she must have felt like after what she went through in her life and what ended up being the effect of it.

"I went to see Jean in Nyack, New York, when she played Eleanor Roosevelt in a one-woman show. This was the early 1990s. I brought flowers and asked one of the theater workers after the show to tell her who I was. She wanted to see me. It was like seeing my aunt. She always made time for us."[7]

Michael Hill of the *Sun* wrote, "Ms. Stapleton is the perfect choice to play this working-class hero. There's a lot of Edith Bunker there, and a lot of Jean Stapleton."[8]

Notes

1. Kay Mills, "Aunt Mary story filmed in Calif.," *Baltimore Evening Sun*, May 1, 1979, C1.
2. Michael Hill, "'Aunt Mary,'" *Baltimore Evening Sun*, December 5, 1979, B1.
3. Michael Jaffe, telephone interview, December 28, 2022.
4. Cecil Smith, "They Still Love Lucy," *Los Angeles Times*, May 23, 1977, 79.
5. Peter Werner, telephone interview, March 7, 2022.
6. Robbie Rist, telephone interview, February 3, 2023.
7. Telephone interview with Robbie Rist, February 3, 2023.
8. Hill, "'Aunt Mary.'"

"She was always looking for publicity for the team and herself. She was a great lady."[31]

Indeed, she was. Dobkin's legacy lasted through generations. "But my greatest joy is the boys who are now grown up and are bringing their own kids to practice," she said in a profile for the *Sun*. "Some of them are my best coaches."[32]

By 1982, Dobkin was estimated to have undergone 180 operations.[33] Her building—3899 in the Claremont Homes public housing complex located at 3885–4047 Sinclair Lane in East Baltimore—was a long-time destination for generations of kids to visit, whether after a game or to say hi to the woman known as Aunt Mary. After suffering a stroke, Dobkin lived in Levindale Hebrew Geriatic Center and Hospital's nursing home section for the last months of her life.[34]

Mary Dobkin died on August 22, 1987. Her obituary was a front-page story for the *Sun*. Former Orioles manager Earl Weaver said, "Just to see the look on the kids' faces when they had Mary Dobkin Night at the stadium and they'd present her with a trophy was special. She touched a lot of lives."[35]

There is a baseball field named after Dobkin in East Baltimore. Given her selfless devotion to the Orioles and the city, there ought to be a statue of her at Camden Yards and an annual night dedicated to her where the O's wear uniforms with the Dobkin's Dynamites logo. ■

Acknowledgments

I want to highlight the invaluable assistance of Margaret Gers in the Periodicals Department at the Enoch Pratt Free Library in Baltimore. Margaret provided several archival articles from the *Baltimore Sun* and *Baltimore News-American* in addition to biographical information about Mary Dobkin.

Notes

1. The Pirates were down 3–1, then battled back to win the World Series in seven games.
2. Beth Ann Krier, "Aunt Mary: Still Going to Bat for Baseball," *Los Angeles Times*, June 1, 1979, E1.
3. Krier.
4. "Mary Dobkin Honored Tonight," *Baltimore Sun*, December 11, 1966, A2.
5. "Miss Mary's Baseball Teams To Go 'Big League' At Stadium," *Baltimore Sun*, June 21, 1954, 28.
6. "Miss Mary's Baseball Teams"; Thomas McNelis, "'Aunt Mary' Lone Woman Pilot Here," *Baltimore Evening Sun*, May 27, 1954, 51.
7. "Club House Appeal Made," *Baltimore Sun*, May 9, 1958, 8.
8. "Look and Listen with Donald Kirkley," *Baltimore Sun*, January 20, 1958, 8; "End of the Rainbow," Internet Movie Database, https://www.imdb.com/title/tt13159768/; "John Crosby's Radio and Television," *Baltimore Sun*, January 22, 1958, 34.
9. Hope Pantell, "To View," *Baltimore Evening Sun*, January 28, 1958, 20.
10. "Club House Appeal Made," *Baltimore Sun*, May 9, 1958, 8.
11. Don Gamber, telephone interview, March 2, 2022.
12. Travis Kidd, "Aunt Mary Dobkin's Hopes Fade," *Baltimore Evening Sun*, January 14, 1960, 1.
13. Newspaper ad, *Baltimore Sun*, March 6, 1960, 46.
14. Travis Kidd, "Aunt Mary Dobkin Overcomes Setbacks in Providing Aid," *Baltimore Evening Sun*, June 24, 1960, 25.
15. "The Forum: Letters to the Editor—Thanks from Mary Dobkin," *Baltimore Evening Sun*, January 23, 1964, A12.
16. Robin Frames, "Aunt Mary Brings Cheer To Many Young Lives," *Baltimore Evening Sun*, March 10, 1964, B1.
17. Irvin Nathan, "Piloting Cubs No Problem To Veteran Mary Dobkin," *Baltimore Evening Sun*, July 29, 1964, D4.
18. Jim Elliot, "Tribute Is Paid To Mary Dobkin," *Baltimore Sun*, December 12, 1966, C1.
19. Josephine Novak, "'Special Baltimoreans' Being Cited For Contributions To Life Quality," *Baltimore Evening Sun*, September 19, 1973, C1.
20. Peggy Cunningham, "Aunt Mary," *Baltimore News-American*, December 5, 1979, 1C.
21. Cunningham.
22. Krier, "Aunt Mary: Still Going to Bat for Baseball."
23. Isaac Rehert, "Mary Dobkin, baseball coach on crutches, to get 'Bunker' treatment in Hollywood," *Baltimore Sun*, April 10, 1979, B1.
24. Michael Wentzel, "'This is all real,' says 'Aunt Mary' as she watches 'repeat' at home," *Baltimore Evening Sun*, December 6, 1979, A1.
25. Wentzel.
26. Michael Hill, "'Aunt Mary,'" *Baltimore Evening Sun*, December 5, 1979, B1
27. John J. O'Connor, "TV: Jean Stapleton as Manager of a Baseball Team," *The New York Times*, December 5, 1979, C29.
28. Robert A. McLean, "'Aunt Mary' just couldn't miss," *Boston Globe*, December 4, 1979, 47.
29. Hill, "'Aunt Mary.'"
30. Bill Carter, "Aunt Mary's TV hometown: Baltimore shot in L.A.," *Baltimore Sun*, December 5, 1979, B1.
31. Karen Herman, "Jean Stapleton discusses the TV movie 'Aunt Mary,'" Television Academy Foundation Interviews, November 13, 2015. Interview conducted November 28, 2000, https://www.youtube.com/watch?v=vuZ9Vke__JE (accessed January 24, 2023).
32. Rehert, "Mary Dobkin, baseball coach on crutches."
33. Morton I. Katz, "Aunt Mary: 80 Years Young," *Baltimore Sun*, October 9, 1982, A11.
34. Margaret Gers, personal conversation, February 7, 2023. The city of Baltimore demolished the complex in 2004.
35. Rafael Alvarez, "Cronies recall 'Hot Rod Mary' and her love for life," *Baltimore Sun*, August 24, 1987, 1A.

Major and Minor League Occupancy at Cleveland's League Park, 1914–15

Alan Cohen

In 1914 and 1915, for the only time in baseball history, two baseball teams, one a major league team and the other a minor league team, played a full schedule of games in the same ballpark.[1] It came about in an unusual fashion.

A Federal League club, managed by Cy Young, had played at Cleveland's Luna Park in 1913. In that season, the Federal League was considered an independent league. It was in its first season and had started out as a six-team Midwestern league with modest goals. The Cleveland Green Sox finished second in the league with a 64–54 record. Most of the players were unknown and were not a part of the scene beyond 1913 in Cleveland or anywhere else.

Only four members of the 1913 Green Sox 30-man roster were heard from again. John Potts, an outfielder who batted .341 in 92 games, played the 1914 season with Kansas City when the Federal League was recognized as a major league. Frank Rooney, a first baseman who batted .300 in 100 games, played 12 games with Indianapolis in the Federal League the following season. Harry Juul, a pitcher who went 7–7 in 1913, went 0-3 for the Federal League Brooklyn Tip-Tops in 1914. Gil Britton, after batting an unremarkable .211 in 21 games with Cleveland in 1913, completed that season with the Pittsburgh Pirates, appearing in three games. He was hitless in 12 at-bats.

In 1914, the Federal League expanded to eight teams and declared itself a major league, adding teams in Baltimore, Brooklyn, and Buffalo to the holdovers from Chicago, Kansas City, Indianapolis, Pittsburgh, and St. Louis. The Federal League's attempt to put a team in Cleveland in 1914 was pre-empted by owner Charles W. Somers of the Cleveland Naps (now the Guardians) of the American League. Somers had been an owner in the American League since it came to Cleveland in 1900 as a minor league, led the drive that brought Sunday baseball to Cleveland in 1911, and was an early proponent of the farm system. By the end of the 1913 season, the Cleveland minor league chain included teams in Toledo; New Orleans; Portland, Oregon; Ironton, Ohio; and Waterbury, Connecticut. He had

developed a working relationship with manager Walter McCredie of Portland in 1908 and had obtained ownership stakes in the other teams over the next five years.[2]

Somers' intent was to keep a Federal League team with big-league caliber players out of Cleveland. He did not want to compete for the Cleveland fan base. The preemptive move by Somers was to relocate his Toledo team in the minor-league American Association to Cleveland and have two teams—one major league and one minor league—share the fourth incarnation of League Park. The American Association team, known as the Bearcats in 1914 and the Spiders in 1915, had several players with major-league experience. None of them had played with the 1913 Cleveland Green Sox.

In 1914 and 1915, not only did the two teams coexist, but some of the players went back and forth between them. One of those players, Sad Sam Jones, after going 10–4 for the Bearcats in 1914, went on to play 22 seasons in the American League with a career record of 229–217. He went 16–5 for the World Series champion Boston Red Sox in 1918 and 21–8 for the New York Yankees in 1923, their first world championship season.

Somers, along with preempting a Cleveland entry in the Federal League, had been a combatant in the war between the new major league and Organized Baseball. Before the 1914 season, he'd had all he could handle in fighting off the Federal League raid on his pitching staff. The raiders were particularly after his top three pitchers, who had gone a collective 58–33 in 1913. He retained most of his players with higher than usual salaries. The most substantial loss was that of pitcher Cy Falkenberg, who had gone 23–10 in 1913. He went to Indianapolis in the Federal League in 1914. After Falkenberg's departure, rumors circulated that three other pitchers would jump to the new league. Somers opened his wallet and signed Vean Gregg in March. Gregg had been 20–13 in 1913 and would go on to a 9–3 record in 1914.

The most controversial case was that of pitcher Fred Blanding, who had gone 15–10 for the Naps in 1913. Blanding had jumped to Kansas City of the

Federal League but, before the ink was dry, he had second thoughts and returned to Cleveland, setting off a firestorm of legal maneuvering. Kansas City sought to have its contract with Blanding honored but did not prevail in court.[3] Blanding went 4–9 for Cleveland in 1914.

Another pitcher, George Kahler (5–11 in 1913), appeared to have been lured away by the Buffalo team in the Federal League but sent back the advance money and stayed with the Naps. In 1914, he went back and forth between the two Cleveland teams. After starting the season with the Naps and only appearing in two games, he was sent to the American Association, where he went 15–11.

The Naps were coming off a 1913 season that saw them finish third in the American League. Nap Lajoie was still with the team and, at age 38, had batted .335. The top player was Shoeless Joe Jackson, who had batted .373 with 63 extra-base hits.

But the success of 1913 would not carry over.

The Naps began the 1914 season losing their first seven decisions (five in a row by one-run margins) and never recovered. Lajoie was 39 years old and his career, which had begun in 1896, had experienced an inevitable downturn. He joined Cleveland in 1902 and his batting average was .345 in his first 12 seasons with the team.

After opening the season with an 0–7 road trip, the Naps played 12 of their next 15 games at home. When they left Cleveland and turned the ballpark over to the American Association team, their record stood at 7–14 (there had been a 3–3 12-inning tie against the St. Louis Browns on April 30). In the last game before departing, they defeated the Browns and former teammate Bill James, 4–0.

James ((William Henry James, not to be confused with William Lawrence James, who spent four seasons with the Boston Braves), had gone 2–0 in two starts against his former mates in the past two weeks. In 1911 and 1912 with Cleveland, he had done little to distinguish himself. The *Cleveland Plain Dealer* implied that he had spent more time in transit between Cleveland and Toledo than he had spent pitching for the Naps. James was on the long end of the decision in his next game in Cleveland as the Browns won, 10–5, on June 1. During that game, Jackson had his only League Park homer of the season. Unfortunately, his defensive lapses that day contributed to the Browns win.

It was the Deadball era, but the Naps's home run output, especially at home, was anemic even by contemporary standards. They were last in the league in homers with 10, only four of which were hit at League

Park. Jackson's homer on June 1 was the only one that went over the fence. The team finished last with a 51–102 record. It was Cleveland's first season with more than 100 losses since joining the American League in 1900. The franchise did not lose as many games in a season again until 1971.

THE 1914 CLEVELAND SCOUTS, SPIDERS, WARRIORS, SHECKS, AND, FINALLY, BEARCATS

The Mud Hens identity was left in Toledo when the team moved to Cleveland, and it took a while for the club to settle on a name.[4]

They were known as the Scouts, Spiders, Warriors, and Shecks (for manager Jimmy Sheckard) before they officially became the Bearcats on June 21.[5] Cleveland was competitive after getting off to a slow start. The Bearcats, to use the name they settled on, played 24 games on the road at the beginning of the season, and by the time of their home opener on May 14, they were in last place with an 8–16 record. They then proceeded to win 27 of their next 39 to pull within a game of first place.

Due to scheduling issues (the initial schedule was drawn up before the move from Toledo) and park availability, the Bearcats played only 65 of their 166 games at League Park in 1914, of which they won 40. Only six American Association homers were hit at the venue that season (four by the home team), but if the balls did not go a long way, some of the games did—in innings, that is. And runs were scored—most of the time.

In a wild encounter on May 20, the first homers of the American Association League Park season were hit. In a 12-inning win by the unwieldy score of 15–14, Denney Wilie homered for Cleveland (they were the Scouts at the time), and Bunny Brief homered for the Kansas City Blues. Brief's two-run homer capped a five-run second inning that gave Kansas City an early lead. Wilie's three-run homer came in the bottom of the second and closed the gap to 5–4.[6]

Wilie homered again six days later in a losing cause against the Milwaukee Brewers. He played parts of three seasons in the majors and had two big-league homers, both at the Polo Grounds in New York. He was one of the players who shuttled between the American Association and the American League during the 1914–15 period without having to pack a suitcase. In August 1915, he was promoted to the Cleveland American League team, by then known as the Indians. He batted .252 in 45 games as the Indians limped to a 57–95 finish, good for seventh place.

Alfred "Greasy" Neale was hardly a renowned slugger. His only homer of the 1914 season came in his debut, on June 28, in a 5–2 Bearcats win. It was gift-wrapped. Columbus Senators left fielder Bill Hinchman allowed a line drive to "percolate through his legs."[7] Neale is remembered not for his prowess on the diamond but for his genius on the gridiron, where he coached the Philadelphia Eagles to back-to-back NFL championships in 1948–49. But that win in which he homered put Cleveland within two games of first place.

Among the players that Somers kept for the Naps when the Federal League teams were making tempting offers was Jack Lelivelt, the team's top pinch-hitter (9-for-23) in 1913. The Naps brought him into the fold in January 1914.[8] While with the Yankees in 1912, Lelivelt had torn a muscle in his leg. He was limited to pinch-hitting when he joined Cleveland in June 1913. In 1914, he returned to the outfield for the Naps.

On June 25, Lelivelt was sent to the Cleveland Bearcats, becoming one of several players to take the field for each of the two Cleveland teams from 1914 through 1915. Lelivelt was batting .328 when he was sent down, but the minor-league squad had some chance of winning, as opposed to the Naps, whose 1914 season was an unqualified disaster from start to finish. Lelivelt was not happy with the change of team (if not the scenery) and did not report right away. He sat out four games. With the Bearcats, Lelivelt played first base and batted .295 in 92 games. He never returned to the majors.

When Lelivelt began to play, the immediate results were unsatisfactory. The Bearcats lost successive games to the Indianapolis Indians by scores of 9–3 and 15–2. The latter game resulted in a somewhat comedic article by C.L. Kirkpatrick in the *Cleveland Plain Dealer* with the headline "Indians Win in Real Comedy." The first paragraph included a note that "loyal fans enjoyed the merry swat, swat of bat against leather and the sizz and zang of wildly hurled balls" and went on to make light of the lopsided game.[9] Then Louisville came to town and the Bearcats won consecutive doubleheaders on July 4–5 to move into second place. Up and down movement in the standings became an everyday thing, with six teams within 4½ games of each other.

On July 19, the Bearcats were in second place, a game behind Milwaukee, as the Brewers came to Cleveland for a doubleheader. The largest crowd of the season, 10,000, went home happy as the Bearcats won the doubleheader to move into first place by percentage points.[10] When they lost a doubleheader to Milwaukee two days later, they slid to third place. They then went on the road for almost a month and lost further ground, dropping 18 of 30 games and slipping to fifth place. They came home to sparse crowds in September, drawing as little as 200 fans to a doubleheader played in cold weather on September 8. The Bearcats finished the season in fifth place with an 82–81 record.

THE NAPS' FRUSTRATIONS CONTINUE

The Naps were on the road beginning on May 12 and were away from League Park for all but four games before returning home for a long homestand on June 6. They started the homestand in eighth place with a 14–28 record and proceeded to pour gasoline on their own fire, losing five straight. When they defeated the Philadelphia A's, 3–0, on June 11, only 955 fans were in attendance. Bill Steen was the winning pitcher in his only shutout of the season. Writing in the *Cleveland Plain Dealer*, Henry P. Edwards joked that manager Joe Birmingham "was forced to call upon his entire pitching staff, as Bill Steen worked throughout the nine innings."[11] He was not far off the mark: The

League Park as seen from the air. Note the large bleacher section in left field.

STRONGSVILLE PUBLIC LIBRARY/PUBLIC DOMAIN

win was his third in four decisions, and his three wins from May 30 through June 11 were the club's only victories against 10 losses. After the win on June 11, his record stood at 3–3 with an earned-run average of 1.09. Over the full year, he was 9–14 with a team-leading ERA of 2.60.

The Naps were going nowhere in the standings and looked for help from their farm system. Not only were players shuttled back and forth between the Naps and the Bearcats, but Somers drew on his relationships with other minor-league teams, including the one in Waterbury, Connecticut.

Elmer Smith was 21 years old in 1914 and began the season with Waterbury in the Class B Eastern Association. He batted .332 in 93 games and was promoted to the Bearcats on August 19. He played in 23 American Association games and batted .311. Smith's ascendance was complete when he advanced to the Naps and made his major-league debut on September 20. He appeared in 13 games with the Naps and batted .321. He had two or more hits six times and, on September 29, his three hits led the Naps to a 10–4 win over the Chicago White Sox. Unfortunately, his performance had nominal impact as the Naps only improved to 50–100 with that victory.

As the 1914 season drew to its close, Lajoie was closing in on his 3,000th hit. In the first game of a doubleheader on September 27 at League Park, he went 2-for-3 with a pair of doubles as the Naps defeated the Yankees, 5–3, bringing his career hit count to 3,001.[12]

They were his last hits with Cleveland. He was given the second game off. Three days later, in his Cleveland swan song, he appeared as a pinch-hitter against Chicago and walked.

The first game on September 27 was notable for another reason. Pitcher Guy Morton, who had begun the season on the Waterbury farm club, posting an 8–1 record, earned his first win with the Naps—after 13 losses. He had been promoted in June and, despite posting a 3.23 ERA, had lost 13 decisions in 24 appearances. The following season, Morton improved to 16–15.

Toward the end of the 1914 season, there was speculation, fueled by an article in *Sporting Life*, that the Federal League's Kansas City Packers would move to Cleveland.[13] The speculation was just that. The Packers stayed put in 1915.

The biggest change in 1915 involved financial reversals suffered by Cleveland owner Somers. Money woes plagued the ballclub as they drew only 185,977 fans in 1914 (worst in the American League), and Somers still had to cover the expenses of the American Association team. Not only had his Cleveland baseball

teams not done well in 1914, but his non-baseball interests, particularly in the coal industry, experienced a reversal of fortune. His liabilities were estimated in the range of $1.75 million.[14] A committee of bankers from Cleveland, Buffalo, and Elyria, Ohio, moved to establish cost-cutting measures to keep Somers afloat. Lajoie was sold to the A's, which cut the team payroll. Somers also cut the scouting staff, dismissing Charlie Hickman, Bill Reidy, Jack McAllister, and Bade Myers.[15] The 1915 payroll was only $50,000.

After two years in the Eastern Association, Somers sold off his interest in the Waterbury team.[16] The decision had come before Somers' financial woes became public. The *Hartford Courant* wrote on September 6, 1914: "The Cleveland club is tired of its bargain and is anxious to dispose of the franchise, and it will be on the market this fall waiting for a buyer. Moreover, it is hinted that it will not take any great lump of money to secure the franchise."[17] Baseball-wise, Waterbury had been a success. The team finished 70–61 in 1913 and 69–51 in 1914. Five members of the 1914 team moved up to the Indians, including manager Lee Fohl, who became a Cleveland coach in 1915.

On January 16, 1915, the Bearcats became the Spiders, and the Naps were renamed the Indians. The teams again shared League Park, which was renamed Somers Park. The Spiders had a new manager in 1915: Jack Knight replaced Sheckard at the helm. The Indians retained Joe Birmingham.

On the way back from spring training, the teams played each other in Louisville, and the Indians won, 3–2. Missing from the Indians lineup was Jackson, who had sprained his ankle. He healed in time to play in every regular-season game through June 1. Once up north, both teams got off to bad starts. The Spiders, plagued by bad pitching, were in sixth place for a good part of the season. Nick Carter and Lefty James (yet another Bill James: William L. James) were the only reliable pitchers.

The Spiders were the first of the Cleveland teams to play at Somers Park in 1915 and began the season with a 3–3 homestand. When they took to the road, their fortunes worsened, and by the time they returned to Cleveland for a Memorial Day doubleheader, they were 14–17. After losing the holiday pair to Indianapolis, another road trip beckoned. They limped home with a record at 14–21.

They then feasted on home cooking, winning seven of eight games, including five in a row from June 6 through June 11. This boosted their record to 21–22. On June 9, they staged a spectacular ninth-inning rally to defeat Minneapolis, 12–11. In that game, Billy

LIBRARY OF CONGRESS BAIN COLLECTION

Sad Sam Jones, after going 10–4 for the Bearcats in 1914, pitched for the Cleveland Indians in 1914 and 1915. In all he spent 22 seasons in the American League with a career record of 229–217.

Southworth had two triples and two singles, one of which drove in a run in the six-run ninth inning.[18] After that, Southworth, who was batting .336 through his first 40 games, was promoted from the Spiders to the Indians. The need for the immediate promotion was fueled by arm problems that had caused Jackson to be out of the starting lineup since June 4.[19] The Indians defeated Philadelphia on June 9, but they, like the Spiders, were under .500. Southworth joined a team that was in sixth place with a 19–24 record.

Amid reports that the Spiders were being transferred back to Toledo, they went on a road trip in mid-June during which they lost two no-hitters. However, they won 10 of the 16 games on the trip and came home at the beginning of July to sweep Columbus in two straight doubleheaders and climb to the dizzying heights of third place. The move to Toledo fell through and so did the move to the first division: The Spiders went on a long road trip in July, and when they returned to Cleveland, they were in sixth place once again.

The Indians, having finished last in 1914, got off to a bad start in 1915. Jackson was batting .358 through 28 games but he was just about the only bright spot in the lineup. After starting the year 7–9, the Indians began a long homestand on May 1. They dropped seven of the first 12 games of that stand, and Birmingham was fired as manager on May 21.

Owner Somers was in no rush to replace him. When speculation arose that he would choose George McBride, then with the Washington Nationals, Somers said, "For the present, I am in no hurry to appoint a manager for my ball club. I am willing to admit that I have talked to [Clark] Griffith about McBride, but we have come to no terms."[20] Coach Lee Fohl ran the team in the interim. Reports had Somers considering Spiders skipper Knight as a replacement, but Fohl stayed on as manager into the 1919 season.

CONTINUING FRUSTRATIONS FOR SPIDERS

Long road trips were the norm for the Spiders in 1915, and like their nineteenth century namesake that finished the 1899 season with a 20–134 record (11–101 on the road), they played far more games outside of Cleveland than at home. *The Sporting News* on July 15 wrote:

> Knight's team has played a great many of its games on the road. The Spiders practically haven't a home town. Cleveland fans are not strong for them by any means and they were always compelled to play second fiddle to the American League team. Then the talk about transferring the club to Toledo was brought up and then the players' salaries were sliced. Outside of that, Knight didn't have a thing to buck up against, and yet he has had his men fighting day in and day out.[22]

The original 154-game schedule called for only 65 Spiders home games due to the lack of local interest and the club losing money. Even some of those games were switched to opponents' cities, meaning only 50 games were played in Cleveland, with the Spiders posting a 24–26 record. Just as it had been in 1914, the long ball was all but invisible at Somers Park for the American Association games. Only four homers were hit there all season, two by the Spiders.

The first homer at Cleveland during the American Association season came off the bat of Southworth on April 20. Southworth spent the bulk of his career in the National League, and each of his 52 career big-league homers was hit in the National League. In July 1913, he was acquired by the Naps and appeared in one game before being sent to Toledo. He spent 1914 with the Bearcats. After joining the Indians following his terrific start with the Spiders, he batted .220 in 60 games. By the end of August, when he was sent to Portland of the Pacific Coast League, the Indians were 46–74 and battling for sixth place with the St. Louis Browns.

Adding to the Indians' on-field woes had been the loss of outfielder Jack Graney, who broke a bone in his leg against Washington on July 20 and was out of the starting lineup until August 21. By then, the team's fate in the standings was pretty much a certainty. There was some talk of moving Billy Nixon, who had played under Fohl at Waterbury, up from the Spiders, but Nixon never got an opportunity to play in the big leagues.[23]

The Indians lost successive doubleheaders to the Detroit Tigers at Somers Park on August 16–17 to fall to 41–66.

At that point in the season, the crowd of 4,150 fans who showed up for the first of those doubleheaders constituted a mob, and they were treated to classic inefficiency by the home team. In the first game, the Tigers stole eight bases, victimizing Cleveland catcher Ben Egan, and won, 6–2.

The second game featured one of the best pitching performances of the season—albeit by Detroit pitcher Bernie Boland. The Tigers, helped along by a Bill Wambsganss error when Egan finally found the range with one of his throws to second base, took a 2–0 lead in the fourth inning, and the Indians scored one in their half. Ray Chapman was hit by a pitch, the ball bouncing off his head and into the grandstand. Chapman stole second and advanced to third on a passed ball by the Detroit catcher. After Jackson walked, putting runners at the corners, Cleveland tried a double steal. Tigers shortstop Donie Bush intercepted the throw from the catcher and threw to third. The throw went over everything, and Chapman scored.[24]

Boland did not allow a hit until there were two outs in the eighth inning, and the hit came from an unlikely source. Nineteen-year-old Ben Paschal, who had spent his first professional season with Dothan, Alabama, in the Class D Florida-Alabama-Georgia League, had just been called up by the Indians. He was sent up to pinch-hit for pitcher Rip Hagerman. In his second major-league at-bat, Paschal singled to center field. It was the only hit of the game as Detroit won, 3–1.

The following day, Detroit won by scores of 10–3 and 7–3 in front of 2,462 fans.

At the conclusion of play on August 20, a white-washing at the hands of Washington, Somers, to survive financially, traded Jackson to the Chicago White Sox.[25] Jackson was batting .327 at the time and the price was estimated at $25,000 plus three White Sox players.[26]

By the time the Indians left Somers Park for a road trip at the end of August, they were in seventh place with a 45–74 record. The Spiders stayed on the road and did not return to Cleveland until September 12. They limped home in seventh place with at 62–78.

After taking two of three from St. Paul, the Spiders welcomed Kansas City and old friend Lelivelt for a doubleheader on September 15. The Spiders won the first game, 4–1, to give them a 3–1 record for the homestand. In the nightcap—a real nightcap as darkness due to an impending storm caused play to be stopped after seven innings—the Spiders lost, 4–2. The second Somers Park homer of the 1915 minor-league season was hit in the second game by Lelivelt.

The final two Somers Park minor-league homers were belted in the Spiders' last home game, against Minneapolis on September 18. Cleveland manager Knight, who would lead his team with four homers, hit one as his team lost, 9–4, in a game that clinched the pennant for Minneapolis. Wally Smith homered for the victorious Millers. The Spiders played the balance of the schedule on the road and finished in seventh place with a 67–82 record.

Jay Kirke was perhaps the longest-tenured player to play for both the Bearcats/Spiders and Naps/Indians. His career began in 1906 in the low minors. He made his first big-league appearance in 1910 in a handful of games with Detroit. In both 1914 and 1915, he began the season with Cleveland in the American Association and was called up to the majors in midseason. Other than 17 games with the New York Giants in 1918, Kirke spent the rest of his career in the minors, retiring after the 1927 season.

The Indians spent most of the last month or so of the 1915 season on the road, playing only five games at home after August 29, with estimated attendance figures of ranging from 650, twice, to 2,150. They finished the season in seventh place with a 57–95 record. Total attendance for the season was 159,285, sixth in the American League.

BEYOND 1915

After the season, the Federal League disbanded as two owners bought AL/NL franchises (Chicago Cubs and St. Louis Browns), and a financial settlement was reached with the other Federal League owners. In Cleveland, with no potential threat from the Federal League and Somers under mounting financial pressures, it was decided that he would give up his interest in the Spiders.[27] In 1916, the Spiders returned to Toledo. Somers continued as owner of the Indians—but not for long.

Somers' problems had not been helped by the record of his American League team in 1914 and 1915. After finishing in third place with an 86–66 record in 1913, the team had fallen on hard times, with 102- and 95-loss seasons the next two years. Even with the absence of a Federal League rival, the attendance plummeted, and Somers' woes did not abate.

Remember Joe Birmingham? The manager fired by Somers sued for $20,000 in back wages and damages. The matter was settled out of court in late February 1916. By that point, Somers was no longer the owner of the team.[28]

It was announced on February 17, 1916, that railroad executive James C. Dunn would head up a group that would purchase the club, which had fallen into receivership. On March 11, it was announced that the new ownership would abandon its farm system.[29] Somers' advocacy of the practice was long forgotten when Branch Rickey built his Cardinals powerhouse on the farm system in the upcoming decades.

Somers' legacy was unintended. The hiring of Lee Fohl, the only manager he could afford (Fohl's pay did not change when he was promoted from coach to manager), wound up working out well for the Indians. When Dunn bought the team, he retained Fohl. As the Indians improved in 1916, reaching sixth place and the .500 mark, writer Frank Menke remarked, "Fohl, with the genius that is his, rooted out the dissension that had wrecked the club earlier, brought order out of chaos, cured the 'soreheads,' and brought about harmonious conditions."[30]

Fohl was fired in 1919 after starting the season 44–34, and was replaced by Tris Speaker. In 1920, Speaker, as both manager and star center fielder, led the Indians to the World Series championship, the first in the history of the franchise. ■

Acknowledgment

The author thanks Don Jensen for his review of the initial manuscript of this story.

Sources

In addition to the sources shown in the endnotes, the author used Baseball Reference, Retrosheet, and:

"Kilfoyl Quips Naps – Sells Share to Somers, Latter Now Owning Club Alone," *Washington Post*, July 27, 1910, 8.

Menke, Frank G. "Big Question of Day is Whether Fellow Magnates Will Help," *Oregon Sunday Journal*, January 17, 1915, 19.

Rainey, Chris, "Guy Morton," SABR, https://sabr.org/bioproj/person/738c6571.

Schuld, Fred. "Charles Somers," SABR, https://sabr.org/bioproj/person/ee856cc8.

Wancho, Joseph. "Greasy Neale," SABR, https://sabr.org/bioproj/person/6481237f.

Notes

1. Other cities have had major-league and minor-league baseball at the same time but in different ballparks. Five cities (Indianapolis, Kansas City, Buffalo, Baltimore, and Newark) had both a Federal League and minor-league presence at the same time.

2. "Portland's Friend in Major Leagues," *Oregon Sunday Journal*, December 7, 1913, 3–2.

3. "Somers Makes Answer to President Gilmore," *Hartford Courant*, March 4, 1914, 16.

4. Toledo, despite the move of its American Association team, did have professional baseball in 1914. The newly founded Southern Michigan League put one of its 10 teams in Toledo, and Somers owned that team as well as the teams in Cleveland. See "Toledo Franchise in Southern Michigan League Said to be Owned by Charles Somers," *Cincinnati Enquirer*, March 20, 1914, 6. The Toledo Mud Hens finished in eighth place and did not return to the Southern Michigan League in 1915. The league itself did not have prolonged success, folding in July 1915. Other than 1956–64, the 1915 season was the only one in the twentieth century during which Toledo did not have professional baseball.

5. "'Bearcats' New Name for Sheckard's Crew," *Cleveland Plain Dealer*, June 22, 1914, 10.

6. C.L. Kirkpatrick, "Scouts Take Real Batfest," *Cleveland Plain Dealer*, May 21, 1914, 11.

7. Kirkpatrick, "Bearcats Win, then it Rains," *Cleveland Plain Dealer*, June 29, 1914, 9.

8. "Sweeney Joins Feds," *Cincinnati Enquirer*, January 24, 1914, 6.

9. Kirkpatrick, "Indians Win in Real Comedy," *Cleveland Plain Dealer*, July 4, 1914, 9.

10. Kirkpatrick, "Bearcats in First Place by Twice Beating Brewers," *Cleveland Plain Dealer*, July 20, 1914, 9–10.

11. Henry P. Edwards, "Naps Reward Small Bank of Loyal Fans by Winning," *Cleveland Plain Dealer*, June 12, 1914, 13.

12. "Lajoie Third Player to Make 3,000 Hits," *Cleveland Plain Dealer*, September 28, 1914, 9.

13. Ed Bano, "Plea for Peace: The Cleveland Club an Object Lesson as to the Cost of War - Why the Organized Ball and Federal League Powers Should Get Together," *Sporting Life*, August 29, 1914, 9–10.

14. "Ball Club Owner Fails," *The New York Times*, January 1, 1915, 12.

15. "Timely Baseball Bits," *Hartford Courant*, February 5, 1915, 20.

16. "O'Rourke Boosting Waterbury Club: Somers, Owner of Franchise, Has Gone into Bankruptcy," *Hartford Courant*, January 2, 1915, 20.

17. "O'Rourke Blind to M'Cann's Methods," *Hartford Courant*, September 6, 1914, 2–3.

18. Kirkpatrick, "Terrific Rally in Ninth Inning Defeats Millers," *Cleveland Plain Dealer*, June 10, 1915, 13.

19. "Southworth Goes; Spiders Get Player," *Cleveland Plain Dealer*, June 10, 1915, 13.

20. William Peet, "George McBride Slated to Manage the Indians," *Washington Herald*, May 22, 1915, 9.

21. Edwards, "Somers May be Watching Knight for Indian Pilot," *Cleveland Plain Dealer*, May 30, 1915, 15.

22. George Biggers, "Grand Upset for Association Fans," *The Sporting News*, July 15, 1915, 2.

23. "Nixon May be Seen with Naps," *Hartford Courant*, July 23, 1915, 16.

24. Edwards, "Indians Twice Beaten in Double Bill by Detroit," *Cleveland Plain Dealer*, August 17, 1915, 9. This was, of course, a foreshadowing of a similar beaning of Chapman in 1920 that resulted in his death.

25. Edwards, "Comiskey is Kind Indeed to Somers," *The Sporting News*, August 26, 1915, 4.

26. Edwards, "Joe Jackson Goes to White Sox in Baseball Deal," *Cleveland Plain Dealer*, August 21, 1915, 10.

27. Edwards, "Fellow Magnates Rally to Somers," *The Sporting News*, December 23, 1915, 1.

28. "Joe Settles with Cleveland Indians," *Grand Rapids Press*, February 26, 1916, 14.

29. "Will Cut Out Farms," *Washington Evening Star*, March 12, 1916, 5–2.

30. Frank G. Menke, "Busher Manager Proves a Master," *Omaha Sunday Bee*, September 3, 1916, 4-S.

The Ill-Fated Dodgers and Indians World Baseball Tour of 1952

Matthew Jacob

Abe Saperstein is best known as the founder of the Harlem Globetrotters basketball team, but he also was deeply involved in baseball. During the 1930s, Saperstein worked as a promoter, publicist, and agent who booked barnstorming games for Negro Leagues teams. He was also a co-owner of the Birmingham Black Barons.[1] Saperstein is known by baseball historians for his role in helping Satchel Paige become the first Black pitcher in the American League in 1948.[2] This article details one of Saperstein's most ambitious but ill-fated schemes: a baseball world tour at the height of the Cold War.

In 1950, Saperstein validated his basketball team's name by leading his squad on the first of many trips abroad. Overseas tours by the Globetrotters and other Black athletes were actively supported by the US State Department, which saw these trips as a subtle way to counter communist rhetoric that highlighted racial discrimination in the United States.[3] With the State Department's cooperation, Saperstein drafted plans for a similar tour by big-league baseball teams in 1952, but his bold idea has been largely forgotten.

Indeed, the profile of Saperstein that the Society for American Baseball Research published in 2017 does not mention his proposed tour—a trip that one sports editor called "the most ambitious barnstorming tour in the history of baseball."[4]

Bill Veeck, Hank Greenberg, and Abe Saperstein.

DOLPH BRISCOE CENTER FOR AMERICAN HISTORY

Saperstein's plan called for the Brooklyn Dodgers and Cleveland Indians to play a series of 22 games over a 60-day schedule.[5] The tour was to begin in Hawaii during the autumn of 1952 and continue in Japan, India, Egypt, Australia, and North Africa.[6] Hideo Kurosaki, a Japanese baseball official, said the two-team tour "would do more to help baseball in Japan than tours by all-star groups."[7]

The tour idea had been contrived in 1948 by Indians owner Bill Veeck, a longtime Saperstein pal.[8] That year, while Saperstein worked for the Indians as a scout of Negro League players, he and Veeck discussed a tour abroad that would feature the Indians playing the New York Giants. Yet the Indians won the pennant and the World Series that year, and the suspense of that season distracted the duo from advancing their plan.[9]

Three years later, in the spring of 1951, Veeck was no longer in Cleveland. The succeeding general manager, Hank Greenberg, was interested in pursuing Saperstein's tour, but discussions between the Indians and Giants did not bear fruit.[10] By the following year, the Giants' enthusiasm had waned. However, Saperstein learned that the Dodgers were interested.[11]

The Indians and Dodgers emerged as the teams for the 1952 tour based largely on Saperstein's connections. But the Globetrotters owner also knew these two teams would be welcomed by the State Department. After all, the Dodgers and Indians had been the first racially integrated teams in their respective leagues. This was the height of the Cold War, and Secretary of State Dean Acheson referred to this dynamic as a key reason why the government would back the proposed tour. Because both teams had players "of every nationality, creed, and color," he wrote, the trip would attest to America's democratic values.[12] By the start of the that season, only six teams in the American and National Leagues had integrated.[13] And the Dodgers and Indians featured six of the 13 Black players who were on league rosters in 1952.[14]

State Department officials believed the Dodgers-Indians tour was so relevant to US foreign policy that they briefed Joseph Feeney, a close aide to President

Harry Truman. In a memo to Feeney, the department wrote that the baseball tour should give foreign nations a positive impression similar to the one created by recent Globetrotters trips.[15] The memo added that the tour "would contribute materially to 'The Campaign of Truth' campaign," an initiative launched by Truman to counter Soviet propaganda.[16]

The Sporting News described Saperstein as "the leg-man on the deal, having done most of the work in setting up the itinerary."[17] He viewed sports tours as a vehicle to reduce friction during the Cold War. "It doesn't make any difference whether it's in this country or overseas," he said. "Sports ease tensions."[18] Saperstein contended that a Dodgers-Indians tour "could do a lot to restore whatever prestige we have lost in foreign countries."[19]

The Dodgers-Indians tour would have been the first prolonged tour abroad by two big-league teams since 1913–14, when the Giants and Chicago White Sox played a series of games that began in Tokyo and concluded in London.[20]

Saperstein tried to manage the teams' expectations, stating publicly that the tour's expenses would be too high to generate a profit. "But it will do baseball a lot of good and do the country a lot of good," he said, adding that the trip would be a "high class" venture.[21]

The cost of the tour was estimated at $500,000, and the owners of the Dodgers and Indians wanted the games to generate sufficient revenue to at least cover their expenses.[22] "We would like the trip to carry its own load," said Dodgers President Walter O'Malley.[23]

Saperstein's effort faced challenges from all directions. Soon after he publicly disclosed his plans, attempts were made to change the itinerary.

Perhaps inspired by his ancestral roots, O'Malley wanted the tour to start in Brooklyn and conclude in Dublin, Ireland. During a discussion that April, Saperstein countered with a compromise itinerary, but O'Malley left the meeting sounding pessimistic about the tour, citing concerns that his players might have "other commitments" after the 1952 season.[24]

As the summer of 1952 began, momentum seemed to build for the tour. Commissioner Ford C. Frick expressed his support for the trip.[25] And a journalist reported that President Truman had given the tour his "blessing."[26] Grandiose ideas were floated among State Department officials and with Saperstein. There was even talk of adding a game in Rome and arranging for Yankees star Joe DiMaggio to make an appearance in the Eternal City.[27]

Yet Italy wasn't the only country the State Department wished to add to the itinerary. Mexico, the

Philippines, and Spain were among the nations that diplomatic leaders wanted to include.[28] Records from the National Archives reveal a steady stream of cables between the State Department and US diplomats abroad, exploring the potential for playing baseball games in a variety of countries where the population knew little or nothing about the sport. These documents reveal the numerous financial and logistical hurdles that complicated the tour.

US embassy staff informed the State Department that in many countries the Dodgers and Indians would not be able to convert the local currency they received into US dollars. In addition, the Dodgers and Indians would have to pay luxury taxes and other surcharges—such as Spain's "protection of minors" tax—before departing these nations.[29] Obviously, these dynamics would make it difficult for the teams to cover their expenses.

Attendance was another major concern among diplomats. For example, the US embassy in Lisbon conveyed a message of caution: "In view of fact that baseball is virtually unknown in Portugal, there are doubts [about] possible financial returns of venture."[30] Greeks were unfamiliar with baseball, prompting the US embassy in Athens to project that a local Dodgers-Indians game would produce no more than $700 of revenue.[31]

Adding Cuba to the tour would have given the Dodgers and Indians a baseball-loving audience, but the US embassy in Havana reported that leasing a stadium and paying other costs might leave the teams with no more than 47 percent of the box office revenue.[32]

While discussions continued about the itinerary, Commissioner Frick announced on the eve of the 1952 All-Star Game that baseball owners had voted to authorize the trip. They also relaxed a rule that prohibited players from participating in barnstorming tours more than 30 days after the end of the World Series.[33] The owners' unanimous vote, wrote a sports editor, was a tribute to Saperstein: "It proved the high regard and respect major league moguls have for the portly promoter." O'Malley said he was "elated" by the vote, and the Indians' Greenberg added: "I can hardly wait to get going."[34]

However, the ballplayers had not yet weighed in. A *Detroit Free Press* columnist explained why the players should be enthused about the tour, using language that was common in that era. "Fact is," he wrote, "up to right now the biggest selling point the whole deal offers the players is that they not only will be given a two-month trip around the world but will be allowed to take their wives with them to forestall any screams of loneliness which would be certain to come if the little woman were left at home."[35]

Meanwhile, as the summer progressed, Saperstein and the State Department encountered several non-financial challenges, including logistics.

In one cable, embassy officials in Beirut, Lebanon, informed the State Department that "only curious wld be attracted; without traditional Amer peanuts and crackerjack environment." More significantly, the embassy explained that no existing facility in Beirut could accommodate baseball, and a hastily built ballpark would be "costly, very inferior, and physically dangerous" for players.[36] In Athens, the only suitable stadium for baseball would have provided a distance of only 210 feet down one foul line.[37] A feast for hitters but a nightmare for pitchers.

Although the State Department recommended that a game be played in Singapore, US diplomats there warned that the tropical weather conditions were unpredictable year-round. The diplomats cautioned that heavy rain showers "sometimes drench parts of city [while] leaving others sunny."[38]

Efforts to schedule one or more baseball games in the Philippines were undermined by a controversy surrounding the man hand-picked by Saperstein to serve as the tour's local sponsor. The embassy in Manila disclosed that the sponsor "is well-known throughout [the Philippines] as head of notorious gambling syndicate," and for this reason, embassy officials wanted to stop exploring the feasibility for a game to be played there.[39]

Yet of all the obstacles, the one that primarily doomed the tour arose in Cleveland. In late August, Indians officials presented the tour plans to their team, and several players objected.[40] It isn't known which of the team's players said they would not participate and what reasons each of them gave, but newspaper articles offered some clues. Earlier that summer, Al Rosen, Bob Lemon, Bobby Avila, and Jim Hegan had voiced concerns about the trip. Rosen said the tour's departure date conflicted with his wedding plans.[41] A United Press journalist wrote that Lemon and Avila "expect to become fathers before long and prefer to stay in this country."[42] Press reports did not disclose why Hegan frowned on the trip.[43] *The Sporting News* suggested that some players might have preferred the revenue that would come from a domestic barnstorming tour.[44]

While future Hall of Famer Bob Feller was supportive of the tour, the four known objectors on the Indians roster were key players. Rosen and Avila made up half of Cleveland's infield and were crucial weapons for the team's offense. Rosen had driven in over 100 runs in each of the previous two seasons, and

Abe Saperstein, sports entrepreneur, created the Harlem Globetrotters and is widely credited with pioneering the three-point shot in basketball.

DOLPH BRISCOE CENTER FOR AMERICAN HISTORY

Avila led the Indians in batting average in 1951. Lemon anchored Cleveland's pitching staff and had won at least 20 games in three of the past four seasons.[45]

After his team voted, Greenberg reported that only seven of the Indians players were willing to commit to the tour.[46] Even if that number had been higher, it would have been unthinkable for Cleveland to participate in the tour without Rosen, Lemon, Avila, and Hegan.

Because the players on each team had to give their approval, the Indians' resistance created a roadblock.[47] Still, Saperstein wasn't ready to give up. O'Malley and the Dodgers remained willing to embark on the trip, so Saperstein turned his attention to finding a team to replace Cleveland on the tour. While Saperstein was a stockholder of the St. Louis Browns, he probably assumed the Dodgers would not be enthused about playing weeks of baseball against that struggling club. The Browns had averaged 98 losses over the previous four seasons.

In August, Saperstein set his sights on the Yankees to fill the Indians' slot. If the Bronx Bombers weren't interested in the tour, the persistent Saperstein had a backup plan. "If not [the Yanks], I think we can round up a representative group of American Leaguers and make it a Brooklyn vs. American League all-stars deal," he suggested. Saperstein's optimism was contagious, prompting a national sportswriter to assert that "an all-star team is sure to be recruited."[48]

It isn't known whether the Yankees owners or players ever gave the tour serious consideration. The logistical hurdles of forming an all-star squad to travel with the Dodgers were too formidable, and Saperstein's tour plans disintegrated.

Although the original cost of the tour was estimated at $500,000, that total rose to $700,000 after Saperstein and his contacts more closely evaluated likely expenses.[49] On September 3, O'Malley issued a statement to the media saying the Dodgers wouldn't participate in the tour. Instead of citing the objections of Cleveland's players and the inability to find a replacement team, O'Malley cited financial issues. "The many economic problems cannot be solved in the short time available," he said.[50] O'Malley told the State Department he wanted to carry out the overseas tour in 1953, but the plan never regained momentum.[51]

While Saperstein was disappointed that his idea died, he had no time to dwell on the bad news. When O'Malley released his statement, Saperstein was traveling with the Globetrotters abroad and seeking,[52] as he once put it, to "do a job of propaganda for the American way."[53] ■

Notes

1. Neil Lanctot, *Negro League Baseball: The Rise and Ruin of a Black Institution* (Philadelphia: University of Pennsylvania Press, 2004), 114, 145.
2. Lanctot, 336.
3. Damion L. Thomas, *Globetrotting: African American Athletes and Cold War Politics* (Urbana: University of Illinois Press, 2012), 45–50.
4. Norm King, "Abe Saperstein," in *Bittersweet Goodbye: The Black Barons, the Grays, and the 1948 Negro League World Series*, ed. Frederick C. Bush and Bill Nowlin (Phoenix: SABR, 2017), https://sabr.org/bioproj/person/abe-saperstein; Joe Anzivino, "Dodgers-Indians Honolulu Series Planned for Next October," Honolulu Star-Bulletin, February 6, 1952, 20.
5. Red McQueen, "Why Brooks Dropped World Tour," *Honolulu Advertiser*, September 10, 1952, 10.
6. Mark Langill, "Dodgers— International Baseball Overview," WalterOMalley.com, https://www.walteromalley.com/en/dodger-history/international-relations/Overview_Page-1.
7. Anzivino, *Honolulu Star-Bulletin*, February 6, 1952.
8. Lyall Smith, "Dodgers, Indians Set for Grand Tour of World," *Detroit Free Press*, July 9, 1952, 16.
9. Jimmy Cannon, "Jimmy Cannon Says," *Newsday* (Hempstead, New York), July 11, 1952, 42.
10. "Flock May Tour Australia," *Brooklyn Eagle*, March 18, 1952, 15.
11. Cannon, *Newsday*, July 11, 1952.
12. Memorandum for Mr. Joseph Feeney: Proposed 1952 World Tour of the Cleveland Indians and Brooklyn Dodgers Baseball Clubs, May 15, 1952, National Archives, 811.4533/5-1552.
13. Bill Ladson, "These players integrated each MLB team," MLB.com, August 14, 2020, https://www.mlb.com/news/players-who-broke-color-barrier-for-every-team.
14. Peter Dreier, "The Real Story of Baseball's Integration That You Won't See in 42," *The Atlantic*, April 11, 2013, https://www.theatlantic.com/entertainment/archive/2013/04/the-real-story-of-baseballs-integration-that-you-wont-see-in-i-42-i/274886/. Dreier states that only six big-league teams had any Black players by 1952: the Dodgers, Giants, Braves, White Sox, Browns, and Indians. Although a total of 20 players had crossed the color line by then, only 13 were active that season, with some having left/retired by then, while others were in military service.
15. Memorandum for Mr. Joseph Feeney, National Archives.
16. Memorandum for Mr. Joseph Feeney, National Archives; Harry S. Truman, Address on foreign policy at a luncheon of the American Society of Newspaper Editors, April 20, 1950, Harry S. Truman Library & Museum, https://www.trumanlibrary.gov/library/public-papers/92/address-foreign-policy-luncheon-american-society-newspaper-editors.
17. Oscar Ruhl, "From the Ruhl Book," *The Sporting News*, July 23, 1952, 16.
18. Cannon, *Newsday*, July 11, 1952.
19. Smith, "Dodgers, Indians Set for Grand Tour of World."
20. Tom Clavin, "The Inside Story of Baseball's Grand World Tour of 1914," *Smithsonian*, March 21, 2014, https://www.smithsonianmag.com/history/inside-story-baseballs-grand-world-tour-1914-180950228/.
21. Cannon, *Newsday*, July 11, 1952.
22. Cable from US State Department to US embassies, July 19, 1952, National Archives, 811.4533/7-1952.
23. Langill, "Dodgers— International Baseball Overview."
24. Oscar Ruhl, "From the Ruhl Book," *The Sporting News*, April 2, 1952, 14.
25. Associated Press, "Majors Plan Bonus Study," *Fort Worth Star-Telegram*, July 8, 1952, 29.
26. Jim Schlemmer, "Leagues OK Indian-Dodger World Tour," *Akron Beacon Journal*, July 8, 1952, 50.
27. Cable from US embassy in Rome, Italy, to the US Secretary of State, July 18, 1952, National Archives, VR-351.
28. Airgram from Dean Acheson to American Legation, Beirut, Lebanon, July 31, 1952, National Archives, 811.4533/7-3152.
29. Cable from the US Embassy in Madrid, Spain, to the US State Department, July 30, 1952, National Archives, 811.4533/7-1952.
30. Cable from US embassy in Lisbon, Portugal, to US Secretary of State Dean Acheson, July 30, 1952, National Archives, 811.4533/7-2452.
31. Cable from the US Embassy in Athens, Greece, to the US State Department, July 29, 1952, National Archives, 811.4533/7-1952.
32. Dispatch from US embassy in Havana, Cuba, to US State Department, July 29, 1952, National Archives, 811.4533/7-2952.
33. Langill, "Dodgers—International Baseball Overview."
34. Joe Anzivino, "Dodger-Indian World Tour Approved; Plans Include 3-Game Honolulu Stand," *Honolulu Star-Bulletin*, July 22, 1952, 14.
35. Smith, "Dodgers, Indians Set for Grand Tour of World."
36. Cable from the US Embassy in Beirut, Lebanon, to the US State Department, August 16, 1952, National Archives, 811.4533/7-1952.
37. Cable from the US Embassy in Athens, Greece, to the US State Department, July 29, 1952, National Archives, 811.4533/7-1952.
38. Cable from US embassy in Singapore to US Secretary of State Dean Acheson, August 13, 1952, National Archives, 811.4533/7-1952.
39. Cable from US embassy in Manila, Philippines, to US Secretary of State Dean Acheson, September 4, 1952, National Archives, 811.4533/032511.96.
40. Tom Siler, "Mama Likes Football—If Junior Doesn't Get Hurt; Faust Scouts Tide Again," *Knoxville News-Sentinel*, August 27, 1952, 16.
41. United Press, "World Tour for Two Clubs," *Greenville* (Ohio) *Daily Advocate*, July 8, 1952, 9.
42. United Press.
43. Schlemmer, "Leagues OK Indian-Dodger World Tour."
44. "State Department Clears Dodgers' Proposed Tour," *The Sporting News*, August 27, 1952, 2.
45. "Cleveland Guardians Team History and Encyclopedia," Baseball Reference, https://www.baseball-reference.com/teams/CLE/.
46. Jack McDonald, "Yanks Now Sought for Globe Tour," *The Sporting News*, August 27, 1952, 1.
47. International News Service, "Indians-Brooklyn World Tour OK'd by Commissioner," *Sandusky Register Star News*, July 8, 1952, 12.
48. Jack McDonald, "Yanks Now Sought for Globe Tour," *The Sporting News*, August 27, 1952, 1.
49. Red McQueen, "Why Brooks Dropped World Tour," *Honolulu Advertiser*, September 10, 1952, 10.
50. Memorandum from Marilyn C. Jones to Files, US State Department, September 4, 1952, National Archives, 811.4533/9-452.
51. Memorandum from Marilyn C. Jones to Files, US State Department, September 4, 1952, National Archives, 811.4533/9-452.
52. Don Doane, Associated Press, "Globetrotters Spread Gospel of Basketball on World Tour," *Standard Star* (New Rochelle, New York), September 4, 1952, 24.
53. John Mooney, "Pioneered Hawaii Junket," *Salt Lake Tribune*, December 27, 1953, 19.

"Death to Flying Things"

The Life and Times of a Spurious Nickname

Richard Hershberger

"Death to Flying Things" is one of the all-time great baseball nicknames, routinely included in lists of such things. Indeed, it serves double duty, attributed to two players: Robert Ferguson and John Chapman. Ferguson joined the Atlantic Club of Brooklyn in 1866 and played for various clubs through 1884. He managed clubs into 1887 and died in 1894, aged 49. Chapman was of the same generation. He also played for the Atlantics in the 1860s. He had a shorter playing career, through only 1876, but a longer managerial career, running various major- and minor-league clubs up to 1899, dying in 1916, aged 73.

Sadly, neither Ferguson nor Chapman was called "Death to Flying Things" during their playing careers, or for many years after. The nickname is entirely spurious. This article will attempt to explain where the supposed nickname came from in the first place, and how it got assigned to two different persons.

HOW WE KNOW THE NICKNAME IS SPURIOUS

First, we must establish that it is indeed spurious. In one sense, this is unknowable. Stating that it was not used during either player's career just means that no examples have been found. This does not, in principle, mean that they might not be found in the future. Nonetheless we can have high confidence that no such examples are waiting to be found. This comes from the nature of baseball nicknames. When we talk about players' nicknames, we really mean two distinct varieties: the baseball version of ordinary nicknames, and colorful sobriquets that replace the player's real name. "Death to Flying Things" is of the latter sort, which has distinct and readily identifiable characteristics.

The first variety acts like an ordinary nickname, used in place of the person's given name and suitable for ordinary speech. Both Ferguson and Chapman had ordinary nicknames: "Bob" and "Jack" respectively. It is entirely likely that they were called these in ordinary speech, both referring to them and directly speaking to them. The baseball version is somewhat more colorful, but still plausibly used in everyday speech. It does not stretch the credulity that Adrian Anson's players might have called him "Cap," that George Ruth's teammates might have called him "Babe," or that any of various southpaw pitchers were called "Lefty."[1]

It can sometimes be difficult to distinguish between a baseball nickname and a nickname that has nothing to do with sports. Taking an example from football, Gus Dorais, the quarterback for Notre Dame during its rise to prominence as a football power, was actually named Charles. He got his nickname from an art history class, attended in those innocent days even by football stars. The class included studying the work of nineteenth-century French artist Gustave Doré. His classmates were struck by the identical pronunciation of Doré and Dorais, and as a joke started calling him Gustave. This was quickly shortened to Gus, and the name stuck.[2] Turning to baseball, it is not immediately obvious if Camp Skinner (real name: Elisha Harrison Skinner), a utility player in the majors in 1922–23, or Duffy Lewis (real name: George Edward Lewis), a Deadball Era left fielder, mostly for the Boston Red Sox, had baseball nicknames, or simply nicknames. Either way, the key is that these act like ordinary nicknames, used similarly to and in place of the formal given name.

Then we come to colorful nicknames. These are journalistic inventions, not generally used in everyday speech, and whose use is distinctly different from or-

John C. Chapman might have been called "Young Jack," or perhaps Al Spink made that up, as well.

SABR/RUCKER ARCHIVE

dinary nicknames. It is hard to imagine a teammate telling Ted Williams, "Hey, Splendid Splinter! You're up next." This is not their function. Their purpose is to enliven a newspaper article or headline. To the extent that they are used in real life, they displace the entire name, not merely the given name: "The Splendid Splinter," not "Splendid Splinter Williams." If used with the real name, the nickname is used as an aside: "Walter 'Big Train' Johnson."

"Death to Flying Things" falls solidly into the colorful category. This is why we can be confident that it was not in fact used while either Ferguson or Chapman was active. The careers of both are well documented in the contemporary press, and these press accounts have been studied by modern researchers. Use in newspaper reports is the whole point of a colorful nickname like this. It is very unlikely that it would have gone unnoticed. Nor should we be surprised by this absence. Colorful nicknames were very rare during Ferguson and Chapman's playing heydays. The only clear example is that of George Zettlein, whom contemporary accounts often called "The Charmer." This establishes that such nicknames were not entirely unknown, but "the Charmer" is the exception that proves the rule.

THE ORIGIN OF THE NICKNAME

So if it was not a contemporary nickname, when did it finally appear and where did it come from? The first of these questions turns out to be straightforward. The earliest known attestation is from *The National Game*, published in 1910 by Alfred Spink, the editor of *The Sporting News*. Spink was of the same generation as Ferguson and Chapman, but where they came out of the Brooklyn baseball fraternity, Spink was a westerner. He was born in Canada, his family emigrated to Chicago in 1867, when he was 14, then in 1875 he relocated permanently to St. Louis. There he was a sports reporter for various newspapers and in 1886 founded *The Sporting News*, establishing himself as one of the leading baseball journalists in the country.[3]

Buried in a discussion of the Capitoline Grounds of Brooklyn, in a list of players who appeared there, is this:

> Here John C. Chapman of the Atlantics, "Young Jack," as he was then called, often surprised the natives by his wonderful running one-hand catches and earned the name of "Death to Flying Things."[4]

Given the *Sporting News* connection, we might suspect that the nickname can be found there, but this seems not to be the case. The expression simply does not occur—at least not within the limitations of optical character recognition. Nor, as we shall see, does it occur in the years following. The 1910 use is a one-off.

We do not know precisely where Spink got the name from, but there are some hints. The Eckford and Atlantic clubs played September 22, 1868. A reporter praised Dave Eggler, the Eckford center fielder: "Eggler at centre field covered himself with glory. He was 'sure death' to any 'fly' that went towards centre field, and is entitled to the highest credit for general good play."[5]

Six years later, a reporter for the Middletown *Constitution*, assessing the lineup for the new Hartford club, praised outfielder Jim Tipper: "He is regarded among the ball-playing fraternity as one of the most promising players in the country, and is 'death on fly-balls.'"[6]

Neither of these is cast as a nickname, but they show that the metaphor of a catch being death to a fly ball was in use, if not widespread, during Chapman's playing career. There is no evidence that it was ever applied to him, much less as a nickname, but these uses hint that Spink may have had a distant memory of the metaphor and, for unknown reasons, applied it to Chapman.

THE CHAPMAN YEARS

The nickname would be ascribed to Chapman alone for over half a century after Spink's imaginative invention. But not often, and not until decades later. The next known use would not be until 1947, in a history of baseball by Robert Smith. He has an account of early sportswriter Henry Chadwick, who

> had met and known such pioneers as Catcher Bob Ferguson, Asa Brainard (the bearded pitcher), and outfielder John Chapman (called, in the stilted catch phrase of that naive day, 'Death to Flying Things').[7]

The 37-year gap is understandable. Spink's 1910 book was one of several baseball histories published within a few years, most notably Albert Spalding's *America's National Game* in 1911 and Francis Richter's *History and Records of Base Ball* in 1914. These works collectively established a conventional narrative of early baseball history. While Spink's book was unquestionably influential, details could easily get lost in the mix. The book is densely written, not particularly well organized, and printed in small type. Both Spalding's and Richter's books compare favorably in ease of use for the reader. The supposed nickname, for all that it is striking, was buried in the mass of verbiage.

The nickname remained obscure after 1947. The next known ascription to Chapman is again from Robert Smith, this time from 1961:

"Young Jack" Chapman, left fielder for the Philadelphia Athletics in the 1860s, brought kranks to their feet with his one-handed catches, his fleetness of foot, and the strength of his throws. Such sensation did his one-handed catches create (remember, most players still caught balls with their wrists together and fingers extended toward the ball) that Chapman earned, in print at least, the name of "Death to Flying Things."[8]

There is a lot wrong in that excerpt, starting with Smith confusing the Athletics of Philadelphia, whom Chapman never played for, with the Atlantics of Brooklyn, his club of many years. This is followed by the anachronistic use of "kranks," a piece of baseball slang from the 1880s. The repetition of the "Death to Flying Things" tale only incrementally adds to the problems.

There is one other use, sandwiched between Smith's contributions. This middle contribution is neither a Chapman nor a Ferguson example, but rather is openly fictional. It comes from *The Sunlit Field*, an obscure baseball novel by Lucy Kennedy published in 1950. The story is set in Brooklyn in a fictionalized version of the early amateur era. Many of the players have colorful, and ahistorical, nicknames such as "Bushel Basket" and "Twinkle Toes." Kennedy picked up on "Death to Flying Things" and added it to her roster:

A tall lanky man with a rectangular jaw, wearing butternut shirt and breaches, a long whip stuck in his boot top, was standing up, arguing angrily. Brian said it was Hank Collins, a teamster at Quimby's, and left fielder, called "Death-to-Flying-Things" because he could catch anything passing through the air.

THE FERGUSON ERA

The nickname was, outside Kennedy's purely fictional context, only applied to Chapman, and only rarely. This changed in 1969. The nickname suddenly burst forth, cited by numerous sportswriters across the country, inevitably applied to Ferguson. Here is a typical example:

Many nicknames are included for old-timers and maybe the fact our modern stars don't use them much is one of the reasons the game seems to sometimes now lack color.

I mean like, Hawk Harrelson is OK, but could it ever compare with Joe "Horse Belly" Sargent, or Doggie "Calliope" Miller, Jack "Stooping" Gorman, Bill "Barnyard" Henderson, Joe "Ubbo Ubbo" Hornung, Dain "Ding-A-Ling" Clay, Nick "Tomato Face" Cullop, Pat "Whoops" Creeden?

Or how about my all-time favorite, Bob "Death to Flying Things" Ferguson who played nine years as an infielder in the 1800's?[10]

This set the pattern to the present day. The nickname turns up from time to time, often in the context of sepia-tinged discussions of baseball nicknames of an earlier era, where it is assigned to Ferguson far more often than Chapman.

The source for the nickname spreading to Ferguson is clear from the 1969 citations. It came from *The Baseball Encyclopedia*, published that year and familiarly known (speaking of nicknames) as "The Big Mac." This work is rightly famed for bringing rigor to baseball's statistical record, but it included ancillary material as well. This included player nicknames, presented in a format to accommodate the peculiarities of the genre. Each entry in the player register has up to three different names listed. The front matter explains the system: The main listing is a shortened version of the name most familiar to the fans, followed by the player's full name, and finally any nickname or nicknames.[11] The main listing is shortened in that it has the surname and either a single given name or a single nickname. If the latter, it will be of the less colorful variety, which can be used in place of the given name. What the introductory matter calls the player's nickname is what I have been calling here the colorful nickname. Taking the most famous example, the three entries for the longtime home run king lists "Base Ruth," "Ruth, George Herman," and "The Sultan of Swat."[12]

This is essentially the same format still used in modern online sources such as Baseball Reference. Retrosheet omits the colorful nickname but keeps the main listing and full name distinction: Babe Ruth and George Herman Ruth. Baseball Reference not only includes the colorful nickname, but will provide a longer list: Babe, the Bambino, the Sultan of Swat, Jidge, the Colossus of Clout or the King of Crash.

Alas, while the Big Mac's statistical record was exquisitely researched, it did not bring this rigor to its nickname listings. Indeed, this would hardly be possible. The statistical record is a synopsis of discrete events. To the extent that our knowledge of these events is complete, the statistical record is objective fact. The name entries, on the other hand, necessarily are fuzzy editorial judgments. How do we determine which is the name most familiar to the fans? It may be obvious, but some are borderline cases. What are the criteria for inclusion of colorful nicknames? How often does it have to be used? By how many reporters? This is before we even consider editorial bias. Adrian Anson is listed as "Cap Anson," which is fair enough, but surely his list of nicknames should include "Baby Anson," which was more common through much of his career and not meant as a compliment.

Put together, we have research ancillary to the Big Mac's main purpose, in a domain that is necessarily subjective. In this light, it is unsurprising that pure errors crept in. This is where we get the expanded use of "Death to Flying Things." There not only was no serious examination of the authenticity of the nickname, it was mistakenly assigned to Ferguson rather than Chapman.

The publication of the Big Mac was a huge event in baseball history. It brought attention to earlier players, with authoritative data about them. The difference in rigor between the statistical data and the nicknames was a nuance that went unnoticed, which contributed to errors writers made in articles reviving colorful nicknames of the past. Some writers eventually noted that Chapman also had the same nickname, but this has generally been taken at face value. Baseball Reference lists "Death to Flying Things" as nicknames for both players.[13]

CONCLUSION

"Death to Flying Things" is not going to go away. It is too good a nickname for that. It is, in the big picture, a harmless myth. A reasonable person might believe that Ferguson or Chapman or both were called this, while still maintaining a solid grounding in early baseball history.[14] Compare this with, for example, the Abner Doubleday and Alexander Cartwright myths. These are not mere peccadilloes that can exist within an otherwise sound grasp of early baseball history, but incompatible with it.

It is, nonetheless, worthwhile to keep in mind that "Death to Flying Things" is folklore, not history. Keeping this distinction is always beneficial, and in this instance it can serve as a cautionary tale about how we understand early baseball. It is no coincidence that the supposed nickname makes its appearance just five years after the Doubleday and Cartwright myths make theirs.[15] The modern understanding of early baseball came out of the early twentieth century. Its creators, even when well-intentioned, often indulged in the telling of tales. And, not a few times, the grinding of axes. Rigorous fact checking and analysis did not enter in. These narratives established themselves as the baseline for early baseball history. They often do not stand up to modern scrutiny, yet they're hard to dispel.

One might, in a burst of sunny optimism, think that "Death to Flying Things" proving an early twentieth-century fantasy might give onlookers pause, inducing them to consider what else was equally inventive. ■

Notes

1. On the other hand, Allen Wood states that Ruth's teammates usually called him "Jidge," a variant of George. Allen Wood, "Babe Ruth," SABR, https://sabr.org/bioproj/person/babe-ruth/.
2. Joe Niese, *Gus Dorais: Gridiron Innovator, All-American and Hall of Fame Coach*, with Bob Dorais, (Jefferson, NC: McFarland, 2018).
3. Bill Pruden, "Alfred Henry Spink," SABR, https://sabr.org/bioproj/person/alfred-henry-spink/.
4. Alfred H. Spink, *The National Game* (St. Louis: National Game Publishing Co., 1910), 10.
5. "The National Game." *New York Herald*, September 23, 1868. There is no byline, as is typical in this era, but it probably was Michael J. Kelly, the *Herald*'s regular baseball reporter.
6. "The Hartford Base Ball Club," *The Constitution* (Middletown, Connecticut), March 18, 1874. This was brought to the attention of the author by David Arcidiacono.
7. Robert Smith, *Baseball: A Historical Narrative of the Game, the Men Who Have Played It, and Its Place in American Life* (New York: Simon & Schuster, 1947), 79.
8. Robert Smith, *Baseball in America* (New York: Holt, Rinehart and Winston, 1961), 25–26.
9. Lucy Kennedy, *The Sunlit Field* (New York: Crown Publishers, 1950), 57.
10. Jack Patterson, "Baseball Buffs Get A 'Bible.'" *Akron Beacon Journal*, December 28, 1969.
11. *The Baseball Encyclopedia*, (New York: Macmillan, 1969), 495.
12. The author has a longstanding suspicion that the underlying motivation for this format is to avoid an entry headed by "George Ruth."
13. Baseball Reference also lists the nickname for twenty-first century outfielder Franklin Gutierrez. Seattle Mariners broadcaster Dave Niehaus hung the throwback nickname on him during his years with the club.
14. The exception is the "vintage base ball" historical reenactment community, who have embraced the colorful nickname far more than can be supported.
15. Richard Hershberger, "The Creation of the Alexander Cartwright Myth," *Baseball Research Journal*, 43, no. 1 (Spring 2014).

Shining Light on the Smiling Stan Hack Mirror

A Bill Veeck Gamesmanship Ploy—Was It Real or Mythical?

Herm Krabbenhoft

Stan Hack, who spent his entire big-league career (1932–47) with the Chicago Cubs, was one of baseball's all-time top leadoff batters.[1] In 1931, playing with the Sacramento Solons, he compiled a .352 batting average and earned the nickname "Smiling Stan." As Edward Burns wrote in the Rochester *Democrat and Chronicle*, "No matter how hard the coaches rode the rookie, Stanley would beam his contagious smile."[2] The sobriquet stuck with Hack throughout his baseball career as both a player and a manager.

Bill Veeck Jr. worked for the Cubs from 1934 to 1941. His roles included serving as a liaison between fans and executives, a statistician, an office staffer, and the treasurer.[3] In 1962, after stints as the principal owner of the Milwaukee Brewers (1941–45), the Cleveland Indians (1946–49), the St. Louis Browns (1951–53), and the Chicago White Sox (1959–61), Veeck wrote his autobiography, *Veeck As In Wreck*. In a chapter about gamesmanship, Veeck defined the term as "the art of winning without really cheating." He provided an example:

> During my days with the Cubs, we had a great third baseman, Smiling Stan Hack. I well recall that in 1935, the sale of 'Smile-with-Stan-Hack' mirrors was exceptionally brisk to the bleacherites. Now that I think of it, it was rather strange how the makeup of female bleacherites seemed to need attention when the opposition was hitting. …And if a beam of light occasionally shone in the batter's eye on a particularly important pitch…well, what better pitch to choose? Unladylike? Of course. Unsporting? Perhaps. In-effective? Oh no. Awfully, awfully effective. And, until it happened too often, perfectly legal.[4]

This account also appeared verbatim in a newspaper article published shortly after the book.[5]

After retiring as a player following the 1947 season, Hack went on to coach and manage several minor league teams, in addition to managing the Cubs from 1954 to 1956. During the 1960–1964 seasons, he took time off from baseball to operate the Stan Hack Land-mark restaurant with his wife in Grand Detour, Illinois. After returning as a manager for the 1965 and 1966 seasons, Smiling Stan permanently retired from base-ball and continued operating the restaurant.[6] Hack passed away at age 70 on December 15, 1979. In the next day's *Chicago Tribune*, David Condon quoted Veeck telling the same story, but situating it in a different year:

> "Right now I can see Stan's smile," said Bill Veeck, an old friend who had kept in close con-tact with Hack. "It inspired one of my first zany ideas in baseball. I think it was the year after the 1932 World Series and I was determined to cap-italize on Hack's popularity and his smile. I believe it was after we'd sent him down to the minors for a short spell," continued Veeck. "Anyhow, I thought up the slogan 'Smile with Stan Hack' and a concessionaire made me some mirrors with a grinning picture of Stan on the back. They were sold, on target day, in the bleachers. We still [?…thought?…felt?…hoped? …expected?…?] that fans should not only enjoy Stan's smile, but they should take advantage of the sunshine and reflect the mirrors in the faces of opposing batsmen. I believe we were playing Pittsburgh. Anyhow, the other team was furious. Umpires stopped the game, confiscated the mir-rors, and threatened a forfeit if any more turned up. I've always hoped Stan saved one of those mirrors so he could occasionally look at it and enjoy his own smile as so many of us did."[7]

THE STAN HACK MIRROR

According to the description provided in a 2016 auction, the mirror is 2.25 inches in diameter. The manufac-turer was Parisian Novelty Co, Chicago. "The image is printed on fabric substance with a very fine texture."[8] See Figure 1 (and Appendix A, available on the SABR website).

Figure 1. The Stan Hack Mirror

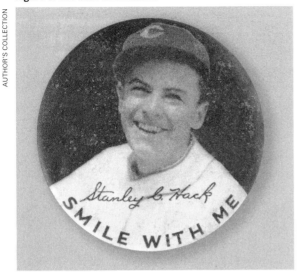

AUTHOR'S COLLECTION

BILL VEECK'S CLAIMS ABOUT THE STAN HACK MIRROR

Two questions immediately jump out from Veeck's claims: In what season, and in which specific game (or games) did the events take place? In addition to the date, I have endeavored to determine the details of the game: the inning, the players and managers, the umpires, the duration of any delay, whether there were any ejections, and whether the game was played under protest.

Hack debuted with the Cubs on April 12, 1932, and played in 72 games that season. In 1933, he appeared in three games (each as a pinch-runner) before being sent down to the Albany Senators of the Class AA International League. Hack played in 137 games for Albany before returning to the Cubs on August 29.[9] He became a full-time player in 1934, slashing .289/.363/.366 over 111 games. Bill Veeck Jr. was employed by the Cubs from January 1934 through June 22, 1941. Therefore, Veeck's claim that, "I think it was the year after the 1932 World Series" is not tenable. In 1933, Hack spent virtually the entire season in the minors, and Veeck was not with the Cubs. The earliest possible season for the Stan Hack Mirror Game is 1934.

The events are extraordinary, and would almost certainly have been reported in the Chicago press, the press of the victimized team's hometown, and *The Sporting News*.

RESEARCH PROCEDURES

1. Examine multiple game accounts for every Cubs home game during the 1934–41 seasons (the years Veeck was employed by the Cubs). This was achieved by searching Newspapers.com, GenealogyBank.com, and *The Sporting News*, with an emphasis on the key terms of Veeck's claims: *mirror, confiscate,* and *forfeit*.[10] Scrutinize the Hack and Veeck files available at the National Baseball Library.

2. Peruse books on the history of the Chicago Cubs.

3. Speak to people with knowledge of the Stan Hack mirror.

EXAMINATION OF GAME STORIES OF CUBS HOME GAMES (1934–41)

Table 1 summarizes my examination of game accounts from the 1934–41 seasons.

Out of the nearly 2,700 newspaper accounts I examined, only one mentioned spectators using mirrors: the Cubs-Giants game on June 7, 1938.[11] Marvin McCarthy, the Sports Editor of the *Chicago Daily Times* wrote, "mirrors figured only briefly—for about two innings." There was no mention of Stan Hack, and there was no mention of the umpires stopping the game, confiscating the mirrors, or threatening a forfeit. Following up on McCarthy's article, accounts from 12 other major daily Chicago and New York newspapers were examined in search of additional information.[12] None mentioned anything about mirrors or any of Veeck's claims. That these items were not mentioned at all seems unusual and surprising in light of the importance of the game. It was the first of a four-game series between the first-place Cubs and the second-place Giants, who were separated by just half a game in the standings.

Since the Cubs emerged with a 4–2 triumph, it is surprising that the Giants manager, Bill Terry, would not have played the game under protest. It is even more incongruous considering the fuss he

Table 1. Game Stories Examined for Stan Hack Mirror for Cubs Home Games (1934–41)

Season	Home Dates (Games)	Chicago Newspaper Stories	Opposing Team Newspaper Stories
1934	69 (77)	164	204
1935	68 (77)	164	194
1936	70 (77)	171	212
1937	68 (78)	167	179
1938	66 (77)	168	181
1939	69 (80)	172	205
1940	66 (77)	164	191
1941 (thru 6–22)	26 (29)	64	75
Total	**502 (572)**	**1,234**	**1,441**

Figure 2. June 7, 1938 Game Story

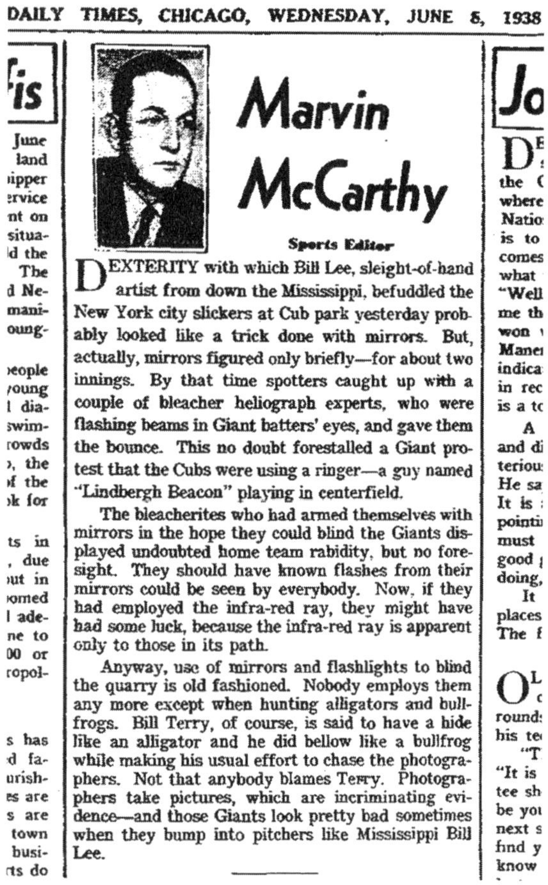

AUTHOR'S COLLECTION

DAILY TIMES, CHICAGO, WEDNESDAY, JUNE 8, 1938

Marvin McCarthy

Sports Editor

DEXTERITY with which Bill Lee, sleight-of-hand artist from down the Mississippi, befuddled the New York city slickers at Cub park yesterday probably looked like a trick done with mirrors. But, actually, mirrors figured only briefly—for about two innings. By that time spotters caught up with a couple of bleacher heliograph experts, who were flashing beams in Giant batters' eyes, and gave them the bounce. This no doubt forestalled a Giant protest that the Cubs were using a ringer—a guy named "Lindbergh Beacon" playing in centerfield.

The bleacherites who had armed themselves with mirrors in the hope they could blind the home team displayed undoubted home team rabidity, but no foresight. They should have known flashes from their mirrors could be seen by everybody. Now, if they had employed the infra-red ray, they might have had some luck, because the infra-red ray is apparent only to those in its path.

Anyway, use of mirrors and flashlights to blind the quarry is old fashioned. Nobody employs them any more except when hunting alligators and bullfrogs. Bill Terry, of course, is said to have a hide like an alligator and he did bellow like a bullfrog while making his usual effort to chase the photographers. Not that anybody blames Terry. Photographers take pictures, which are incriminating evidence—and those Giants look pretty bad sometimes when they bump into pitchers like Mississippi Bill Lee.

---

made in the first inning about photographers stationed along the first base line in front of the Giants dugout. The *Chicago Tribune* related the incident:

> Soon after the game started, seven photographers went into a flying wedge formation just back of first base when [New York's leadoff batter] Joe Moore came to bat the first time. Terry went roaring out of the Giant dugout. "I can't see anything that's going on," he shouted at Umpire Larry Goetz, who was stationed at first base. He motioned for Umpire Babe Pinelli, who was officiating back of the plate. "Throw 'em all off the field," the roaring Mr. Terry demanded. There was a pow wow and a compromise. The photogs stayed on the field, but had to break up the flying wedge formation, thus affording an opening through which the arrogant Giant boss was able to view the proceedings.[13]

OTHER SEARCHES FOR DETAILS ABOUT THE STAN HACK MIRROR GAME

I conducted several other searches in addition to those previously detailed. I searched *The Sporting News* for the years 1934 through 1941, employing the search terms *mirror, mirrors, forfeit, forfeited, confiscate*, and *confiscated*. I also searched for the years 1934 through 2003, using the search term *smile* with *stan*. I found no mention of the Stan Hack mirror or the events detailed by Veeck. (See Appendix B-1.)

I searched Newspapers.com for Cubs home games during the 1934–41 period, employing the search terms *mirror, mirrors, forfeit, forfeited, confiscate*, and *confiscated*. I found no mention of the Stan Hack mirror or the events detailed by Veeck. (See Appendix B-2.)

I found no mention of the events in the Stan Hack and Bill Veeck Jr. files available at the National Baseball Library at the National Baseball Hall of Fame and Museum.

I found no mention of the events in several books on the history of the Chicago Cubs. (See Appendix C.)

Fortunately, thanks to further searching on Newspapers.com and GenealogyBank.com for the 1942–2022 period, I did get six relevant hits, two of which are presented here. (See Appendix D for the other four.)

The first appeared on page 176 of the *Chicago Tribune* on April 1, 2001. It was a "Flashback" article by Nancy Watkins, whose source was "Tribune archives." It essentially reiterated the claims in Condon's 1979 *Chicago Tribune* article, although in this version Veeck himself was the one selling the mirrors:

> 'Smiling Stan' Hack was one of the most popular players of his day. Once, Bill Veeck Jr. walked the Wrigley Field bleachers selling mirrors featuring a grinning picture of the third baseman on the back with the slogan, 'Smile With Stan Hack.' The fans began shining the mirrors into opposing batters' eyes, and the items were promptly confiscated.[14]

The second hit was a response to the first, appearing on page 164 of the *Chicago Tribune* on May 20, 2001. It was a letter to the editor with the heading "Reflections," and it provided support for the claims in Watkins' article:

> I was happy to see the article about Stan Hack [Flashback, April 1]. I have one of those mirrors. As Nancy Watkins' article stated, Bill Veeck Jr. sold them, or passed them out, to the bleacher fans, and they would flash them into the eyes of the opposing batters. The umpires halted the game and served notice that the mirrors go, or the Cubs forfeit! As I remember, only a limited number of the mirrors were made by 'Parisian

Novelty Co. Chicago' (the company name is on the rim of the mirror). Rudy Drnek/Brookfield[15]

INTERVIEWS OF PEOPLE WITH KNOWLEDGE OF THE STAN HACK MIRROR

In 2023, I had the opportunity to speak with Jim Drnek, Rudy Drnek's son.[16] The Drneks have been Cubs fans for generations. Rudy, who passed away at age 92 in 2012, would have been 18 years old on June 7, 1938. Jim recalls his dad recounting the story of the Stan Hack mirror, as well as the fact that he sold the mirror in his later years. Jim does not know how his dad, who was not a collector of baseball memorabilia, obtained the mirror. Although Rudy Drnek did not state that he had attended the game, it's entirely possible that he was there. Jim Drnek has likened this uncertainty to the famous question involving Babe Ruth's called shot: "Did he point?"

I also had the opportunity to speak with two members of Stan Hack's family. I asked Stanford Hack, one of Stan's five children, about his recollections of his dad and the Stan Hack mirror in early 2023.[17] Stanford related that his dad did not have one of the mirrors, and that he does not recall him ever mentioning the incident. Stanford first learned the story by reading about it after his dad passed away.

Grandson Richard Stephens, the son of Hack's daughter Barbara Dee (Hack) Stephens, had never heard of the mirror until I mentioned it to him.[18] He said his mother would have told him about the story if she had known about it. Richard also mentioned that he asked his aunt, Beverly Pearl (Hack) Berti, if she had any knowledge or recollections of the mirror. She told him she didn't.

Lastly, I had the opportunity to speak with Mike Veeck, Bill's son, in February, 2023.[19] Mike never saw the Stan Hack mirror and didn't recall the topic ever coming up. Mike said that Stan Hack was Bill Veeck's favorite Cubs player. Mike recalled his dad telling him that he would bring Hack four or five hot dogs between the first and second games of doubleheaders.

DISCUSSION

There are several items about the Stan Hack Mirror Game that merit discussion. First and foremost, the reality of the Stan Hack mirror is incontrovertible, as demonstrated by the 2016 auction and Rudy Drnek's letter. Second, Bill Veeck Jr. twice made claims about heliographic events—extraordinary events, in my opinion—surrounding the mirror. Third, as demonstrated in Appendix D, (at least) seven other people have subsequently published articles in which it appears that they merely rephrased Veeck's claims without providing the specific date of the game.

Fourth, I have carried out a virtually exhaustive search for independent, contemporary evidence in support of Veeck's claims. I found only one game in which it was reported that "heliograph experts" used mirrors to reflect sunlight into the eyes of opposing batters: the Cubs-Giants game on June 7, 1938. Whether or not the mirrors employed were Stan Hack mirrors was not stated. Therefore, it is not known for certain whether that was the Stan Hack Mirror Game. Fifth, I did not find any independent documentation which lends credence to any of Veeck's claims:

1. There being a game in which fans used Stan Hack mirrors to reflect sunlight into the faces (eyes) of the visiting players (batters).

2. There being such a game in which the umpires stopped the game.

3. There being such a game in which the umpires confiscated the Stan Hack mirrors.

4. There being such a game in which the umpires threatened to forfeit the game.

Thus, the June 7, 1938, Cubs-Giants game does not align with the claims made by Veeck.[20] The Cubs won, and Bill Terry did not object to "heliograph experts" hindering his batters by playing the game under protest. This suggests that the impact of the use of mirrors was actually insignificant, if even noticeable.

I asked Professor (Emeritus) Alan Nathan, a physicist and SABR member, what impact a pocket mirror 2¼ inches in diameter could have on a batter some 350 feet away (the approximate distance between the Wrigley Field bleachers and home plate). Nathan responded, "Without having done any serious analysis, I am skeptical that something that small could reflect enough sunlight at that distance to be an annoyance to the batter."[21]

Another item that merits discussion is the last sentence of Veeck's version: "And, until it happened too often, perfectly legal." This statement suggests that some rule was subsequently enacted—after "it happened too often"—making the use of mirrors by fans to reflect sunlight onto a player's face illegal. It is not known what Veeck meant by "too often." Too many games, or too many times in one game? Two of the subsequent versions of the story (detailed in Appendix D) also stated that such a (preemptive) rule was enacted.

I checked the official rules for spectator interference for the years from 1934 through 2022 and found nothing about prohibiting the use of mirrors to interfere with the performance of players or umpires.

In summary, my essentially exhaustive effort to elucidate the exact date of the "Stan Hack Mirror Game" described by Veeck appears to have been unsuccessful. Perhaps what Bill Veeck Jr. claimed to have happened didn't actually happen. As such, it could be argued that I am attempting to controvert the longstanding philosophical axiom, "You can't prove a negative." Here are a few additional axioms that are pertinent in this case:

- **Hitchens' Razor**: *"What can be asserted without evidence can also be dismissed without evidence."*[22] Veeck, as well as those who essentially repeated his claims, made his assertion without evidence, i.e., identifying the specific game. Therefore, they may be dismissed without evidence. However, I have provided an abundance of evidence that does not support Veeck's claims.

- **The Sagan Standard**: *"Extraordinary claims require extraordinary evidence."*[23] In my opinion, Veeck's claims are extraordinary. I find it absolutely incredulous that *no* players (particularly those impacted), *no* managers, *no* umpires, *no* journalists covering the game (other than Marvin McCarthy) ever mentioned anything at all that substantiated Veeck's claims.

- "Proving a negative can be accomplished by providing *evidence of absence*, scientific evidence gathered from scientific research that shows absence. At that point the burden of proof shifts to those who claim the positive."[24]

This is precisely what I have accomplished: methodically gathering an abundance of evidence that shows the *absence of evidence* for (a) fans using Stan Hack mirrors to reflect sunlight onto the faces (eyes) of the Cubs opposing players (batters); (b) umpires stopping such a game; (c) umpires confiscating the Stan Hack mirrors in such a game; (d) umpires threatening a forfeit in such a game. Thus, I contend the burden of proof shifts to those who concur with Veeck's claims about the Stan Hack mirror.

CONCLUDING REMARKS

Having stated my contention, I also wholeheartedly endorse the conclusion of Jules Tygiel's article in the 2006 *Baseball Research Journal*, "Revisiting Bill Veeck and the 1943 Phillies". Tygiel discovered evidence to support a different Veeck claim that had previously been (seemingly definitively) debunked by David M. Jordan, Larry Gerlach, and John P. Rossi.[25] Tygiel wrote:

> they had correctly chastised earlier historians for accepting Veeck's narrative at face value and injected a dose of skepticism, replacing unwarranted certainty with healthy debate. Their own rush to judgment, however, offers yet another cautionary tale of relying on an absence of evidence and overreaching one's resources in drawing conclusions."[26]

It is now the responsibility of those who believe Veeck to produce original, independent, contemporary evidence—not hearsay—in support of Veeck's claims. In other words, they must identify the specific Stan Hack Mirror Game. I asked Mike Veeck what he thought about my contention. His response was, quote-unquote, "Perfect." Mike then added that perhaps his dad was winking when he related the story to Condon the day after Hack's passing. The *wink* possibility adds another layer of uncertainty.

Thus, my final words on the Stan Hack Mirror Game are:

- It really did happen, but I was unable to ascertain the date and corroborate the extraordinary claims made by Bill Veeck.

- It did not happen. It's a myth—a tall tale concocted by Veeck and told with a wink. ∎

The Appendices to this article may be found in the digital edition and online at SABR.org.

Acknowledgments
I gratefully thank Jerry Adams, Larry Annis, Jack Bales, Cliff Blau, Bill Deane, Jim Drnek, Stanford Hack, Eric Hanauer, Ed Hartig, Richard Hershberger, Bill Hickman, Steve Hirdt, Cassidy Lent, Gary Livacari, David McDonald, Alan Nathan, Dave Newman, Pete Palmer, John Racanelli, Jeff Robbins, Tom Shieber, Caleb Simonds, Richard Smiley, Cary Smith, Richard Stephens, Don Stokes, Gary Stone, Patrick Todgham, Mike Veeck, and Al Yellon for valuable help and/or discussions.

Notes
1. Herman O. Krabbenhoft, *Leadoff Batters of Major League Baseball* (Jefferson, NC: McFarland & Company, Inc. Publishers, 2006); Herm Krabbenhoft, "Stan Hack: Leadoff Batter Extraordinaire," *The National Pastime* (2023), 78–88.
2. Edward Burns, "Hack, Cubs' Rookie Infielder, Plucked Out of Bank on Coast," *Democrat and Chronicle* (Rochester, NY), January 10, 1932.

3. "Another Bill Veeck With Cubs," *Brooklyn Times Union*, January 31, 1935; Francis J. Powers, "National Loop Bent On Selling Game As Show," *The Daily Argus-Leader* (Sioux Falls, SD), March 19, 1935; Arch Ward, "Talking It Over," *Chicago Tribune*, October 31, 1936; Edward Burns, "New Wrigley Field Blooms in Scenic Beauty—and Scoffers Rush to Apologize," *Chicago Tribune*, September 12, 1937; "Box Seat Supply Dwindles; Will Grandstand Do?," *Chicago Tribune*, October 2, 1938; Irving Vaughan, "Cubs Trading Staff Returns Empty Handed, Hopeful," *Chicago Tribune*, December 17, 1938; "Give Gallagher Cubs' General Managership," *Chicago Tribune*, November 15, 1940.

4. Bill Veeck and Ed Linn, *Veeck as in Wreck* (New York, NY: G.P. Putnam's Sons, 1962), 58.

5. Bill Veeck, "Gamesmanship Helped Indians Win 1948 AL Pennant," *News-Journal* (Mansfield, OH), September 14, 1962.

6. Eric Hanauer, "Stan Hack," SABR Bio Project, last revised April 25, 2022 (accessed December 17, 2022), https://sabr.org/bioproj/person/stan-hack/.

7. David Condon, "Cub fans, smile if you loved Stan Hack," *Chicago Tribune*, December 16, 1979.

8. "Stanley C. Hack/SMILE WITH ME" pocket mirror, Hake's Auctions, March 15, 2016 (accessed December 18, 2022), hakes.com/Auction/ItemDetail/201987/stanley-c-hacksmile-with-me-pocket-mirror.

9. Irving Vaughan, "Rain Again Puts Double Header On Cub Program," *Chicago Tribune*, August 29, 1933.

10. Chicago newspapers examined included the *Chicago Tribune*, *Chicago Daily News*, and *Chicago Daily Times*. Newspapers from the cities of visiting teams included: Boston (*Globe*; *Herald*); Brooklyn (*Daily Eagle*; *Citizen*; *Times Union*); Cincinnati (*Enquirer*; *Post*); New York (*Daily News*); Philadelphia (*Inquirer*); Pittsburgh (*Post-Gazette*; *Press*; *Sun-Telegraph*); St. Louis (*Globe-Democrat*; *Post-Dispatch*; *Star-Times*).

11. Marvin McCarthy, *Daily Times* (Chicago, IL), June 8, 1938.

12. *Chicago Tribune*, *Chicago Daily News*, *Chicago Evening American*, *Chicago Herald-Examiner*, *New York Daily Mirror*, *New York Daily News*, *New York Herald-Tribune*, *New York Journal American*, *New York Post*, *New York Sun*, *New York Times*, and *New York World-Telegram*.

13. French Lane, "Dizzy Finds a Snap; Relief Duty for Lee," *Chicago Tribune*, June 8, 1938.

14. Nancy Watkins, "Flashback 1939—Smile Baseball's Back," *Chicago Tribune*, April 01, 2001.

15. Rudy Drnek, "In-Box—Reflections on baseball," *Chicago Tribune*, May 20, 2001.

16. Jim Drnek, telephone interviews, January 4 and February 8, 2023; email exchanges January 5, January 13–15, February 1, and February 10, 2023.

17. Stanford Hack, telephone interviews, January 20–23, 2023; email exchanges January 20–22, January 31, February 6, February 8, and February 10, 2023.

18. Richard L. Stephens, telephone interview, February 14, 2023; email exchange, February 14, 2023.

19. Mike Veeck, telephone interview, February 9, 2023; email exchange January 27 and February 10, 2023.

20. Thank you to an anonymous peer reviewer, who wrote, "I know a Cincinnati game, September 22, 1937, was interrupted by a fan with a mirror. The 1937 incident was minor, but could be/should be mentioned as a predecessor to this 1938 'promotion.'" Here's what I was able to find reported about this incident: Lou Smith, "Nose Dive Taken By Reds," *Cincinnati Enquirer*, September 23, 1937: "A female Redleg-hater shined a mirror in the eyes of our hitters until Umpire Sears spotted her in the window in a building back of the bleachers and shook his huge ham-like fist at her." *The Sporting News*, September 30, 1937: "Evidently a young woman who lives in a building back of the bleachers at Crowley Field in Cincinnati does not care much about the Reds. During the September 22 game with the Phillies, Cincy batters, who had trouble seeing the pitches of Claude Passeau, anyway, complained that somebody was shining a mirror in their eyes when they were at the plate. Investigation disclosed that the shafts [of light] were from the nearby window. There wasn't much the umpires could do about it, but the young woman disappeared from the window, mirror and all, when Ziggy Sears shook a fist at her."

21. Alan Nathan, email exchange, February 21, 2023.

22. Christopher Hitchens, *God Is Not Great* (New York: Twelve, 2007), 161.

23. Carl Sagan, *Broca's Brain* (New York: Presidio Press, 1974) 73.

24. Thomas DeMichael, "You Can't Prove a Negative—MYTH," July 26, 2017; last updated March 1, 2021 (accessed February 08, 2023), http://factmyth.com/factoids/you-cant-prove-a-negative/.

25. David M. Jordan, Larry Gerlach, and John P. Rossi, "A Baseball Myth Exploded: The Truth About Bill Veeck and the '43 Phillies," *The National Pastime* 18 (1998), 3. See also: Paul Dickson, *Bill Veeck, Baseball's Greatest Maverick* (New York, NY: Walker & Company, 2012), 357; Norman L. Macht and Robert D. Warrington, "The Veracity of Veeck," *Baseball Research Journal*, Volume 42, (2013), 17.

26. Jules Tygiel, "Revisiting Bill Veeck and the 1943 Phillies," *Baseball Research Journal*, Volume 35 (2003), 109.

Teenage Umpires of the Nineteenth Century

Larry DeFillipo

Baseball tradition before the Civil War favored the selection of respected, senior members of the community as umpires, to interpret rules and resolve disputes between opponents typically grateful for their help. Interjecting themselves only now and then into the conduct of games, umpires were pampered; "given easy chairs, placed near home plate [and] provided with fans on hot days…their absolute comfort…uppermost in the minds of the players."[1] By the late-1860s, deference gave way to disrespect in the treatment of many umpires, as their role had evolved to passing judgment on nearly every pitch, often leaving one side or the other feeling wronged. The rise of professional baseball, and the subsequent popularity of gambling on the outcome of games, brought about more virulent reaction to umpiring decisions. With that, arbiters became younger. They needed to be athletic enough to move about the diamond during the action and better suited to handling physical confrontation.

Youth was clearly favored in the selection of National League umpires in its inaugural season, 1876. Based on Retrosheet's game logs and biographical databases, the median age of the 61 umpires that officiated games that year was 25.[2]

At least three, and as many as four of those umpires were just 19 years old. Over the next two decades, another seven umpires under the age of 20 officiated major league games, as listed in Table 1. All toiled in either the NL or American Association. Neither the Players' League nor the Union Association played a regular season game with a teenage umpire.

TEENS IN THE AMERICAN WORKPLACE

By present-day definition, 18- and 19-year-olds are "teenagers," a term rarely used before the 1940s. But in the late 1800s, their place in society was vastly different than it is today. Secondary education was compulsory in few communities before 1900, so many children began working full time while in their early teens or younger. According to the 1870 US census, one in eight American children between the ages of 10 and 15 were members of the workforce. In 1880, 43% of white males between the ages of 10 and 19 were members of the workforce.[3] Many nineteenth-century teenagers worked to help sustain family households and had done so since an early age.[4] With fewer than one in 40 Americans aged 18–24 enrolled in institutions of higher learning by 1900, it was commonplace in many walks of life to see teenagers working along-

Figure 1. Age distribution of 1876 National League umpires (ages based on year of birth only)

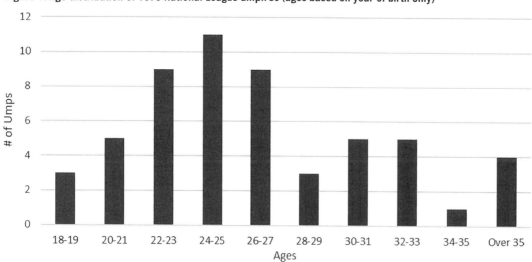

Table 1. Nineteenth-Century Major League Umpires Known to Be Teenagers

Name	Date of Birth	Place of Birth	Date of Umpiring Debut	Age at Debut	League	Games Umpired as a Teen	Baseball Affiliation at Debut
John Morris	7/8/1857	Kentucky	7/8/1876	19y, 0m, 0d	NL	4	Amateur
John Cross	2/2/1857	Providence	8/5/1876	19y, 6m, 3d	NL	1	College
Norman Fenno	3/10/1857	Chelsea, MA	8/7/1876	19y, 4m, 28d	NL	1	Scorer
Bill Gleason	11/12/1858	St. Louis	10/1/1877	18y, 10m, 19d	NL	1	Lower-level professional
Dan Stearns	10/17/1861	Buffalo	6/29/1881	19y, 8m, 12d	NL	3	Former MLer
Adonis Terry	8/7/1864	Westfield, MA	8/2/1884	19y, 11m, 26d	AA	1^	Active MLer
Morgan Murphy	2/14/1867	E. Providence, RI	9/15/1886	19y, 7m, 1d	NL	1	Lower-level professional
Ice Box Chamberlain	11/5/1867	Buffalo	9/25/1887	19y, 10m, 20d	AA	1	Active MLer
Kid Carsey	10/22/1872**	New York	9/7/1891	18y, 10m, 16d	AA	1*	Active MLer
Ed Conahan	5/6/1877	PA or DE	8/8/1896	19y, 3m, 2d	NL	10	Umpire

* Umpired for the first two innings only
** In the SABR BioProject entry on Carsey, Stephen V. Rice contends that Kid was born in 1870, a revision that Retrosheet and MLB have not adopted.
https://sabr.org/bioproj/person/kid-carsey/.
^ Umpired a second game that season, after his 20th birthday

Table 2. Nineteenth-Century Major League Umpires Who May Have Been Teenagers

Name	Date of Birth	Place of Birth	Debut	Age at Debut	League	Games Umpired as a Teen (possibly)	Notes
William Walker	1856*	Cincinnati	6/24/1876	19/20	NL	Up to 18	Amateur
Cliff Megrue	1856**	Cincinnati	8/10/1876	19/20	NL	1	Amateur

*Possibly January
**Possibly 1857 or 1858

side adults.[5] Many luminaries of that age got their start as teens, like inventor Thomas Edison, who began working at age 12 and was a telegraph operator at 19; lawman Wyatt Earp, who transported cargo as an 18-year-old teamster; and author Mark Twain, who started his working life around age 12 and at 16 was a typesetter. The advent of professional baseball in the 1860s inspired many teenagers, but only a handful were lucky enough to be direct participants. Roughly 7% of the ballplayers who played in the inaugural season of the National Association in 1871 were under the age of 20 (eight of 115). Even fewer of that age served as umpires during the NA's five-year existence; seven or eight according to the Retrosheet database. So while the idea of a teenage major league umpire may seem ill-advised in the present day, to fans and ballplayers in the 1870s, their presence was infrequent but not unheard of.[6]

UMPIRE SELECTION AND DEMOGRAPHICS

During its inaugural seasons, the NL delegated responsibility to home teams for the selection of umpires, subject to approval of the visiting nine. Clubs relied heavily on umpires with no previous experience at the highest levels of the sport (e.g. in the defunct National Association), presumably because not enough experienced umpires or ballplayers were available. That opened the door for the NL's three known teen umpires in 1876: John Morris, a Louisville amateur

ballplayer; John Cross, a Rhode Island collegian; and Norman Fenno, a Boston Reds non-playing employee.

Table 3. Previous Experience of 1876 NL Umpires

Background	Number
Active NL player	10
Active NL manager	2
Former NA umpire	1
Former NA player with no NA umpiring experience	6
Former NA player with NA umpiring experience	11
No NL or NA playing or umpiring experience	31

As was typical for NL umpires that year, Morris, Cross, and Fenno worked few games; four, one, and one, respectively. With teams cobbling together umpiring coverage from inexperienced hands, former NA ballplayers, and active ballplayers, two-thirds of 1876 NL umpires (41 of 61) worked no more than twice. All labored alone, as NL rules called for only one umpire to oversee games. Except for a few isolated trials with two-man crews, NL umpires worked solo until the 1898 season.[7]

The NL continued to allow home teams to select umpires for regular-season games in the 1877 and 1878 seasons, tweaking the process with regard to visiting team rights of refusal so as to reduce the likelihood of a biased umpire. During that time, only one umpire under the age of 20 worked an NL game,

18-year-old Bill Gleason, a member of a lower-level local professional team selected by the St. Louis Brown Stockings to work one of their games.

In 1879, NL President William Hulbert defined a pool of prospective umpires from which home teams, with concurrence of their opponents, could select arbiters for games. The average age of NL umpires rose to 27, with none under the age of 22. Not until 1881 did another umpire under the age of 20 work an NL game. In 1881, the Buffalo Bisons engaged a young player they'd released earlier that season, 19-year-old Dan Stearns, to umpire a three-game series for them.

Shortly after the American Association opened for business in 1882, it went a step further than the NL had in centralizing league umpires. It maintained a cadre of umpires "hired, paid, and assigned to games by the league itself."[8] The NL followed suit in 1883. With their umpiring corps now league-controlled, the median age of major league umpires topped 28.

The median age of major league umpires continued to rise throughout the nineteenth century, reaching 35 in 1900. Yet across the four major leagues that were in operation between 1876 and 1900, the median age of *new* umpires was only 25, as shown in Figure 3. During the twentieth century, the NL and AL collectively favored new umpires who were more ma-

Figure 2. Median age of NL and AA umpires for selected seasons from 1876 to 1900 (ages based on year of birth only)

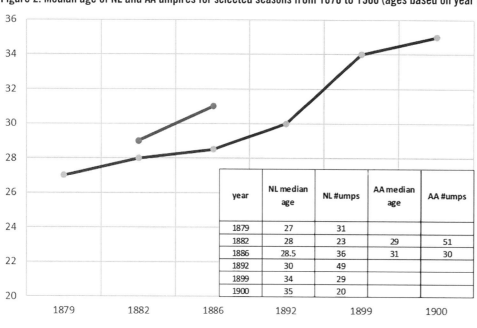

year	NL median age	NL #umps	AA median age	AA #umps
1879	27	31		
1882	28	23	29	51
1886	28.5	36	31	30
1892	30	49		
1899	34	29		
1900	35	20		

Figure 3. Median age of major league umpires in their debut season, by epoch[9] (ages based on year of birth only)

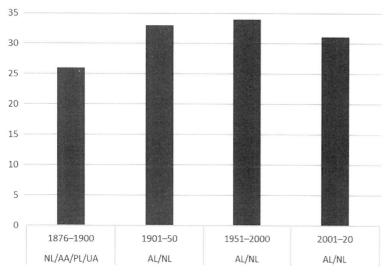

ture. From 1900 to 1950, median new umpire age across the two leagues was 33, rising to 34 in 1950–2000. In the first two decades of the twenty-first century that trend reversed, with the median umpire age over that period falling to 31.

Going back to 1879, when the NL first centralized the umpiring pool, when an umpire selected from Hulbert's list became suddenly unavailable (due to illness or other circumstance), the home team bore the burden of finding a replacement. Otherwise it faced canceling scheduled games and losing gate receipts. In those situations, teams turned to players on their rosters who they could afford to have out of the lineup (typically pitchers unavailable that day or fielders nursing an injury), local amateurs (including college players), or club employees who worked behind the scenes (scorekeepers, ticket takers, etc).

Exactly how many replacement umpires were needed for major league games in the nineteenth century is unknown. Using the number of umpires who worked only one or two games in a season as approximating the number of replacement umpires, approximately 6% of major league games in 1879 were officiated by a replacement umpire. That number fell to as low as 1% in 1899, a year in which 95% of the league's games were worked by two-man umpiring crews.

It was as a replacement that the next few teenage major league umpires came on the scene. In 1884, 19-year-old Brooklyn Grays pitcher Adonis Terry became the American Association's first teenage umpire when he was inserted as an emergency replacement for an assigned umpire who'd taken ill. Two years later, Morgan Murphy was a local ballplayer inserted as an emergency replacement for an NL arbiter who'd come up sick. In 1887, 19-year-old Louisville pitcher Elton "Ice Box" Chamberlain worked an AA game, presumably as a replacement umpire. The next-to-last teenage major league umpire of the 1800s, 18-year-old Washington Nationals hurler Wilfred "Kid" Carsey, who also proved to be the youngest, subbed for an AWOL umpire in the AA's final season, 1891.

Five years later, the last teenage major league umpire of the nineteenth century made his debut, but not as a replacement. Edward Conahan, a 19-year-old ump in a New Jersey semipro league, was hired into the umpiring corps by NL President Nick Young. Though he was heralded in his first few games, scathing newspaper critiques of his subsequent work triggered his dismissal after just 10 games. More than 80 years went by before the NL had another umpire under the age of 20, once again a temporary replacement. Conahan remains the one and only teenage umpire known to have been in the employ of a major league.

THEIR STORIES

In this section, the circumstances surrounding each teenage umpire's first assignment are described, including what is known about how they came to be selected, game results, reviews from the press, and highlights from the balance of their days. Players are listed in the order in which they first appeared as major league umpires.

KNOWN TO BE TEENAGE UMPIRES
John Morris, 19 years exactly
Debuted 7/8/1876 (NL)

The first teenage major league umpire of the nineteenth century was Kentucky native John Stuart Morris. The son of a prominent Louisville businessman, Morris was a player with Fall City's first organized baseball club, the amateur Louisville Base Ball Club.[10] During the same summer that the United States celebrated its centennial, Morris umpired a quartet of games for Louisville of the newly formed National League. The first took place at Louisville Base Ball Park, on Morris's 19th birthday, July 8, 1876. For reasons that the *Louisville Courier-Journal* called "inexplicable," the Louisvilles and their opponents, the visiting Mutuals of Brooklyn, found experienced umpire Mike Walsh an unacceptable choice to umpire their contest and settled on Morris as an alternative.[11] Louisville erased a four-run deficit in the bottom of the ninth to send the hard-fought

Table 4. Percentage of Nineteenth-Century NL and AA Games Possibly Worked by Replacement Umpires

Year	AA # Games Worked by Umps Who Worked 1–2 Games on the Year	# of AA Games that Year	%	NL # Games Worked by Umps Who Worked 1–2 Games on the Year	# of NL Games that Year	%
1879	–	–	–	19	322	6%
1882	13	234	6%	44	339	13%
1886	15	558	3%	24	496	5%
1892	–	–	–	41	922	4%
1899	–	–	–	11	924	1%
1900	–	–	–	15	570	3%

game into extra innings, and Morris had to halt the action after 15 innings on account of darkness. The *Courier-Journal* called the game "unparalleled in the history of professional baseball-playing," and singled out Morris for his hand in it. "We venture to say that no umpire ever gave more satisfaction to both sides in a long fifteen-inning game as he gave yesterday," adding that Morris's "judgment on balls and strikes was excellent, and also in points of base running. His decisions were quickly made and adhered to, and if his umpiring failed to satisfy the Mutuals we can only say that we have given them as good as we've got in the shop."[12]

Morris umpired three more Louisville matches during the summer of 1876, each opposite the Chicago White Stockings. On August 5, he filled in for Charlie Hautz, who was upset that the NL office had reversed his decision to award the White Stockings a win over Louisville in a game Hautz had stopped two days earlier.[13] Once again, Morris's work drew raves. "Mr. Morris umpired the game intelligently and impartially. His decisions were correct in every instance, and, on the whole, he is as fine an umpire as there is in the West at the present day."[14] Later in life, Morris took his prowess as a baseball arbiter and applied it to the worlds of business and civic affairs. He served as the director of Louisville's Commercial Club, a businessman's society, and built a career working for the city of Louisville as an auditor for various municipal departments.[15]

John Cross, 19 years, 6 months, 3 days
Debuted 8/5/1876 (NL)

Shortly after completing their first homestand of the 1876 season, the Boston Red Stockings lost a match in Providence against the independent New Havens.[16] The umpire for that late April game was John Alexander Cross, a Providence native and the regular catcher for Brown University's nine.[17] Two months later, the Red Stockings had Cross umpire an NL game with the Athletics of Philadelphia at Boston's South End Grounds. The Athletics also invited a Boston amateur to help that day, John Bergh, a local catcher who filled in for their regular and backup catchers, who were both out with injuries. Struggling early, Bergh switched positions with the Athletics' banged-up backup, Whitey Ritterson, who was playing center field. After Ritterson was struck in the wind pipe by a foul tip, Bergh returned behind the plate for the balance of the game, which Boston won.[18]

Two years later, Cross, who'd left Brown to help his father run the family textile mill, returned as an NL umpire. In the first of nine games he worked that year,

on May 8, 1878, he called what may have been the first unassisted triple play in NL history. After catching a low line drive on a dead run, Providence center fielder Paul Hines raced to third base, where he put out two Boston Red Stockings baserunners; or possibly just one.[19] Differing accounts of the play make it impossible to know for sure whether Hines retired all three himself, but without question it was Cross who rung them all up.[20]

Norman Fenno, 19 years, 4 months, 29 days
Debuted 8/7/1876 (NL)

The growth of professional baseball's popularity in the late 1860s and early 1870s was accompanied by a voracious public appetite for statistics. Numbers allowed fans to compare the teams and players they might not be able to see with those they could, or imagined they could. For fans of the Boston Red Stockings, it was Norman Fenno, who compiled team statistics for public consumption.[21] On August 7, 1876, Fenno, the heretofore "efficient and obliging official scorer of the Reds," was drafted to umpire a contest between Boston and the visiting Athletics.[22] The Red Stockings had employed several different umpires in recent home games, suggesting that with Fenno they were simply trying another. The *Boston Globe* mentioned that Fenno had made a few wrong calls in the game, won by Boston, 6–5. Referring to *Beadle's Dime Base-Ball Player*, the bible of baseball rules edited by Henry Chadwick, the *Globe* went on to suggest, "A brief study of Chadwick would help matters amazingly with him."[23]

Over the next few years, Fenno turned his facility with numbers into N.F. Fenno & Company, a banking and brokerage firm.[24] In February 1879, Fenno went over to the dark side, disappearing with $16,000 in cash and securities borrowed from his customers.[25] Newspaper reports presumed he had fled to Europe, but three years later, he turned up as an agent of the Louisville and Nashville Railroad, living in Little Rock, Arkansas. Typhus took Fenno's life at the age of 27.

Bill Gleason, 18 years, 10 months, 20 days
Debuted 10/1/1877 (NL)

Before he became a strong-armed, aggressive shortstop for the St. Louis Browns team that dominated the American Association in the 1880s, Bill Gleason played for the Minneapolis Browns of the League Alliance. A few weeks after the Browns had completed their 1877 season, Gleason umpired an October 1 NL contest between the Brown Stockings of St. Louis and Louisville.[26] Gleason's performance didn't draw any comments from newspapers that covered that game, but multiple box scores misidentified him as a member of the St. Paul Red Caps, the rival of his Minneapolis squad.[27] Before the month was out, two Grays who appeared in the game that Gleason umpired, left fielder George Hall and pitcher Jim Devlin, were expelled from the NL for their involvement in a scheme to fix games that came to be known as the Louisville Scandal.[28] Fourteen years later, after Gleason had completed a major league career in which he collected over 900 hits, he umpired his second and last major league game, on Opening Day of what turned out to be the American Association's final season.[29]

Dan Stearns, 19 years, 8 months, 12 days
Debuted 6/29/1881 (NL)

In 1880, Daniel Eckford Stearns became the first major league ballplayer born during the Civil War. A weak-hitting reserve with the Buffalo Bisons, he went unsigned until the first week of the 1881 season, when the Detroit Wolverines gave him a chance.[30] Released a week later, Stearns joined the Buffalo fire department.[31]

At the end of June, Stearns took a break from wrestling a horse-drawn steam pumper to umpire a three-game series between the Bisons and the Boston Red Stockings. Buffalo downed Harry Wright's squad in the opener, behind a 19-hit attack and the pitching of Pud Galvin. The *Buffalo Commercial* called the match "a roaring, red-hot game," but chided Stearns for failing to reign in excessive kicking from both sides. "Never before have we seen such outrageous conduct towards a man chosen to act as referee in a game of ball," claimed the *Commercial*, adding "Stearns was weak in not appreciating the dignity of the position he occupied."[32] After the next game, the *Buffalo Morning Express* gave Stearns a D for expertise but an A for effort. Stearns "tried hard to treat one side as justly as the other," the Express reported, suggesting "the only blame that Buffalonians could offer to his work yesterday was that he did not increase the League treasury" by fining a pair of ill-mannered Red Stockings.[33] For reasons unexplained, Boston objected to Stearns umpiring the finale, but relented.[34] In a major league career spent with five teams over parts of seven seasons in the NL and the American Association, Stearns was perhaps best known for making the final out for the Cincinnati Red Stockings in Louisville hurler Tony Mullane's no-hitter on September 11, 1882, the first in Association history.[35]

Adonis Terry, 19 years, 11 months, 26 days
Debuted 8/2/1884 (AA)

William H. Terry, later known as Adonis, was the American Association's first teenage umpire. An 18-year-old

pitching prodigy for the 1883 Brooklyns of the Interstate Association (16–9 with a 1.38 ERA) Terry had a dismal 10–16 record on August 1 of the following year, having lost six of his last seven starts for Brooklyn.[36] The next day, Brooklyn manager George Taylor tabbed Terry to fill in for scheduled umpire John Valentine, who'd taken ill before Brooklyn's home game with the Baltimore Orioles at Washington Park. The *Brooklyn Eagle* reported that Terry, five days away from his 20th birthday, umpired the game, won by Brooklyn in front of 3,000 "gratified spectators," "with thorough impartiality."[37] The day after his 20th birthday, Terry umpired for a second and final time that season. He umpired 10 times during a 14-year major league career in which he won 197 regular season games and three World Series games.[38] Hired as an NL umpire in 1900, Terry worked 39 games that year, including a July 12 no-hitter thrown by Cincinnati's Noodles Hahn against the Philadelphia Phillies.[39]

Morgan Murphy, 19 years, 7 months, 1 day
Debuted 9/15/1886 (NL)

Morgan Murphy burst onto the Boston baseball scene in the spring of 1886 as a catcher for the Boston Blues of the New England League. In late-August, the *Boston Globe* called Murphy "the pluckiest catcher in the New England League," describing his work behind the plate as "beautiful," "unsurpassed," and "magnificent, and at times simply superb."[40] Two weeks after that assessment, Murphy umpired an NL tilt at Boston's South End Grounds between the Red Stockings and the visiting Philadelphia Phillies, subbing for Chick Fulmer, a member of the league's umpiring corps too sick to officiate. Boston won the game, 5–3, with pitcher Bill Stemmyer holding off a Phillies rally in the bottom of the ninth. The game ended as would Ernest Thayer's as-yet-unwritten classic; with Casey (in this case Stemmyer's opposite number, *Dan* Casey) at the bat.

Unlike the nameless ump that eternally draws the ire of Thayer's imaginary patrons, no threats on Murphy's life nor claims of trickery were reported during the real Casey's final at the bat, which ended of course with a strikeout. According to the *Globe*, Murphy did well throughout the contest. "His judgment on balls and strikes was good, and of the two questionable decisions he made…neither affected the score."[41] Four years later, Murphy reached the major leagues as a player, backstopping for the Boston Brotherhood Club of the Players League.[42] Over an 11-year major league career, Murphy umpired five more games and became one of only six ballplayers to play in the Players League, National League, American Association, and American League.

Ice Box Chamberlain, 19 years, 10 months, 20 days
Debuted 9/25/1887 (AA)

Nicknamed "Ice Box" for his ability to stay calm under pressure, Elton Chamberlain was one of a small group of nineteenth-century hurlers known to have pitched with either hand.[43] In 1887, the 19-year-old Chamberlain, along with 22-year-old southpaw Toad Ramsey and veteran Guy Hecker, gave the American Association Louisvilles a formidable pitching staff expected to challenge the two-time defending pennant winner and reigning World Series champion, the St. Louis Browns.

As Louisville dropped out of the pennant race in late August, they fell into turmoil. Ramsey was suspended for thuggish conduct and Chamberlain accused the widely unpopular Hecker of threatening "to freeze him out of the club."[44] The *Louisville Courier-Journal* reported a "mutiny brewing," with everyone on the team wanting Hecker gone.[45] In Ramsey's second start back after cooling his heels for a week, he faced the last-place Cleveland club at Louisville's Eclipse Park, with Hecker at first and Chamberlain doing the umpiring.[46] Three thousand "heartily disgusted" fans saw Louisville "succumb to the Cleveland tailenders" by a 14–4 score. Ed, as the *Courier-Journal* called him, "umpired satisfactorily."[47] By all accounts, Hecker and Chamberlain had no altercations in the game nor during the rest of their time playing for Louisville. A winner of 157 major league games in 10 seasons, Chamberlain found his way into NL record books for two pitching performances at the tail end of his career. On September 23, 1893, he authored a darkness-shortened no-hitter against the Boston Beaneaters. Eight months later, Boston second baseman Bobby Lowe clubbed four home runs off Chamberlain, becoming the first major leaguer to do so in a game.

Kid Carsey, 18 years, 10 months, 17 days
Debuted 9/7/1891 (AA)

The youngest nineteenth-century major league umpire was Wilfred "Kid" Carsey, a rookie pitcher for the 1891 Washington Nationals. No American Association pitcher lost more games or threw more wild pitches that season than Carsey did. His 37 defeats for the last-place Nationals were 10 more than the second-place finisher, Phil Knell of the Columbus Buckeyes.

On Labor Day, 1891, the Nationals and Buckeyes squared off at Washington's Boundary Field for a doubleheader. At game time for the morning opener, scheduled umpire John Kerins was absent, his whereabouts unknown. Washington manager Dan Shannon agreed with his Columbus counterpart, Gus Schmelz, to form a two-man replacement umpiring crew with one player

from each team.[48] Carsey, six weeks shy of his 19th birthday, was chosen to umpire from behind the plate, with Knell selected to umpire from the field. The responsibility for calling balls and strikes rested not with Carsey, but instead alternated between the two; Carsey handled that duty when his teammates came to bat, and Knell did the same when Columbus was on offense.

Washington elected to bat first, as Association rules then allowed home teams to do, with Carsey overseeing the offerings of hurler Hank Gastright. When Nationals pitcher Martin Duke first took the field, Knell "waltzed up to the rubber and essayed to call balls and strikes."[49] In the bottom of the second, Columbus put together an 11-run rally, during which Kerins, the day's scheduled umpire, finally appeared. After the third out, he relieved the two substitute umpires of their responsibilities.

According to a play-by-play in the *Washington Evening Star*, Carsey entered the game in the eighth inning, grounding out as a pinch-hitter.[50] Thus, he both officiated and played in the same game; a feat rare and maybe even one of a kind. Over the next ten years, Carsey appeared in 268 major leagues games as a player and four as an umpire. Never again did he do both in the same contest.

Ed Conahan, 19 years, 3 months, 3 days
Debuted 8/8/1896 (NL)

Conahan took to umpiring early, working amateur baseball games in his hometown of Chester, Pennsylvania at the tender age of 14.[51] By 1896, the 19-year-old had moved up to umpiring in the independent South Jersey League.[52] In early August of that year, he earned an umpiring appointment from NL president Nick Young.[53] Conahan debuted on August 8, officiating a contest at Philadelphia's Ball Park (later known as Baker Bowl) between the hometown Phillies and the Boston Beaneaters.[54] In its retelling of the Phillies win in the midst of an oppressive heat wave, the *Philadelphia Inquirer* dubbed Conahan's efforts "the bright particular feature of the game,[55] adding that "he's got a great voice and renders his decisions promptly and intelligibly—a boon which will be readily appreciated by the great army of ball goers."[56] After Conahan's next umpiring assignment six days later, the Inquirer said, "The new umpire, Conahan, unearthed by Nick Young in the wilds of Jersey," was "a peach." "He's a nice accommodating lad too. He runs around and picks up the catchers' masks for them and with deferential bow delivers himself: 'Illustrious Sir, allow me.'"[57]

Glowing with praise for Conahan's first four games as an umpire, reviews soon turned sharply negative. Multiple accounts describe Conahan's performance in his fifth game, on August 19, as subpar.[58] Things snowballed from there. Following a doubleheader split the next day between the Phillies and the Louisville Colonels, the *Philadelphia Times* called Conahan's umpiring "of the rankest kind," adding that his decisions were so confounding they "would make an angel forget his vows."[59] The *Times* continued its condemnations the next day, calling Conahan's efforts in a Phillies win "yellow work."[60] The *Inquirer* called for Conahan's dismissal.[61] A twin bill on August 22 between the Phillies and St. Louis Browns proved Conahan's last games as a major league umpire. Once again, the *Times* brutalized Conahan, calling his work "slovenly," and the "the worst ever seen on local grounds." The *Inquirer* reported that Conahan "gave a weird exhibition all through," with one call so rotten it triggered an argument that got St. Louis's umpire-baiting shortstop Monte Cross unfairly ejected.[62]

Three days later, Conahan was fired.[63] He went back to umpiring amateur games in Chester and eight years later was umpiring professional baseball in the independent Pennsylvania League, New York State League, and Eastern League. He signed on as an American League umpire for the 1906 season, but was let go before the start of the regular season.[64] Conahan later umpired in the Western League, the minor league American Association, the International League, the Southern Association, and the Tri-State League.[65]

MIGHT-HAVE-BEEN TEENS

Two umpires in the National League's inaugural season are identified by Retrosheet as born in Cincinnati on an unknown date in 1856; William E. Walker and Enoch Clifford Megrue. Research suggests they were on either side of 20 when they first umpired major league games in the summer of 1876.

The 1900 US Census lists Walker, at that time still a Cincinnati resident, as born in January 1856. Age data in census rolls of that era can be faulty, but Walker's entry suggests that he turned 20 months before umpiring his first NL game. A newspaper account of Megrue's death in September of 1893 claimed he was 35-years-old, implying he might have been as young as 17 when he first officiated.[66] Walker and Megrue crossed paths on a baseball diamond, both as players and as umpires, with Walker's early success at umpiring opening a door for Megrue. In 1876, William E. Walker was both manager and substitute for the amateur Ludlow Base Ball Club of Ludlow,

Kentucky.[67] Located across the Ohio River from Cincinnati, Ludlow frequently played other amateur teams in the Queen City. One of those was the Cincinnati Junior Reds, whose left fielder was Enoch Clifford Megrue, a son of Cincinnati's fire chief.[68] Walker debuted as an NL arbiter in a match between the Boston Red Stockings and the Reds on June 24. Apparently pleased with his work, the Reds called Walker back to umpire a mid-July contest, and five of the Reds next six home games as well. But on August 10, Walker wasn't available; he was working a game in Louisville. Replacing Walker for the contest at Cincinnati's Avenue Grounds was Megrue. Accounts of the game with the Chicago White Stockings, in which Al Spalding shut out Cincinnati, were silent on Megrue's performance.[69] Walker went on to umpire a total of 29 NL games across three seasons, and after his baseball days, became a theatrical publicist.[70]

Megrue's future exploits were decidedly less entertaining. He inherited a substantial sum of money after his father's death in 1881, but squandered it over the next decade. Reduced to living on the charity of relatives, he died of alcoholism while in his 30s.[71]

A CASE OF MISTAKEN IDENTITY

In addition to the youngsters described above, Retrosheet's database identifies one other teenage major league arbiter in the nineteenth century: Michael Joseph Sullivan, a pitcher with the NL Washington Nationals, is listed as having umpired a game on October 2, 1889, several weeks before his 19th birthday. That game, held at Chicago's West Side Park between the Nationals and the White Stockings, was in fact umpired by another Sullivan: 33-year-old Chicago-native *David* Sullivan. An umpire for the Union Association in 1884 and the National League in 1885, David was filling in for league umpire Pat Powers that day, according to the *Chicago Tribune*.[72] A summary published in the *Chicago Inter-Ocean* also names David as the umpire for that game.[73]

POSTSCRIPT

Of the hundreds of major league umpires who've worked a regular season game since the turn of the twentieth century, only one is known to have been a teenager: 19-year-old Roger Dierking, an emergency replacement during the one-day umpires strike in 1978.[74] An airline employee and part-time college umpire in Chula Vista, California, he was two months shy of his 20th birthday when he umpired at first base for a game between the San Diego Padres and the visiting New York Mets on August 25, 1978, at Jack Murphy Stadium.

In 2018, the average major league umpire was 46 years old, with 13 years of professional experience. In reporting the results of a Boston University study on the correlation between umpire age and accuracy in calling balls and strikes during that season, Fanbuzz noted that the 10 most accurate umpires were over a decade younger than average, with a decade less experience.[75] Eye-opening as that finding may be, the inevitable switch to "robo umps" will make that particular distinction irrelevant in the not-too-distant future. ■

Notes

1. Peter Morris, *A Game of Inches* (Chicago: Ivan R. Dee, 2006), 22.
2. Median age value excludes a half-dozen umpires whose dates of birth are unknown. Retrosheet's database includes 549 individuals who debuted as umpires in one of the four major leagues that were in operation during the nineteenth century (National League, American Association, Union Association and Players' League). Of that group, 7% (36) have unknown dates of birth, with only the year of birth known for another 15% (80). https://www.retrosheet.org/boxesetc/index.html#Umpires.
3. Robert Whaples, "Child Labor in the United States," Economic History, https://eh.net/encyclopedia/child-labor-in-the-united-states/, accessed December 22, 2023.
4. Lauren Bauer, Patrick Liu, Emily Moss, Ryan Nunn and Jay Shambaugh, "All School and No Work Becoming the Norm for American Teens," the Hamilton Project, July 2, 2019, All School and No Work Becoming the Norm for American Teens.
5. Thomas D. Snyder, ed., *120 Years of American Education: A Statistical Portrait* (Washington: U.S. Department of Education National Center for Education Statistics, 1993), 76, https://nces.ed.gov/pubs93/93442.pdf.
6. Richard J. Bonnie, Clare Stroud, and Heather Breiner, eds., *Investing in the Health and Well-Being of Young Adults* (Washington: National Academies Press, 2015), 36, https://www.ncbi.nlm.nih.gov/books/NBK284782/, accessed August 25, 2023. As a result of facing profound physical, cognitive, and emotional changes in an ever-changing world, adolescents, according to the National Institute of Health, "tend to be strongly oriented toward and sensitive to peers, responsive to their immediate environments, limited in self-control, and disinclined to focus on long term consequences, all of which can lead to compromised decision-making skills in emotionally charged situations." Behaviors that are the very opposite of those desirable in a professional umpire.
7. Morris, *A Game of Inches*, 254.
8. Larry R. Gerlach and Bill Nowlin, *The SABR Book of Umpires and Umpiring* (Phoenix: SABR, 2017), 161.
9. The number of umpires debuting in each epoch for whom their year of birth is known was 513 in 1876–1900; 246 in 1901–50; 354 in 1951–2000; and 92 in 2001–20.
10. "Louisville Base Ball Club," Protoball, https://protoball.org/Louisville_Base_Ball_Club, accessed August 28, 2023.
11. "Pull, Duck; Pull, Devil!" *Louisville Courier-Journal*, July 9, 1876, 1. Walsh, who had worked a half-dozen National Association games the year before and nearly 20 to that point of the 1876 NL season, had umpired two games between the Grays and Mutuals earlier that week.
12. "Pull, Duck; Pull, Devil!"
13. "Who Says We're Pie?" *Louisville Courier-Journal*, August 6, 1876, 1; Brian Flaspohler, "Charlie Hautz," SABR, https://sabr.org/bioproj/person/Charlie-Hautz/; "Base Ball," *Evansville* (Indiana) *Journal*, August 4, 1876, 1.
14. "Who Says We're Pie?"
15. "Water Company Auditor, 63, Dies." *Louisville Courier-Journal*, May 27, 1921, 3.
16. "New Haven vs. Boston," *New York Clipper*, May 6, 1876, 45.
17. See, for example, "Brown vs. Amherst," *New York Clipper*, June 26, 1875, 101; and "Yale vs. Brown," *New York Clipper*, June 3, 1876, 75.
18. Two days later, when Ritterson's hands gave out late in a contest with the Hartford Dark Blues, there was nobody willing or able to catch, forcing Lon Knight of the Athletics to pitch the last inning *without a catcher*. Larry DeFillipo, "August 10, 1876: Short-handed Athletics borrow substitute from Mutuals, as both teams careen toward expulsion," https://sabr.org/gamesproj/game/august-10-1876-short-handed-athletics-borrow-substitute-from-mutuals-as-both-teams-careen-toward-expulsion/; "The Bostons Vanquish the Athletics Again," *Boston Globe*, August 7, 1876, 2c.
19. "Ball Games," *Boston Globe*, May 9, 1878, 1; Kathy Torres, "May 8, 1878: Three in one? Paul Hines' unassisted triple play," SABR, https://sabr.org/gamesproj/game/may-8-1878-three-in-one-paul-hines-unassisted-triple-play/.
20. Cross's officiating performance earned him an invitation to become a regular NL umpire for the 1879 and 1880 seasons, but he declined, preferring to run the family mill instead. "Resignation of a League Umpire," *Providence Evening Bulletin*, March 14, 1881, 1; "1878-NON," *Providence Journal*, May 18, 1942, 8.
21. Following the 1873 National Association season, Fenno provided the *Boston Globe* with 28 "interesting" rows that described each player's contributions to the two-time defending champions' 43–16 season. "Interesting Items—The Bostons' Record for 1873," *Boston Globe*, November 10, 1873, 5.
22. "Record of the Champions," *Boston Post*, November 16, 1874, 3.
23. "Base Ball," *Boston Globe*, August 8, 1876, 1.
24. "N.F. Fenno & Co," *Boston Golden Rule*, December 11, 1878, 3.
25. "Eastern Massachusetts," *Springfield Republican*, February 6, 1879, 7.
26. "Base Ball," *Minneapolis Tribune*, September 5, 1877, 2.
27. "The Game," *St. Louis Globe-Democrat*, October 2, 1877, 7; "Base Ball," *Louisville Courier-Journal*, October 2, 1877, 1.
28. "Why the Men Were Expelled," *St. Louis Globe-Democrat*, October 31, 1877, 3. For more information on the fixing scandal, see Daniel E. Ginsburg, "The Louisville Scandal" in *Road Trips: A Trunkload of Great Articles From Two Decades of Convention Journals* (Phoenix: SABR, 2004), 71–72, https://sabr.org/journal/article/the-1877-louisville-grays-scandal/.
29. "The Base-Ball Season Opened," *St. Louis Globe-Democrat*, April 9, 1891, 9. The contest featured the St. Louis Browns hosting Cincinnati, a short-lived team that would soon be dubbed Kelly's Killers. In that game, the team's namesake, captain and catcher Mike "King" Kelly, grew infuriated over four walks Gleason granted to Browns batters. Kelly tore off his glove and stormed off the field. Gleason allowed the petulant Kelly to bat in the next half-inning but barred him from returning to the field.
30. "Today's Game," *Buffalo News*, May 5, 1881, 9.
31. "Sporting Notes," *Buffalo Commercial*, June 9, 1881, 3.
32. "Sporting News," *Buffalo Commercial*, June 30, 1881, 3.
33. "Ill-Mannered Bostons," *Buffalo Express*, July 1, 1881, 4. The Boston players thought deserving of fines were Jack Burdock and Pat Deasley.
34. "Sporting News," *Buffalo News*, July 4, 1881, 1.
35. Charles F. Faber, "Dan Stearns," SABR, https://sabr.org/bioproj/person/dan-stearns/.
36. Based on a game log of Terry's pitching appearances compiled by the author.
37. "The Home Nine Wins," *Brooklyn Eagle*, August 3, 1884, 2.
38. Larry DeFillipo, "Adonis Terry," SABR, https://sabr.org/bioproj/person/adonis-terry/.
39. "Hahn," *Cincinnati Enquirer*, July 13, 1900, 4.
40. "Bunched Hits," *Boston Globe*, August 31, 1886, 2; "If 'Murph' Had Been Well?" *Boston Globe*, August 27, 1886, 3; "The Lynns Get Left," *Boston Globe*, August 25, 1886, 5.
41. "Willie is a Daisy," *Boston Globe*, September 16, 1886, 5.

42. The others were Bill Hallman, Billy Hoy, Gus Weyhing, Hugh Duffy, and Lave Cross.
43. Other ambidextrous pitchers of the nineteenth century included Larry Corcoran and George Wheeler, and possibly Tod Brynan. Charles F. Faber, "Ice Box Chamberlain," SABR, https://sabr.org/bioproj/person/ice-box-chamberlain/.
44. "Ramsey Suspended," *Louisville Courier-Journal*, August 28, 1887, 5; "Hecker Must Go," *Louisville Courier-Journal*, September 19, 1887, 3.
45. "Hecker Must Go."
46. "Six to Four," *Louisville Courier-Journal*, September 23, 1887, 3.
47. "King Tom No More," *Louisville Courier-Journal*, September 26, 1887, 2.
48. "Lost By Poor Fielding," *Washington Evening Star*, September 7, 1891, 3.
49. "Lost By Poor Fielding."
50. "Lost By Poor Fielding." Carsey was hitting for pitcher Ed Cassian, who'd relieved Duke in the disastrous second inning. The accompanying box score doesn't show Carsey batting, but it was common for box scores of that era to omit statistics for pinch-hitters.
51. "Houston Wins from Upland," *Philadelphia Inquirer*, August 2, 1891, 3.
52. See, for example, "Millville, 7; Bridgeton 6," *Philadelphia Inquirer*, June 24, 1896, 5.
53. "The Beaneaters Downed with Much Trouble," *Wilkes-Barre Sunday News*, August 9, 1896, 1.
54. "More Like It," *Philadelphia Inquirer*, August 9, 1896, 8.
55. "More Like It"
56. "More Like It." The front page of the next day's *Philadelphia Times* listed nine heat-related deaths. The heat wave, which affected the eastern half of the US, lasted 10 days and took the lives of an estimated 1,500 people. "Heat Kills Nine More," *Philadelphia Times*, August 9, 1896, 1.
57. "Couldn't Hit Gumbert," *Philadelphia Inquirer*, August 15, 1896, 5.
58. "More Like the Real Stuff," *Philadelphia Inquirer*, August 20, 1896, 5; "Between the Innings," *Philadelphia Times*, August 20, 1896, 8.
59. "We Won and Lost to the Colonels," *Philadelphia Times*, August 21, 1896, 8.
60. "Louisville Was Again a Victim," *Philadelphia Times*, August 22, 1896, 8.
61. "Passed Balls," *Philadelphia Inquirer*, August 22, 1896, 5.
62. "Passed Balls," *Philadelphia Inquirer*, August 23, 1896, 8.
63. "Conahan Gets the Dinky-Dink," *Philadelphia Inquirer*, August 26, 1896, 5.
64. "Gossip for the Fans," *Plainfield* (New Jersey) *Courier-News*, November 20, 1905, 5; "Conahan Released," *Scranton Times-Tribune*, March 5, 1906, 3.
65. "Conahan, Veteran Umpire, Dies After Operation," *Brooklyn Eagle*, July 14, 1929, 3.
66. "In Bed," *Cincinnati Enquirer*, September 12, 1893: 4.
67. "Reorganization of the Ludlows," *Cincinnati Enquirer*, May 17, 1876, 1.
68. See, for example, "Junior Reds vs. Ludlow," *New York Clipper*, June 10, 1876, 85; "In Bed," *Cincinnati Enquirer*, September 12, 1893, 4.
69. "Six to Nothing," *Cincinnati Enquirer*, August 11, 1876, 5; "The Chicagos at Cincinnati," *Chicago Tribune*, August 11, 1876: 5.
70. "'Smiley' Walker Stricken," *Cincinnati Enquirer*, February 8, 1909, 8. Going by the name of "Smiley," Walker's most renowned client was Fanny Davenport, an actress who favored roles created for future silent film star Sarah Bernhardt.
71. "Dizzy from Drink," *Cincinnati Enquirer*, July 29, 1891, 4; "In Bed," *Cincinnati Enquirer*, September 12, 1893, 4.
72. Powers had worked the two previous games of the series. "Their Last Encounter," *Chicago Tribune*, October 3, 1889, 6.
73. Box scores in the *St. Louis Globe-Democrat* and *Cincinnati Enquirer* further support that it was David handling the umpiring chores. Each listed the game's umpire as "D. Sullivan." "Hard Knocks for Krock," *Chicago Inter-Ocean*, October 3, 1889, 6; "Chicagos, 9; Washingtons, 7," *St. Louis Globe-Democrat*, October 3, 1889, 8; "Very Poor Game," *Cincinnati Enquirer*, October 3, 1889, 2.
74. *Chula Vista* (California) *Star-News*, May 5, 1974, B-1; Dave Distel, "Umpires Missing, So Is Hitting by Padres," *Los Angeles Times*, August 26, 1978, III-1.
75. John Duffley, "Study Finds that Old Men with Experience are Actually the Worst MLB Umpires," Fanbuzz, July 7, 2022, https://fanbuzz.com/mlb/worst-mlb-umpires-study/.

The International Association of 1877–80

The Third Professional Baseball Organization

Woody Eckard

Organized professional baseball began in the 1870s with three independent entities. The first was the National Association, which operated from 1871 to 1875. This was followed in 1876 by the National League, which has operated continuously to the present day. The third was the International Association, so called because it initially included Canadian teams. It operated from 1877 to 1880, albeit with an 1879 name change.

While the International Association was overshadowed by the National League, it nevertheless saw itself as a counterpoint, aspiring to approximate parity, and many contemporaries viewed it in the same light. As David Nemec notes, the organizers of the International "in no sense viewed themselves as 'minor' operators." According to the contemporary *New York Clipper*: "Just as the rivalry of the International Association is a benefit to the League, so is the League an advantage to the Association. Each spurs the other on."[2] Tom Melville quotes one period newspaper as saying that "international clubs have batted and fielded better than the League teams," and another claiming that "international clubs can play as good a game as the League nines."[3] He also notes that "the International Association…was certainly presenting the National League with a very troublesome, if not outright threatening, challenge to [its] claim as the top baseball organization."[4]

The main purpose of this article is to provide a concise but detailed history of the International Association, "about which little is known and confusion exists."[5] To my knowledge, it is the first such undertaking. Aside from shedding light on a significant early professional baseball organization, it enables a discussion of how close the International Association came to parity with the National League. The author has assembled a database containing the complete game results for all International clubs in each of its four seasons, including the numerous games between International Association and National League clubs. The primary source is the weekly *New York Clipper* newspaper, supplemented by Newspapers.com.[6]

THE FIRST TWO PROFESSIONAL ORGANIZATIONS

The National Association of Professional Base Ball Players (NA) was founded in 1871, although professional clubs had begun operating openly two years earlier.[7] Its main purpose was to provide structure for the national championship competition. The key feature of the NA was its loose-knit, decentralized structure. Membership was open to any club able to pay a nominal entry fee. There were no other restrictions or conditions such as financial backing, management strength, or host city population as a measure of potential fan base. Multiple clubs in the same city were allowed. In addition, while clubs were required to play a series of championship games with each other club, scheduling was generally left to bilateral arrangements among members with no oversight mechanism to assure compliance. There were no other professional organizations during its five-year existence, perhaps in part because of the open entry policy.

The NA's haphazard structure produced operational instability, with many between-season membership changes and midseason failures. It had 25 different clubs, with annual membership ranging from eight to 13. On five occasions, cities had multiple clubs, including three in Philadelphia in 1875. Seventeen different cities were represented, ranging in population from the likes of New York and Philadelphia down to such small towns as Keokuk, Iowa, and Middletown, Connecticut. It was mainly an eastern organization. During its middle three years of operation, there were only two western clubs, meaning west of the Allegheny Mountains.

In 1876, the NA was replaced by the National League of Professional Base Ball Clubs, which addressed many of the NA shortcomings.[8] Six of the NA's best clubs joined, causing it to fold. The NL's largely unanticipated creation was announced in February 1876, too late for another organization to form that season. Entry into the National League was subject to review. Membership was restricted to a single club from cities with populations of at least 75,000 to promote financial viability, although a few early exceptions were made to the population requirement. A $100 annual membership fee was required, equivalent to roughly $3,100 in 2023 dollars.[9] Also, the number of members was limited to six or eight during its first 16 years of operation. In 1877, scheduling was centralized, creating the first fixed schedule, and in 1878, for the first time, all six teams completed their planned 60 games. Importantly, clubs were expected to complete their schedule. As noted by Michael Haupert: "League-created scheduling would become a bedrock upon which the stability of leagues has been built ever since."[10] In the late 1800s, the NL achieved geographical balance in most years by locating an equal number of teams in the East and West.

The National League began as an eight-team circuit. After the first season, the Mutuals of Brooklyn and the Athletics of Philadelphia were expelled for canceling scheduled end-of-season road trips. In 1877 and 1878, the NL operated with six clubs, returning to the eight-club format from 1879 to 1891. In 1877, Cincinnati disbanded in mid-June. However, a second Cincinnati club was quickly organized, beginning play three weeks later, and managed to finish the first club's schedule.[11] In 1879, Syracuse also folded, failing to complete its schedule with 14 games remaining. By modern standards, the National League initially experienced significant membership instability, with 16 different clubs in the first five years. Nevertheless, that improved upon the NA's 25 clubs during its five-year existence and its many more midseason failures.

THE INTERNATIONAL ASSOCIATION

After months of preliminary discussions beginning in the fall of 1876, the International Association (the International) was organized at a Pittsburgh meeting on February 20, 1877.[12] Twenty-one clubs were represented, although only seven later entered the initial championship competition. After the two Canadian clubs departed, the name was changed to the National Association in 1879. Aside from sponsoring the competition, its other main function was to regulate the player market, mainly to prevent contract jumping ("revolving") via mutual contract recognition among all members, including those not contending for the championship. Our focus is on clubs involved in the championship competition.It should be noted at the outset that a national economic depression had begun in 1873 that lasted until the spring of 1879.[13] It no doubt contributed to the International's problems. This was an inauspicious time to be starting a major new economic endeavor.

The International adopted the NA's unstructured organizational model, eschewing the National League model. In fact, it was largely inspired by a rejection of the NL's exclusive entry policy. As we shall see, this decision was a fundamental mistake.

The result was what David Pietrusza described as a "loose confederation" of clubs.[14] Initially, general membership was open to any professional club for a $10 fee, and an additional $15 was required to enter the championship competition.[15] These fees are roughly $310 and $460, respectively, in 2023 dollars. Both memberships were for a single year. There were no other restrictions or conditions. In 1878, each of these fees were doubled. Applications were to be submitted each year by April 1, with the championship season running from April 15 to October 15. Game admission fees were set at 25 cents, in contrast with the National League's 50 cents, respectively about $7.70 and $15.40 in 2023 dollars. Gross gate receipts were to be split evenly, except for a guaranteed minimum of $75 for the visiting team, about $2,300 in 2023 dollars. Geographically, the International was concentrated in the northeastern US, with 13 cities in Massachusetts and New York alone, although no clubs were in Boston, Brooklyn, or New York City. Each championship contender was required to play a specified number of championship games with each other contender. These were to be scheduled by a committee at the beginning of the season, but implementation was haphazard. Instead, bilateral scheduling among clubs seemed to be the norm and, as in the NA, no oversight mechanism existed. In fact, there seemed to be no expectation that clubs would complete their schedule of championship games. For example, an algorithm was defined for adjusting team standings for presumed mid-season departures, of which there were many.

There was substantial instability in the number of championship contenders over the International's four-year existence. Seven clubs participated in the championship competition in the initial year, followed by 13 in 1878 and nine 1879, then only four in the unfinished final season. A total of 23 different clubs competed during the four years, and 22 cities were represented. In 1879 Albany, New York, began the season with two clubs. Also, there were late entrants in 1878 and 1880, and on four occasions clubs relocated midseason. Of the 22 cities, 13 were members for only one year, and another seven for two. The Manchester Club of New Hampshire was in for three years. Only Rochester was represented in all four, albeit with three different clubs.

In-season instability was also a significant problem as many clubs failed to complete their schedules.

Fourteen disbanded for financial reasons, two were expelled for rule violations, and one withdrew voluntarily, completing its season as an independent. In contrast, during this same period, the National League had 14 member cities and clubs and only two failures.

A critical result was confusion regarding the International pennant race. By midseason, newspapers often were reporting multiple standings in the same issue based on various assumptions about how the International's Judiciary Committee would make adjustments for departed clubs. Also, members were allowed to play exhibition games among themselves during the championship season, creating additional confusion about which games counted. As Brian Martin observes, fans "were disappointed when a game believed to be for the pennant turned out to be an exhibition."[16] Last, because of the two membership classes, early in the season there was often confusion about which members were involved in the championship competition. In all three years that a champion was declared, winners were not known for sure until the Judiciary Committee's report at the annual convention several months after the season's end.

A large difference existed between the International Association and the National League in terms of member city population, with the NL in much larger cities. During 1877–80, it had 10 cities with populations exceeding 100,000, while the International had only four.[17] At the other end, all NL cities exceeded 50,000, while the International had no fewer than 11 smaller than that, with three under 10,000. Overall, NL city population averaged about 210,000 during that four-year period, while the International averaged only about a third of that: 69,700. In fact, Ted Vincent argues that "the International…really represented…the organized expression of an immense popularity of baseball in the smaller industrial city."[18] At no point did the International Association and the National League share the same city.

Despite its shortcomings, the International Association was given favorable press by the leading national baseball newspaper of that time, the *New York Clipper*. Its baseball editor, Henry Chadwick, was the top baseball journalist of the era and is a member of the National Baseball Hall of Fame in Cooperstown.[19] The *Clipper*'s coverage of the International was similar to that of the NL regarding the championship competition and the reporting of club standings. Chadwick had taken a strong editorial position critical of the NL's exclusive membership policy immediately upon its inception. He preferred the open entry approach of the NA, which was adopted by the International, and

hoped for the newer league's success. Neil Macdonald describes Chadwick as "the leader of the reportorial minority who opposed [the NL's] creation."[20] One manifestation of Chadwick's antipathy towards the National League was his attempt to undermine the claim that its restrictive business model produced higher quality baseball.[21] To this end, from 1877 through 1880, he periodically published articles in the *Clipper* pointing out that National League clubs lost many of their numerous exhibition games against non-NL opponents. Focusing mainly on games against International clubs, these articles summarized NL losses, but the many more NL victories usually were not reported, a fact that revealed Chadwick's agenda. The result was favorable, if biased, national publicity for the International.

THE NATIONAL LEAGUE REACTION

Although they did not compete directly for fans, the National League was concerned about the International as a competitor for players and prestige, which in turn could indirectly affect home-fan demand. One expression of this concern was the League Alliance, an agreement initiated in February 1877 between the National League and several independent clubs, ostensibly for mutual contact recognition.[22] As Brock Helander notes: "The League Alliance arose as the National League…response to the perceived threat of the International Association."[23] Having expelled clubs in its two largest cities, Brooklyn and Philadelphia, its lineup was reduced to six clubs for 1877, with only two from the much more populous East. As noted above, at this time the NL's future was still uncertain.

The weekly *New York Clipper* first announced the Alliance on January 20, 1877, in the same issue that it first announced the February 20 convention to organize the International Association. A National League representative, described anonymously as "a gentleman from Chicago" (likely Albert Spalding), provided the particulars of the Alliance proposal.[24] Included was a statement strongly suggesting a preemptive motive: Non-NL clubs would "derive far more substantial advantages from this arrangement than from any experimental association that they might organize independently."[25] In fact, a *St. Louis Globe-Democrat* article on the Alliance was headlined: "War Declared Between the League and the Internationals."[26]

While League Alliance member clubs would be protected from player "pirating" by other members, the subtext was that the unprotected players on non-members might be "fair game." Also, independent clubs contemplating International membership might be deterred by fears of retribution by the National League. Concerns regarding NL motives were reinforced by a stipulation in the Alliance agreement that the Judiciary Committee charged with resolving disputes would be composed only of NL clubs, excluding non-league members. Initially, International clubs were not barred from joining. However, in the fall of 1877 the NL added a rule that non-NL clubs belonging to the Alliance could not be members of any other organization, effectively barring International clubs.[27] This, of course, made clear its true purpose as an anti-International vehicle.

Another expression of National League concern was the so-called Buffalo Compact, signed at a meeting in Buffalo on April 1, 1878. It gave preferential treatment to six of the better International clubs in scheduling postseason games with National League clubs and established mutual recognition of player contracts, in effect accepting these clubs into the Alliance.[28] Exceptions were granted to the rule barring membership in other organizations, allowing them to remain as members of the International. Four of the other seven 1878 International clubs reacted by refusing to schedule games with National League clubs, although none resigned over the issue. Both the League Alliance and the Buffalo Compact were generally interpreted as attempts by the National League to undermine the International by preempting possible new member clubs, limiting player availability, and sowing internal discord.[29] However, the International had nobody but itself to blame for its many difficulties.

THE INTERNATIONAL'S FOUR SEASONS

The International Association completed only three of its four seasons. In 1880, at most, four clubs competed at any one time, and that just for a short period. By the end of July, only two clubs remained and the International was effectively history, fading away with no formal announcement of disbanding.

As noted above, numerous intra-International exhibition games and adjustments for failed teams confused the standings. The number of official championship games counted at season's end typically was half or less of the total number of intra-International games. We report both below. Nevertheless, by either measure, in its three full seasons the International's championship competition was reasonably competitive, with no

dominant clubs, unlike the old National Association of 1871–75. Also, only in 1878 was there some totally "out-of-it" teams, when the Alleghenys and Hartfords combined for a 4–40 record in all International games played. In contrast, clubs at both extremes were a problem for the NA.

The 1877 Season

The seven clubs that entered the inaugural championship competition in 1877 were the Alleghenys of Allegheny City (a city later annexed by Pittsburgh); the Buckeyes of Columbus; the Live Oaks of Lynn, Massachusetts; the Manchesters (New Hampshire); the Maple Leafs of Guelph, Ontario; the Rochesters; and the Tecumsehs of London, Ontario[30]. Only Allegheny City, Columbus, and Rochester had 1880 populations exceeding 50,000. Newspaper reports indicated that more were expected to enter, but none did. Several other clubs joined for player contract protection only. The Buckeyes and Live Oaks both disbanded late in the season, in mid-September, while the others completed their schedules.[31] By the standards of the time, this was a successful start. For example, the next professional organization, the minor four-club Northwestern Base Ball League of 1879, disbanded in mid-July after only three months of operation.[32]

The 1877 International standings are shown in Table 1. Each contender was supposed to play four championship games against each other contender, but it wasn't until early September that the International decided that it would be the first four such games that would count.[34] The left panel of Table 1 is the official championship standings as determined by the International Judiciary Committee and made public at the annual convention in February 1878.[35] The committee also resolved an ongoing dispute between the top two contenders regarding which games would count in their championship records. The right panel of Table 1 shows all games between members,

Table 1. 1877 International Association Standings[33]

	Official Final Standings				All IA games					
	G	W	L	AVG	G	W	L	T	AVG	
Tecumseh	18	14	4	.778	30	18	7	5	.683	
Allegheny	16	11	5	.688	22	15	7	0	.682	
Rochester	14	7	7	.500	29	16	12	1	.569	
Manchester	16	6	10	.375	24	12	12	0	.500	
Buckeye	12	4	8	.333	23	9	11	3	.457	Disbanded Mid-September
Maple Leaf	16	4	12	.250	23	5	16	2	.261	
Live Oak	0	—	—	—	19	4	14	1	.237	Disbanded Mid-September

57

including exhibitions and championship games officially excluded because of adjustments for games with the disbanded Buckeye and Live Oak clubs. The Tecumseh Club (Figure 1) was the official champion with a 14–4 record, and the Alleghenys were not far behind at 11–5.

Note that, with the four-game requirement and seven contenders, a full season with all teams completing their schedule would have been only 24 championship games each. As it happened, with the excluded games, only the Tecumsehs had as many as 18 games that counted. The Live Oaks played no games against two members before they disbanded, and so none of their games counted for any team, per the adjustment algorithm.

Meanwhile, the National League had a 60-game schedule, with all teams playing at least 57 games that counted.[36] This was another problem for the Internationals: their infrequent games made it difficult to establish brand identity. As the *Clipper* put it on July 28: "The contest for the championship of the International does not progress very fast, the meetings between the contesting nines being few and far between."[37]

The 1878 Season

The 1878 season saw the addition of eight new clubs, with five holdovers, for a total of 13.[38] Only the Buckeyes and Maple Leafs elected not to reenter.[39] The net increase of six, of course, was a positive sign; the new clubs apparently found the International attractive based on the 1877 showing. The additions were New York teams the Buffalos, the Crickets of Binghamton, the Hornells of Hornellsville, the Stars of Syracuse, and the Uticas; and Massachusetts teams the Lowells, New Bedfords, and Springfields.[40] Of these additions, only Buffalo, Lowell, and Syracuse had populations exceeding 50,000.

On April 20, 1878, the International's Scheduling Committee published in the *New York Clipper* a complete season's schedule of championship games for all 13 members.[41] This was likely inspired by similar set schedules of championship games first announced by the National League at the beginning of the 1877 season. The committee explicitly "permit[ted] clubs to arrange State championship and exhibition games on any open dates" during the championship season.[42] The exhibitions could be with International clubs. And the state championship games in several cases involved other International members, i.e., they were also championship games but not for the International, adding to the confusion.

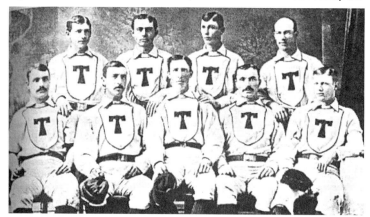

Figure 1. 1877 Tecumseh Baseball Club, International Association Champions

AUTHOR'S COLLECTION

Unfortunately, membership turmoil started almost immediately, and the official schedule became largely a dead letter.[43] First, the New Bedfords withdrew on May 5, shortly after entering, finishing the season as an independent. At that point the New Haven Club entered, picking up the New Bedford schedule. About two weeks later, the New Havens moved to Hartford, adopting the Hartford name. This thread was concluded when Hartford was expelled from the Association on July 17 for failing to pay a visiting International club the required share of proceeds from a home game. The Live Oaks also moved, merging with the existing independent Worcester Club in late May, and adopting that club's name. The combined club remained an International member, assuming the Live Oaks's record and schedule. These disturbances were compounded by several midseason failures. The Alleghenys disbanded on June 8, the Crickets on July 9, the Hornells on August 21, the Tecumsehs in late August, the Rochesters on September 7, and the Worcesters in mid-September.[44] Each of these failures created another round of speculation regarding adjustments to the standings. Confusion about the championship race existed for most of the summer.

On September 21 the *Clipper* observed that "things have become so mixed that the [International] Association Judiciary Committee are likely to become insane before they arrive at a satisfactory conclusion" regarding the standings (Figure 2).[45] A January 4, 1879, *Clipper* review article described the 1878 season as "chaotic," recommending "a tighter rein [on] clubs entering for the championship competition" to exclude those "unable to carry out their engagements."[46] The 1878 tumult stood in sharp contrast to the mostly successful inaugural season.

The final standings are shown in Table 2. As with Table 1, the left panel is the official standings as finally sorted out by the Judiciary Committee and presented at the annual convention of February 19–20, 1879.[47] The right panel shows all games between members, including exhibitions, state championship games, and adjustment exclusions. The Buffalos (Figure 3) were atop the official standings, with a 24–8 record, and the Stars were a close second at 23–9. Of the total of 345 games actually played between International clubs, only 154, less than half, counted in the standings. All of the New Bedford and expelled Hartford games were excluded, with the number counted for remaining clubs varying from 11 to 32. A full season would have been 48 games given the four-game requirement and assuming no departures. Meanwhile, all six National League teams completed their 60-game schedules.

The 1879 Season

The 1879 edition of the International saw nine clubs sign up for the championship competition.[48] The Canadians having withdrawn, it was renamed the National Association. However, we will continue to use the

Figure 2. A clipping from the *New York Clipper* of September 21, 1878

Table 2. 1878 International Association Standings

	Official Final Standings				All IA games					
	G	W	L	AVG	G	W	L	T	AVG	
Buffalo	32	24	8	.750	73	50	21	2	.699	
Star	32	23	9	.719	70	44	24	2	.643	
Tecumseh	20	14	6	.700	55	31	23	1	.573	Disbanded Aug 23
Utica	32	19	13	.594	73	40	30	3	.568	
Manchester	32	18	14	.563	66	34	30	2	.530	
Hornell	20	10	10	.500	52	25	26	1	.490	Disbanded Aug 22
Cricket	11	5	6	.455	39	15	23	1	.397	Disbanded July 9
Rochester	27	12	15	.444	68	38	30	0	.559	Disbanded Sept 11
Lowell	32	13	19	.406	55	26	28	1	.482	
Springfield	32	9	23	.281	48	14	32	2	.313	
LO-Wor	27	7	20	.259	43	14	28	1	.337	Disbanded Sept 12
Allegheny	11	0	11	.000	26	2	24	0	.077	Disbanded June 8
New Bedford	0	–	–	–	4	2	2	0	.500	Withdrew May 5
NH-Hart	0	–	–	–	18	2	16	0	.111	Expelled July 20

Figure 3. 1878 Buffalo Baseball Club, International Association Champions

AUTHOR'S COLLECTION

International name to avoid confusion with the old National Association of 1871–75.

After the chaotic 1878 season, the new lineup saw a major turnover. Nine clubs departed, including the Buffalos and the Stars, who were admitted to the National League. On the plus side, four new clubs joined: the Albanys and Capital Citys, both from New York's state capital; the Holyokes, in Massachusetts, and the Nationals of Washington. Both Albany and Washington had populations exceeding 50,000. The net reduction of five implied a negative market reaction to the 1878 turmoil; the open entry policy also meant "open exit." There is no evidence that the International followed the *Clipper*'s advice to modify the open entry policy or took any other steps to improve its operation. While two of the three newly admitted 1879 cities had large populations, this was most likely happenstance.

As in the previous year, a significant proportion of clubs did not complete their seasons, again creating confusion about team standings.[49] First, the Manchesters and Uticas disbanded in July, as did the Springfields in early September. Second, in early May the Capital City Club relocated to Rochester as the Hop Bitters Club, which then disbanded in mid-July.[50] This thread ended when the International's Judiciary Committee later determined that the relocation had been in violation of its rules in the first place, and therefore retroactively expelled the Hop Bitters.[51] The standings were then adjusted to exclude all their games. On July 26, the *Clipper* reiterated its January 4 recommendation that the International should "limit championship contests to clubs which…carry out their appointed season's programme [*sic*]."[52]

The 1879 standings are shown in Table 3, following the same format as Tables 1 and 2. The Albanys were the champion with a 25–13 record, and the Nationals were

not far behind at 22–16. Both were new members. Note that in the official standings, again as reported in the Clipper, four clubs had 38 games that counted; the "required" number of games against each member had been increased to eight.[53] Once more, less than half of the actual games played between International members counted. And again, the difference can be attributed mainly to exhibition games. The *Clipper* of July 12 argued that those games should be abolished because they "create confusion in making up the record."[54] National League rules prohibited intraleague exhibitions during the championship season.

A second consecutive problematic season for the Internationals may have influenced the National League's decision to implement its player reserve system in the fall of 1879. Perhaps the International was no longer seen as a competitive threat in hiring players. In addition to offering generally lower salaries, men not signing with a winning team likely would be scrambling for a new job by midseason. With the National League, a steady paycheck until the season's end would be much more likely.

Despite its many difficulties, the International Association nevertheless managed to complete three seasons and move on to a fourth. The next new professional organization to achieve this was the major league American Association of 1882–91.

The 1880 Season

As noted above, the 1880 season was a rump affair. Only three clubs initially entered for the International championship.[55] They were the Albanys, the Baltimores, and the National Club. The Albanys and the Nationals were holdovers after finishing first and second in 1879. The International Association clearly was failing after two chaotic seasons. Nevertheless, the championship competition was launched, with newspapers dutifully reporting three-club standings. A newly formed Rochester club joined on June 8 to make it four until the Baltimores disbanded three weeks later.[56] On July 9, the National Club moved to Springfield to reduce travel costs with the remaining Albany and Rochester clubs. Springfield had been an International member in 1878 and 1879. Two other clubs were falsely rumored to have joined midseason, occasionally included in the standings by some newspapers.

The coup de grace occurred when the Albany Club disbanded around July 20, leaving only the Rochesters

Table 3. 1879 International Association Standings

| | Official Final Standings | | | | All IA games | | | | | |
	G	W	L	AVG	G	W	L	T	AVG	
Albany	38	25	13	.658	67	44	21	2	.672	
National	38	22	16	.579	62	32	27	3	.540	
Manchester	13	7	6	.538	42	15	27	0	.357	Disbanded July 6
Springfield	28	15	13	.536	61	35	25	1	.582	Disbanded Sept 6
Holyoke	32	17	15	.531	61	31	26	4	.541	
Worcester	38	16	22	.421	75	41	33	1	.553	
New Bedford	38	12	26	.316	59	22	36	1	.381	
Utica	7	2	5	.286	37	11	26	0	.297	Disbanded July 13
Cap City – Roch	0	–	–	–	30	10	20	0	.333	Expelled late July

and Nationals. On July 24, the *Clipper* published what amounted to an obituary, attributing the International's demise to "bad management," although an almost total absence of management might be closer to the truth.[57] The article further noted that "the Nationals have joined the League Alliance…and thereby have been obliged to resign from the [International] Association…thus ends the 'strange, eventful history' of the Association."[58] There was no published announcement by the International that it had dissolved and apparently no champion was declared. Newspapers, of course, quit publishing standings. Nevertheless, for the record, Table 4 presents the standings for all games between the four 1880 members, as determined by the author. The National Club clearly dominated with a 32–11–3 record, and the other three all under .500.

Table 4. 1880 International Association Unofficial Standings

All IA games

	G	W	L	T	AVG	
National	46	32	11	3	.728	
Rochester	15	7	8	0	.467	
Albany	35	11	21	3	.357	Disbanded July 20
Baltimore	24	7	17	0	.292	Disbanded June 28

THE INTERNATIONAL ASSOCIATION VS. THE NATIONAL LEAGUE

The relative strength of the International and the NL is of interest, given that it was the subject of debate among contemporaries. The most straightforward assessment is to look at the results of the numerous games between clubs in the two organizations. In fact, contemporary newspapers often published summaries of outsider victories over NL clubs for that reason. For example, the *Clipper* of September 28, 1878, reported a detailed analysis of 1878 National League vs International Association games.[59] In evaluating the results of these exhibition games, one must keep in mind that NL clubs often did not have their A-team on the field. Exhibitions were an opportunity to, e.g., provide the "change" pitcher and/or catcher some practice, as well as any reserve players. Also, player motivation was likely lower in these non-championship contests. Nevertheless, NL clubs needed to be careful lest losses to weak clubs damage their brand, including raising suspicions of throwing games, particularly after the Louisville scandal of 1877.[60] Another factor was that these games were usually on the opposing team's home field, often meaning a home team umpire. And its players may have had an extra motivation, perceiving

the game as a tryout for the visiting NL club.[61] Thus, the International's overall performance in these exhibitions must be viewed only as an upper bound on its quality relative to the National League.

Table 5 summarizes interleague game results by year for the 232 such games yielded by our search over the 1877–80 period. During those four years, International clubs were 84–139–9 versus all NL clubs, a .381 winning average.[62] By comparison, the National League's second-division clubs had an almost identical winning average (i.e., vs. all NL clubs) of .376 during the same period. A similar number of interleague games occurred in each year, varying from 54 to 63, the maximum occurring in 1880 despite the International having only four members. The winning average was also similar in each of the four years, varying from .327 to .425. Recall that this comparison yields only an upper bound on the International's relative quality. Accordingly, these data indicate the average International Association club was certainly of lower quality than the average National League club.[63]

Table 5. Aggregate Record of IA Teams Against NL Teams

Year	G	W	L	T	AVG
1877	55	18	37	0	.327
1878	60	24	33	3	.425
1879	54	19	31	4	.389
1880	63	23	38	2	.381
Total	232	84	139	9	.381

It is also interesting to look at the record of individual clubs against the National League. Table 6 presents the seven International teams with at least 10 such games in a single season. The 1880 National Club won the most with 12, but also lost 15 (plus 2 draws). The 1878 Buffalos were 10–8 and in 1879 the Worcester Club was 7–5. The significant number of games played by the Albanys and Nationals in 1880 may have been attempts at auditioning for National League membership, albeit unsuccessfully.

Table 6. Single-season Records of IA Teams vs. NL Teams

	Year	G	W	L	T	AVG
Worcester	1879	12	7	5	0	.583
Buffalo	1878	18	10	8	0	.556
Allegheny	1877	20	9	11	0	.450
National	1880	29	12	15	2	.448
Cap City – Roch	1879	11	4	7	0	.364
Albany	1880	22	7	15	0	.318
Albany	1879	15	4	9	2	.333

Minimum 10 games played

Another consideration is that three International clubs were "promoted" to the National League: the Buffalos and Stars for the 1879 season and the Worcesters in 1880. The Buffalos and Stars were first and second in the 1878 International race, and Worcester finished fourth in 1879. The NL actions here may have been, in part, another attempt to undermine the International by pirating some of its leading teams. Buffalo did well in 1879, finishing third in the NL with a 46–32 record, and Worcester was respectable at 40–43 in 1880, landing in fifth place in the eight-team circuit. The 1879 Stars did poorly, however, finishing in seventh place with a 22–48 record and disbanding before the season's end. Nevertheless, the International provided the NL with half of its six new clubs in 1878–81.

DISCUSSION AND CONCLUSIONS

How close did the International Association come to achieving its aspiration of rough parity with the National League? Its history suggests that any such argument rests mainly on the 232 games against NL teams. Our analysis indicates an overall winning average of .377. However, some International clubs had more respectable individual records, and three were deemed worthy of NL membership. Nevertheless, overall, the average International club was, at most, roughly equivalent to the National League's average second-division clubs.

The remainder of the International's ledger provides little support for parity. First, it was basically regional, mainly confined to eastern US cities, with more than half its clubs in only two states. Columbus, Ohio, was the westernmost member, and that for only a single year, and only four other of its 22 cities qualify as western by 1870s standards.

The International's haphazard operation is a more serious issue. This produced highly unstable membership, muddled championship competitions, and many clubs in cities that were too small to support them. These related problems arose from the adoption of the old National Association (1871–75) organizational model that Pietrusza aptly described as "rather miserable." For example, the open-entry policy yielded 11 clubs in cities with populations under 50,000, while the National League had none. This contributed to high rates of year-to-year membership turnover and midseason failure that were a particular problem for the International. It had 14 failures, while the NL had only two during the same period. In each of its three completed seasons, the championship was in dispute for months after the season ended. In sum,

operationally it was, for the most part, a proverbial train wreck. Per the *Clipper*, "bad management" produced its…"strange history."[65]

Thus, the short answer to the question of how close the International came to parity is: "not very." The International's operating model was not thrust upon it. Also, during its four years of existence, apparently no attempt was made to correct the many shortcomings, despite newspapers not being shy about pointing them out. Had the National League model initially been adopted, or had the International been able to learn from its mistakes, it might have achieved rough parity. Perhaps the International Association's main legacy was that the juxtaposition of its performance on that of the National League's in 1877–80 provided baseball entrepreneurs clear evidence that the NL's operating model was superior. ■

Acknowledgments

The author is grateful for helpful comments from two reviewers.

Notes

1. David Nemec, *The Great Encyclopedia of Nineteenth Century Major League Baseball*, 2nd ed. (Tuscaloosa: University of Alabama Press, 2006), 130.
2. "The International Association," *New York Clipper*, January 4, 1879, 325. The *Clipper* was a weekly newspaper self-described as "The Oldest American Sporting and Theatrical Journal." It was the leading national baseball journal of that period.
3. Tom Melville, *Early Baseball and the Rise of the National League* (Jefferson NC: McFarland, 2001), 104–5.
4. Melville, *Early Baseball*, 104.
5. Brian Martin, *The Tecumsehs of the International Association: Canada's First Major League Baseball Champions* (Jefferson NC: McFarland, 2015), 9.
6. The *Clipper* reported box scores on virtually all professional games. Issues can be accessed via the Illinois Digital Newspaper Collections, University of Illinois Library: https://idnc.library.illinois.edu/?a=cl&cl=CL1&sp=NYC&e=-------en-20--1--txt-txIN----------.
7. For a history of the National Association, see William J. Ryczek, *Blackguards and Red Stockings: A History of Baseball's National Association, 1871–1875*, Revised Edition (Jefferson NC: McFarland, 2016)
8. For histories of the early National League, see Melville, *Early Baseball*, and Neil Macdonald, *The League That Lasted: 1876 and the Founding of the National League of Professional Base Ball Clubs* (Jefferson NC: McFarland, 2004).
9. These and all other conversions to 2023 dollars herein are based on a 19th century Consumer Price Index series available at the Federal Reserve Bank of Minneapolis, https://www.minneapolisfed.org/about-us/monetary-policy/inflation-calculator/consumer-price-index-1800-.
10. Michael Haupert, "In the Face of Crisis: The 1876 Winter Meetings," in Jeremy K. Hodges and Bill Nowlin, eds., *Base Ball's 19th Century "Winter" Meetings: 1857–1900* (Phoenix: SABR, 2018), 140.
11. MLB today recognizes the two as a single combined club, although at the end of the 1877 season the National League excluded both clubs from its official final standings. For example, see Woody Eckard, "The 1877 National League's Two Cincinnati Clubs: Were They In or Out, and Why the Confusion?" *Baseball Research Journal*, Volume 52, no. 1 (2023), 80–85.
12. "The International Association," *New York Clipper*, March 3, 1877, 387.

This article reported the International's founding convention, giving its full name as "International Association of Professional Baseball Clubs," and the *Clipper* used the same name again reporting the second annual convention. A search of newspapers.com yielded only two other contemporary newspaper reports of the founding that included the full name. But both had it as "International Association of Base-Ball Players" ("Baseball: The International Association," *Chicago Tribune*, February 25, 1877, 7; and "The National Game," *Pittsburgh Post-Gazette*, February 22, 1877, 4). The two modern historians with the most extensive coverage of the International both use the same *third* version: "International Association of Professional Base Ball Players" (Martin, The Tecumsehs, 264; and David Pietrusza, *Major Leagues: The Formation, Sometimes Absorption and Mostly Inevitable Demise of 18 Professional Baseball Organizations, 1871 to Present* (Lemurpress.com: Lemur Press, 2020), 48). This is one example of the "confusion" that exists regarding the International, as noted by Martin (see endnote 5). The reader may pick and choose.

13. Per the official business cycle dating of the National Bureau of Economic Research: https://www.nber.org/research/data/us-business-cycle-expansions-and-contractions.

14. Pietrusza, *Major Leagues*, 28.

15. "The International Championship," *New York Clipper*, March 31, 1877, 2. This article contains the complete rules governing the International Association championship competition.

16. Martin, *The Tecumsehs*, 100.

17. This count combines the populations of Allegheny City and Pittsburgh. All population data reported herein are from the 1880 U.S. Census.

18. Ted Vincent, *Mudville's Revenge: The Rise and Fall of American Sport* (New York: Seaview Books, 1981), 142.

19. Chadwick is a Hall member as an "executive," based mainly on his contributions to the development of baseball rules and scoring conventions.

20. Macdonald, *The League That Lasted*, 61.

21. For example, see Woody Eckard, "Henry Chadwick and the National League's Performance vs. 'Outsiders,'" *Baseball Research Journal* 52, no. 2 (2023), 67–76.

22. The League Alliance did not sponsor a championship competition, although newspapers occasionally reported standings. See Brock Helander, "The League Alliance," SABR, https://sabr.org/bioproj/topic/theleague-alliance/, last accessed December 20, 2023..

23. Helander, "The League Alliance."

24. "The League and Its Work," *New York Clipper*, January 20, 1877, 339. See also "Ball to the Bat," *St. Louis Globe-Democrat*, January 15, 1877, 5; "Baseball: Spalding Indulges in a Defense," *Chicago Tribune*, January 28, 1877, 7; and "Spalding's Scheme," *St. Louis Globe-Democrat*, January 28, 1877, 7. Spalding was the star pitcher on the 1876 National League champion Chicago club, and its president, William Hulbert, was also the National League president. Spalding was no doubt acting as his agent.

25. "The League and Its Work," *New York Clipper*.

26. "Ball to the Bat," *St. Louis Globe-Democrat*.

27. For example, see "Ball Talk," *New York Clipper*, December 22, 1877, 306; and "The International Association," *New York Clipper*, December 29, 1877, 314.

28. For example, see Helander, "The League Alliance"; "The Buffalo Conference," *New York Clipper*, April 13, 1878, 21; and "The Buffalo Conference and Its Work," *New York Clipper*, April 20, 1878, 29. The International clubs were the Buffalos, Lowells, Rochesters, Springfields, Stars, and Tecumsehs.

29. See Helander, "The League Alliance."

30. "The International Championship," *New York Clipper*, May 26, 1877, 66. At this time, Allegheny City was a separate polity located across the Allegheny River from Pittsburgh. It was annexed by Pittsburgh in 1907.

31. "The International Championship," *New York Clipper*, September 29, 1877, 210.

32. "The Northwestern League," *New York Clipper*, July 26, 1879, 139.

33. Winning average counts draws as one half of a win each.

34. See "International Championship," *New York Clipper*, September 1, 1877, 179; and "The International Championship," *New York Clipper*, September 8, 1877, 187.

35. "The International Convention," *New York Clipper*, March 2, 1878, 386.

36. "1877 National League Team Statistics," Baseball Reference, https://www.baseball-reference.com/leagues/NL/1877.shtml.

37. "International Pennant Race," *New York Clipper*, July 28, 1877, 138.

38. "International Ass'n Movements," *New York Clipper*, April 6, 1878, 10.

39. The Buckeyes and Maple Leafs had disbanded in September of the previous year, but it was not uncommon at this time for disbanded clubs to reorganize and resume play in the next season or even in the current one.

40. The 1877 Lowells were the top independent club in the country that year, comparable in quality to the National League champion Bostons. See Woody Eckard, "The Lowell Base Ball Club of 1877: National Champions?," *Nineteenth Century Notes* (SABR), Bob Bailey and Peter Mancuso, eds., (Summer 2022), 1–5.

41. "The International Association," *New York Clipper*, April 20, 1878, 29.

42. "The International Association."

43. A detailed summary of club departures can be found in "Baseball—The Buffalos and the League," *The Buffalo Commercial*, November 26, 1878, 3.

44. "Baseball—The Buffalos and the League."

45. "The International Arena," *New York Clipper*, September 21, 1878, 202.

46. "The International Association," *New York Clipper*, January 4, 1879, 325.

47. "The International Convention," *New York Clipper*, March 1, 1879, 386.

48. "The Coming Season," *New York Clipper*, March 29, 1879, 5.

49. "The National Arena," *New York Clipper*, October 11, 1879, 226.

50. Hop Bitters was the name of a patent "medicine" whose manufacturer decided that owning a baseball team would be good advertising. See Tim Wolter, "The Rochester Hop Bitters: A Dose of Baseball in Upstate New York," *The National Pastime* 17 (1997), 38–40.

51. "The Rochester Club," *Brooklyn Daily Eagle*, July 22, 1879, 3.

52. "The National Arena," *New York Clipper*, July 26, 1879, 138.

53. "The National Association Convention," *New York Clipper*, February 28, 1880, 389.

54. "The National Arena," *New York Clipper*, July 12, 1879, 123.

55. "The National Association's Schedule," *New York Clipper*, May 1, 1880, 44.

56. "The National Association Clubs," *New York Clipper*, July 24, 1880, 138.

57. "The National Association Clubs."

58. "The National Association Clubs."

59. "League vs. International," *New York Clipper*, September 28, 1878, 210.

60. Four Louisville players were expelled for throwing games, leading to the club's resignation from the National League. For example, see Melville, *Early Baseball*, 92–93.

61. Excluding the six International clubs that joined the Buffalo Compact of 1878 and thus were protected from National League raiding.

62. Scott Simkus reports International Association results against the National League, apparently for 1877–78, although he does not state the years. He found that the International's record was 35–55–5 (.395), a total of 95 games (Scott Simkus, *Outsider Baseball: The Weird World of Hardball on the Fringe, 1876–1950* (Chicago: Chicago Review Press, 2014), 19). For 1877–78, I found 115 interleague games, with the International record at 42–70–3 (.378), a similar winning average.

63. A t-test rejects the null hypothesis of a .500 winning percentage at the 2% significance level (p = .011), despite the small sample size of four years.

64. Pietrusza, *Major Leagues*, 48.

65. "The National Association Clubs," *New York Clipper*.

The Union Association War of 1884

Richard Hershberger

The Union Association of 1884 can seem puzzling. It is classified as a major league, yet it lasted but one season, with a low level of play, absurdly poor competitive balance within that low level, and an odd selection of cities, several of them changing over the course of the season. Some people question its major league status, and it is not hard to see why. Even apart from its status, the decisions behind it can seem mysterious.

The mystery of these decisions comes from our modern perspective, knowing what we know now about how organized baseball would develop. They make much more sense viewed in the context of 1884. This paper will show that while some of these decisions were wrong, they were not irrational.

BASEBALL IN 1883

Early baseball history featured a series of challenges to the established leagues by various upstarts. The first of these, by the American Association (AA) to the National League (NL), was resolved fairly quickly and painlessly in early 1883, with the AA taking its place alongside the NL as a major league.[1] The peace did not last long. The second war broke out a year later, with the new Union Association (UA) taking on both established major leagues. The first war had been minor and the following peace straightforward. The AA had moved into unoccupied territories and signed players the NL had for the most part passed on. The actual disputes proved not worth losing money over. The UA faced a different reality. It had to fight for territories and players already claimed by the established leagues. This fight was short and ugly.

The AA, the NL, and the minor Northwestern League (NWL) signed the National Agreement of 1883, giving it the nickname of the Tripartite Agreement. This agreement protected the member clubs' territories, player contracts, and reserve lists. The AA and the NL, as befit major leagues, had broad geographical footprints encompassing both the East and the West, which at that time referred to the region east of the Appalachian Mountains and the region between the

Appalachians and the Great Plains. The NWL occupied a smaller geographic footprint with smaller cities, befitting a minor league, with clubs in Michigan, Illinois, Indiana, and Ohio.

To this list of leagues should be added the Interstate Association. While not a signatory to the National Agreement, it allied itself with the AA, protecting its player contracts and making it a de facto party to the agreement. It comprised mostly smaller Eastern cities in Pennsylvania, New Jersey, Delaware, and New York.

The 1883 season was a financial success. The surest sign of this was that the Tripartite Agreement leagues ended the season with the same clubs they opened with. The Interstate Association lost two clubs along the way, but the bulk of the league completed the season. The successful season led to further growth in the fall, with more clubs and more leagues joining in the fun and, hopefully, profit. The NWL grew to 12 clubs, expanding into Wisconsin and Minnesota. A new Eastern League (EL) was formed, replacing the old Interstate Association. The EL was organized first as the Union League, but the name was changed to avoid confusion with the UA.[2] To this we can add lesser leagues. Some of those were outside the geographic region of the major leagues, such as the Western League, centered on Iowa and Missouri. Others, such as the Iron and Oil Association of western Pennsylvania and eastern Ohio, were within the footprint of the majors, but in smaller cities.

The first rumor of the UA came in late August 1883, with word of an "independent base ball association" forming, with clubs from across the country and, most significantly, "to ignore the 'eleven men' rule, now in vogue in the League and the American Association." In other words, it would disregard the established leagues' reserve lists. The first meeting took place on September 12, 1883, with representatives from Chicago, Philadelphia, Baltimore, Washington, Richmond, St. Louis, New York, and Pittsburgh. The meeting resolved to respect signed player contracts but refused to "recognize any agreement whereby any number of ball-players may be reserved for any club for any time beyond the terms of their contracts." That is, it regarded as fair game players under reserve but who had not yet signed contracts for the following season.[3]

The UA included, or would come to include, many experienced baseball men. Among them were Thomas Pratt of Philadelphia, a businessman who had been a star pitcher in the amateur era. A.H. Henderson was a Baltimore businessman with connections to Chicago, where he led the UA club. In the 1870s he had been one of the movers of Baltimore's first professional club. Michael Scanlon had founded the Washington Nationals club, the second of that name, in 1877. After the 1880 season he was double-crossed by the NL, which had promised a franchise to him, inducing him to invest in upgrading the team. The NL went instead with Detroit and trumped up an excuse to raid his team of its best players.[4]

Justus Thorner of Cincinnati had been president of the 1880 Cincinnati club, which the NL expelled on questionable grounds.[5] Finally, there was former star shortstop George Wright, a late addition to the UA. He was by this time retired from the field, and co-owner of the sporting goods firm of Wright & Ditson. The UA was his bid to expand his firm's share of the baseball market.

These were not baseball innocents. They were old baseball hands who went into this with their eyes open.

At the same time, viewed realistically, the UA had modest prospects. Initially, it was a gauzy construct. No one had yet committed serious money. It is entirely possible that nothing would have come of the project, or that the actual league would have been of more modest geographic scale and would have acceded to the established reserve lists. The EL had also initially rejected the reserve lists, but had been brought around in the end and signed the National Agreement.[6] It is likely that the UA would have worked its way around to the same conclusion and retrenched. Then came Henry V. Lucas.

HENRY V. LUCAS

The two salient facts about Henry Lucas are that he was a baseball enthusiast and that he was rich. Not only was he rich, he was old money, at least by St. Louis standards. His grandfather, Jean Baptiste Charles Lucas, had been appointed by President Thomas Jefferson to the newly purchased Louisiana Territory, where he was commissioner of land claims and a judge in the territorial court. He used his position to good effect, coming to be the wealthiest man in St. Louis, owning much of modern downtown. Only two children, a son and a daughter, survived him, keeping the family fortune intact. His surviving son was James H. Lucas. Several of James's sons were involved in early baseball in St. Louis. Robert Lucas, born in 1850, played for the Union Club. This was one of the best, and certainly the most fashionable, of the baseball clubs in St. Louis in the 1860s. John B.C. Lucas, born in 1847, was president of the first professional club in St. Louis, the original Brown Stockings of 1875–77.[7]

Henry was their younger brother, born in 1857. He shared the family passion for baseball. He laid out a diamond on his country estate at Normandy, just outside the city, where he played right field on an amateur club he sponsored. This was all well and good, but he wanted something bigger. He wanted to own a major-league club. There was, however, already a major-league club in St. Louis, and it was not for sale.

The St. Louis Brown Stockings of the American Association were principally owned by Chris Von der Ahe, a colorful German immigrant adept at shrewd business maneuvers and playing the clown. He had been involved in St. Louis baseball since at least 1875, when he was on the board of directors of the amateur Grand Avenue Club. In 1881, as baseball was beginning its recovery from the depression of the late 1870s, Von der Ahe saw where things were heading and managed to gain control of both the only enclosed grounds in St. Louis and the semi-professional club playing there. These were the Brown Stockings, the direct ancestors of the modern Cardinals, and, in 1882, a charter member of the AA.[8]

Von der Ahe was sitting on a gold mine and he knew it. The Brown Stockings would make him rich, carrying him far past the modest prosperity of a local small businessman. Baseball franchise pricing was not yet well understood. The tangible assets of a baseball club were (and still are) comparatively modest. The value was in the intangible assets: the right to compete in a league, the territorial protection this conferred, and the reserve rights to its players. No one knew what these were worth, especially in a major market with bright prospects—which St. Louis was at the time. Purchases are difficult when no one knows the value. Lucas was rich enough that he might have been able to make Von der Ahe an offer so extravagant as to be accepted, but such a valuation of a baseball club was not yet imagined.

Lucas could more realistically have bought into some other existing club. A common ownership model at this time was of many small shareholders, typically local businessmen acting out of civic boosterism and enthusiasm for the game as much as any expectation of making a profit. Lucas might in theory have been able to buy up shares in a club somewhere else, but this was not what he wanted. He was a St. Louis man. That is where he wanted his club.

The incipient UA was the solution to Lucas's problem. His involvement at the initial meetings is not clear. The St. Louis delegate, Ted Sullivan, was another old baseball hand who would go on to manage Lucas's club. He may have been Lucas's agent all along, or they might have combined efforts as the UA began to take form. Either way, Lucas showed his cards by the end of October, openly discussing his new club and dismissing the reserve rule. His wealth, and his readiness to spend on baseball, would strengthen the UA's resolve.[9]

ALTOONA

Seven of the eight clubs that opened the UA season were based in plausible major league cities: Chicago, St. Louis, Cincinnati, Philadelphia, Baltimore, Washington, and Boston. All but Washington already had one or more major-league teams, making this lineup a declaration of war. Seven clubs also left a gap, filled by Altoona, Pennsylvania. Altoona looms large with modern critics of the UA, being the smallest home city in major-league history. The Altoona franchise proved a mistake. The club played only 25 games, 18 of them at home, posting a 6–19 record before disbanding. This was a failed experiment, but there was reasoning behind it that merits examination.

The decision for where to place the eighth franchise was made under two constraints that would not apply today. It had to be a western city, and there had to be local ownership.

It had to be a western city because of how games were scheduled in the railroad era. A league was divided into western and eastern halves. The schedule cycled through the eastern teams going west, the western teams going east, and the teams in each group playing among themselves. This was the only way to minimize non-playing travel days, once the number of games reached a certain point. With 112 games scheduled, the same as the other major leagues, this scheme was necessary. There had to be two geographical groups of four teams.

Filling the western half often was a problem in the 1870s and '80s, as western cities were farther apart than eastern cities, and many in good locations were of marginal size. Chicago, St. Louis, Cincinnati, Pittsburgh, and Louisville were the most stable western baseball cities. Others wandered in and out. Indianapolis had NL franchises in 1878 and 1887–89, and an AA franchise in 1884. Cleveland was in the NL from 1879 to 1884, then in the AA 1887–88. That team then jumped to the NL, where it played 1889–99. Similar histories of intermittent franchises are found in Columbus, Milwaukee, Detroit, and Kansas City.

The American Association expanded to 12 clubs specifically to exacerbate the UA's problem. It brought in clubs in Indianapolis and Toledo (the 1883 NWL champion moving to the AA), which, along with its existing franchise in Columbus, blocked the UA from the mid-sized midwestern cities. At the same time, it gave a franchise to Washington in what would turn out to be a failed attempt to block the UA there, while taking advantage of the situation to bring in Brooklyn, by far the most desirable open market, from the old Interstate Association. This left the UA five flawed possibilities: Pittsburgh, Detroit, Cleveland, Kansas City, and Altoona.

Pittsburgh, Detroit, or Cleveland would seem the obvious candidates. They already had major-league teams, and it is unlikely they were large enough to support two, but they were unquestionably major-league cities that would reasonably fit within the UA's western half. Here we come to the second constraint: local ownership.

Baseball club ownership in the 1880s was extremely local, organized as an association of local businessmen. While the hope was to make money, the reality was to spread the risk. The point was civic pride as much as expectation of profit. A league did not simply decide to place a team in a city. It had to find local owners. Finding money men able and willing to bankroll a club in a distant city was unlikely, and there still would be the problem of getting the operation up and running without any local ties and with only a few months before the opening of the season. This simply was not in the cards.[10]

The UA made an effort to recruit potential owners in Detroit, but nothing came of it. It had a good lead in Pittsburgh in the person of Al Pratt, another old baseball hand, but the AA's Pittsburgh team blocked that effort through the simple, if costly, expedient of renting both available grounds. Cleveland is a cipher. If there was ever a prospective owner approached, it was not reported. In the event, Detroit, Pittsburgh, and Cleveland were all out of the picture.[11]

Kansas City had some distinct advantages. It was small but it was wealthy, its stockyards second only to Chicago's. Baseball enthusiasm also ran high, so much so that in 1886 the Missouri Pacific Railroad would name four of its stations after baseball players. (One survives to this day: the very small town of Bushong, Kansas, named after Albert "Doc" Bushong of the St. Louis club.)[12] Kansas City's location, however, was a major disadvantage. The train ride from

St. Louis took a minimum of 10½ hours under ideal conditions.[13] Travel times between St. Louis and Chicago or Cincinnati were comparable, but St. Louis was a major metropolis that served well as the western anchor of a league. Kansas City could only be an appendage, a costly drag on the league schedule. The result was that Kansas City would be in and out of the major leagues, serving as the fallback for a league that could not find anything better.

Altoona was the ultimate fallback for the UA. It is in the Allegheny Mountains, where it was founded by the Pennsylvania Railroad for a major maintenance facility. Financially, with its railroad money, the town played above its weight class. Its position on the railroad's main line made it convenient for scheduling. The hope was that these would compensate for its small size. This hope was forlorn, but not irrational. It soon became clear that the Altoona club was unsustainable, even with Lucas subsidizing it. He contacted Kansas City backers, who quickly raised the funds necessary as Lucas wrapped up affairs in Altoona and gathered a cadre of players for Kansas City.[14]

RECRUITING PLAYERS

Recruitment of major league–caliber players was the heart of the matter. If the UA was to establish itself in cities that already had major-league teams, it had to put a good—or at least good enough—product on the field

Player recruitment presented a novel problem. When the first professional organization, the National Association, formed in 1871, its membership was made up of clubs that already existed. When the National League formed in 1876, it was largely a reorganization of the National Association clubs that had competed in 1875. When the American Association formed in 1882, it caught the wave of a rising economy, with many plausibly major league–level players available and eager for work. But 1884 was a different matter. With two established major leagues, two high minors, and various lower-level leagues, there were no surplus players to be had.

This was a problem even for the established major leagues. With small rosters, any injury or poor play would require a replacement. It was possible to pay another club to release a player, while simultaneously negotiating a contract with him, but this was slow and expensive. The established major-league clubs tried an experiment of establishing "reserve" teams, and even setting a schedule for them to compete for a pennant: a rudimentary farm system decades before Branch Rickey brought the idea to maturity. The idea was premature. The economics did not support it, and most of the reserve teams were disbanded before the season was over. It is not clear that the experiment was a response to the UA threatening to make replacement players scarcer than they would be otherwise, but it is suggestive that 1884 was the year this was tried.[15]

In the meantime, there was only one possible solution for the UA (and all future challengers to the baseball establishment): Try to hire players away from the established leagues. Everyone preached the principle that a signed contract was sacrosanct. But what about a player who had been reserved, but had not yet signed a contract?

This was not yet the "reserve clause," a part of the player's contract. The reserve was an agreement between owners allowing each club to make a list of a set number of players whom the other owners would not sign. It was, in other words, open collusion. The system had been introduced following the 1879 season, with NL owners each able to reserve five players. This was expanded to 11 in the Tripartite Agreement. Since this was merely an agreement among owners, both players and outside associations would seem to be on firm ground holding that the reserve had nothing to do with them. Leagues not a party to the agreement could sign whom they pleased, and players were under no obligation until they signed a contract.

That was the theory, but not the practice. In reality, when the UA passed a resolution that "we can not recognize any agreement whereby any number of ballplayers may be reserved by any club for any period of time beyond the term of his contract with said club," the established leagues responded vigorously.[16] The NL and AA followed the same manual as the NL had two years earlier in its fight with the AA: refusing to play exhibition games, which were financially important at that time. Both leagues now refused to play exhibitions with any club that played with the UA. The more important weapon was player discipline, with the NL and AA expelling reserved players for signing with the UA. This was done via the Day resolution, proposed by John B. Day, owner of the New York franchises of both the NL and the AA. Here is the version adopted by the NL:

> *Resolved*, That no League Club shall, at any time, employ or enter into contract with any of its reserved players, who shall, while reserved to such clubs, play with any other club.[17]

The Day resolution raised the stakes for any player tempted to join the UA, but not as high as it could have.

It penalized players not for signing a UA contract, but for actually playing in a game on a UA club. The AA and NL would happily take back an errant player who renounced a UA contract before actually playing a game. The talk of signed contracts being a line not to be crossed was pure hypocrisy. The established leagues recognized no contracts but their own.

In the meantime, players could play both sides:

> Hanlon, the left-fielder of the [NL] Detroit Club, has resigned from [sic: should be "signed with"] that organization. He had been reserved by the Detroits, and for a long time refused to sign. When he threatened to go to the Cincinnati Unionists, the Detroits weakened on their bluff and decided to give him the salary he had stipulated. The Lucas Union Clubs may not be successful, but they can be thanked for compelling the League and American Association to pay dearly for passing such an unjust and tyrannical rule as that of reserving eleven players.[18]

The threat also forced the established leagues to measures such as the NL New York club signing pitcher Mickey Welch to a two-year contract, which was nearly unheard of in this era. Even well into the season, the UA was disruptive. In early July, it revoked its earlier policy of respecting NL and AA contracts and renewed its recruitment efforts. "Discipline has gone to the dogs," observed one unidentified NL manager, and the UA was said to have agents in every city making extravagant offers.[19]

The UA tried to make the fight a matter of principle. Players did not like the reserve rule, which often was compared with slavery. Here, an editorial offers a comparatively measured critique:

> Let the eleven men reserve rule be repealed, or else let the players organize and resist its operations. *The Sporting Life* does not counsel any measure that may injure the national game, of which it is one of the most earnest and enthusiastic exponents and supporters. Harmony between managers and players is essential to success. But we do insist that the laborer is worthy of his hire, and that the ball player is a man and a citizen, and not a slave, and as such is entitled to all the rights and privileges of a free man.[20]

The topic offered ample possibilities for those inclined to rabble rousing:

> The reserved players in the League and American Associations should wear high dude collars to hide the iron band put around their neck by the reserve rule.[21]

The UA worked the theme:

> The [UA Philadelphia] Keystone Club enunciates its principles in this, its initial season, by declaring that:
>
> I. Believing it has the right to exist it has come to stay.
>
> II. It recognizes the inviolability of contracts and would refuse the services of the finest player if under agreement with the smallest amateur club in the country.
>
> III. The reserve rule is not part of a player's contract, but is a mere club regulation without the former's consent, to take effect after the termination of such contract.
>
> IV. Its enforcement is exacted by the law of might, not right, and should be resisted by every manly player worthy the privileges of a freeman.
>
> Against such an arbitrary, one-sided, unlawful and un-American violation of the rights of ball players the Keystone club, for itself and colleagues, protests and invokes the approval and support of all the citizens of Philadelphia who love fair play and despise the tyranny of monopolies.[22]

In the end, few players actually made the jump. Regardless of their feelings about the reserve system, the established leagues were the better bet for stable employment. Many players were happy to use the UA as a bargaining chip, even going so far as to sign contracts, but most returned to their clubs. Most of the players, and especially most of the prominent ones, who signed with the UA and stuck with it did so with Lucas's St. Louis club, his wealth allowing him to make offers both extravagant and credible. This led to the competitive imbalance that is a notable feature of the UA, with St Louis ending the season 21 games ahead of second-place Cincinnati.

THE SEASON

The season was neither an artistic nor a commercial success. It could hardly have been otherwise, dominated as it was by competitive imbalance. Cincinnati's second-place finish, 21 games behind St. Louis, fails to capture the state of affairs. Add that Cincinnati held what would, in normal circumstances, be an excellent 69–36 record, and it is more clear how steep was the drop-off.

We have seen that Altoona dropped out at the end of May after 25 games. Its replacement by Kansas City provided stability over most of the summer, but the Keystone club gave up the ghost in early August, reportedly having lost over $10,000. Confidence in the UA nonetheless remained high. Three players, including star shortstop Jack Glasscock, jumped from the NL Cleveland club to the UA Cincinnati club. The Wilmington club jumped from the Eastern League to take Keystone's place.[23]

Chicago was the third club to collapse. It did this in a more complicated way. The club announced on August 19 that it was moving to Pittsburgh. This on its face contradicts the earlier discussion about why the UA could not put a team in Pittsburgh, as it lacked local connections and both local ball grounds, Union Park and Exposition Park, had been secured by the city's AA club. The claim had been that the AA club was going to field a reserve team in Exposition Park while the main team played at Union Park. This might have been true, or it might have been a move to block the UA all along. Either way, by August the club had relinquished its control of Exposition Park. This opened it up for the UA Chicago club to transfer there, splitting the gate receipts with the proprietors, the Exposition Park Association.[24]

This leaves the matter of local ownership. Partly, the transfer was a desperation move improvised on the fly, making thinkable the previously unthinkable. Partly, the Exposition Park Association could be expected to play the role of local ownership. Mostly, there was less here than meets the eye. While this was presented as a genuine transfer, it was timed for when Chicago would play St. Louis, by far the biggest attraction in the UA. They played a five-game series in Pittsburgh, then played the rest of their games on the road, including one nominal home game in Baltimore, again against St. Louis. This looks less like a genuine transfer and more like a marketing stunt to gin up interest in a series at a neutral site. Modern sources take the transfer at face value, but this is generous.

To complete the tale of woe, the Chicago/Pittsburgh club and the Quickstep Club of Wilmington both collapsed in mid-September, replaced by Milwaukee and St. Paul, respectively, who emerged from the wreckage of the Northwestern League's own collapse. Of the original eight UA clubs, five (St. Louis, Cincinnati, Boston, Baltimore, and Washington) completed the season.

It was not all grim for the UA, however. There were some bright spots. The St. Louis club was essentially immune to market forces, backed as it was by Lucas's riches. The UA Cincinnati club also did pretty well. It had stolen a march on Cincinnati American Association club, whose lease on its grounds was set to expire before the 1884 season. The AA club had not anticipated any difficulty renewing the lease, giving the UA club an opening to sneak in. The result was that the UA club had the best playing ground in Cincinnati, while the AA club had to scramble to find a replacement. The UA Cincinnati club came out of the 1884 season solvent and expecting to play in 1885.[25]

The UA Washington club was another success. It beat the AA Washington club into submission while reportedly turning a profit. The two Washington clubs had entered the fray on equal footing. Both were new organizations, with no fan base predisposed to favor either. Neither were good, but the UA team's 47–65 record looked good compared to the AA team's 12–51. The most important difference was their playing grounds. The UA club's ground was immediately north of the capitol, near present-day Union Station. The AA club played on a site over a mile away. While not a terrible location, it could not complete with the UA site for convenience.[26] The AA club disbanded in early August, the UA giving a twist of the knife by holding a benefit game for the AA players who had not been paid. The AA vacancy was filled by the Eastern League Virginia Club of Richmond. Interestingly, the position was initially offered to the Quicksteps, who declined, instead taking the UA vacancy left by the Keystone club a week later.[27]

AFTERMATH

The UA closed the season expecting to return in 1885. Over the course of the fall, ambitions were reduced somewhat. The economics did not support the travel expenses of its large geographic footprint, leading to the anticipation that the eastern clubs would drop out. The rumors proved true. At the annual meeting in December, Baltimore sent a resignation, while Boston and Washington simply did not show up. The Boston and Baltimore clubs would dissolve. The Washington club had a brighter future. After a failed attempt to join the AA for 1885, it settled on the Eastern League. This proved wise, as the following year it joined the National League, where it played 1886–89.[28]

With the loss of the eastern clubs, the plan was to field what today we might call a quadruple-A league, with clubs in St. Louis, Cincinnati, Kansas City, Milwaukee, and St. Paul, plus three more cities to complete the circuit. Toledo, Detroit, and Cleveland were reported to be their target. A meeting was set for a month later to consider applications for membership.[29]

WAS THE UNION ASSOCIATION A MAJOR LEAGUE?

When major league baseball determined to codify its statistical record in the mid-1960s, preparatory to the publication of *The Baseball Encyclopedia*, the Special Baseball Records Committee was created, meeting in 1968 to decide a wide assortment of questions. The most basic was what to include. Which leagues were major?[1]

The Union Association made the cut. This was not a surprise. Earlier histories of baseball had routinely treated it as a major league. The committee simply made this official. This decision has never been officially revisited, but it has been unofficially challenged. By far the most prominent challenge came from Bill James in *The New Bill James Historical Abstract*, with later commentary following James's lead.[2]

James's argument begins with some rhetorical flourishes, giving great weight to the UA's only playing a single season (a critique absent from the discussion of the Players' League of 1890). It then gets down to the heart of the argument: The UA's level of play was poor. James is unquestionably right about this. Later critiques of the UA typically are merely expansions of this theme.

There are two problems with this argument. It is simply assumed that level of play is the appropriate criterion, that a major league, by definition, is good. Even if we accept this standard, showing that the UA was weaker than the established major leagues does not by itself lead to any conclusion about its status.

Taking the second issue first, we can take as proven that the UA was significantly weaker than the NL and AA. So what? Considering any three leagues, it is unsurprising that their quality of play is unequal, and also unsurprising that a new league will be the weakest. If we want to categorize that third league as either major or minor, we need also to have some idea about the level of play of the established minors.

The Northwestern League and the Eastern League were the two high minor leagues in 1884. Was the UA more like these, more like the established majors, or something in between? Neither James nor his successors make any real argument. James nods in this direction by writing, "By 1884 there were actually eight minor leagues, a good many of which probably could have kicked the Union Association's butt and stolen their lunch money."

The statement about eight minor leagues in 1884 is mysterious. It might be defensible, if we are loose about including local semipro leagues, but the claim immediately follows a list of earlier leagues that were defunct by 1884. It seems more likely that James believed they still existed. In any case he makes not even a gesture toward defending the claim that they could "kick the Union Association's butt," and this section is most generously taken as hyperbole. What is needed here is an analysis of the NWL and EL. This would be more work than with the majors, the data being less readily available. But again, so what? Without it, we are left with half an argument.

This is, in any case, getting ahead of things. The discussion of definitions is perhaps tedious, but necessary to establish that everyone is talking about the same thing. What is the definition of a major league? Here James starts on firmer ground. He correctly notes that in modern terms a major league "rests atop a pyramid of organized competition." He follows this by also correctly noting that the structure was just getting organized in 1884.

He then abandons the thread. The issue with analyzing the UA is not that organized baseball in 1884 was inchoate. The major status of the National League and American Association was established, as was the minor status of the Northwestern and Eastern Leagues. The difficulty with categorizing a league such as the UA is that it was not a part of organized baseball. It was an upstart challenger, like the American League would be in 1901 and the Federal League in 1914. Like those leagues, the UA was trying to force its way into organized baseball, and at the top level. Like the Federal League, it would fail.

What does it mean to say that the major leagues "rest atop" the pyramid? What places them in this privileged position? How do they stay there? Why do the minor leagues tolerate this arrangement? These questions suggest a better definition of major and minor leagues: In its mature form, organized baseball is a hierarchy of professional leagues, with the leagues higher up controlling larger markets than the leagues below them, and the higher leagues controlling the flow of players to and from the lower leagues. One or more leagues occupy the top of the hierarchy. This position is the definition of a major league, when considering leagues operating within organized baseball.

This definition has many advantages over simply defining a major league by level of play. If we define a major league as one that is good, this tells us nothing about why it is good, or whether it will stay good. Should we examine each league year by year to decide if it is major that year? Most years, this would be pointless, but we might wonder about 1890, when the Players' League gutted the NL and AA. More to the point, why do leagues' quality of play not drift up and down over the decades? This is exactly what happens in college football, on both the level of conferences and individual schools.

The answer lies in the control of the best markets. This is baked into the structure of organized baseball dating to the National League's original constitution of 1876:

Every club member of this League shall have exclusive control of the city in which it is located, and of the territory surrounding such city to the extent of five miles in every direction, and no visiting League club shall, under any circumstances—not even with the consent of the local League club—be allowed to play any club in such territory other than the League club therein located.[3]

Major leagues have exclusive control of the largest markets, giving them the financial wherewithal to dictate terms to the leagues with smaller markets, and therefore smaller revenue. The practical application of this strength is for major-league clubs to claim—and enforce—the right to take desirable players from minor-league clubs. It is, in this light, obvious why major leagues are good: because they can demand and take the best players. Major leagues are good because they are major, not major because they are good.

Being good is not, however, universally true. We see this on the team level, where a major-league team might be very bad indeed, but the mere fact of membership in a major league allows them to get better. Were the 1919 Philadelphia Athletics better than the 1919 International League Baltimore Orioles? It is hard to say for certain, but the Orioles' collection of past and future journeyman major leaguers looks better than the Athletics' motley crew. But beyond question even at the time was that the Athletics would get better, in later years winning World Series. The Orioles were about as good as they could ever be.[4]

The same was true on the league level. The American Association of 1882 was woefully weaker than the National League, which swept the spring exhibition season games. Four years later, the AA St. Louis Brown Stockings beat the NL Chicago White Stockings in the World Series. The fact of the AA being major meant that its clubs could protect their good players and acquire more good players from the minors. Their quality of play in 1882 was simply beside the point. They were major because they had the financial strength to force the NL to treat them as major. From there, raising the level of play was simply a matter of time to let the logic of the situation run its course.[5] This definition of major league removes any mystery about both why a major league is good, and why it stays good. Its status can only be overturned by a challenger with the finances to muscle in on the action.

This brings us to the question of classifying upstart leagues such as the Union Association or the Federal League. The American League poses less of a question, as its status was resolved when it forced the NL to make peace in 1903. The UA and the FL tried to do the same but fell short. The difference between these and what would later be called "outlaw" minor leagues is the established leagues' response. The established leagues took the UA and FL very seriously, in a way that we don't see with something like the outlaw Carolina League of the 1930s.[6]

The AA added teams to block the UA. The established leagues changed their own rules via the Day resolutions. They were forced to pay higher salaries. The AA Washingtons were run out of town by the UA. The NL Clevelands were brought to the brink and forced to sell out. Finally, the NL paid Lucas off by bringing him into the league, risking renewed war with the AA. In short, we should regard the Union Association as a major league because the National League and American Association regarded it as a major threat. They were in a position to know.

Notes

1. *The Encyclopedia of Baseball*, (New York: MacMillan, 1969), 2,327.
2. Bill James, *The New Bill James Historical Abstract* (New York: Simon & Schuster, 2001), 21–34.
3. Article V. Sec. 2 of the 1876 National League Constitution.
4. The Orioles of 1919 were, of course, completely unrelated to the modern AL Orioles. See Alan Cohen, "Baltimore's Forgotten Dynasty: The 1919-25 Baltimore Orioles of the International League," *The National Pastime* (2020).
5. Richard Hershberger, "The First Baseball War: The American Association and the National League," *Baseball Research Journal* 49, no. 2 (Fall 2020).
6. For the Carolina League, see R.G. Utley and Scott Verner, *The Independent Carolina League, 1936–1938: Baseball Outlaws* (Jefferson, NC: McFarland), 1999.

A bombshell fell before the meeting took place: The UA St. Louis club was joining the National League, the UA Cincinnati club also maneuvering to get in. Rumors had been floating around for weeks, which Lucas had denied. He and Justus Thorner of Cincinnati had been two-timing their UA partners.[30] A rump meeting of the UA came off, only Kansas City and Milwaukee in attendance. They knew what course of action was needed: abject surrender to the established major leagues. They declared the Union Association to be dissolved and set about forming a new Western League that would follow the rules of the National Agreement.[31]

There were various loose ends on the NL side. The admission of Lucas's club was predicated on there being a vacancy. Lucas arranged this by buying out the Cleveland club, $500 down and another $2,000 when his membership in the NL was finalized. (Cincinnati's hopes were based on Detroit's anticipated readiness to also resign, but this hope proved unfounded, and Cincinnati seems not to have offered any financial inducement.) Cleveland had been particularly hard hit by the events of the previous season, with rising salaries and losing players to the UA. They were ready to sell out. They took a parting shot, arranging the transfer of the bulk of their players to the AA Brooklyn club.

This took Lucas by surprise. One account from the time, often repeated nowadays, was that he thought he was buying the reserve rights as well. This is unlikely. The idea of reserve rights being something that could be transferred did not yet exist. Technically, Lucas did not buy Cleveland's franchise, but rather paid it to resign from the league, while separately negotiating with the other NL owners to get the vacant franchise. Such a transaction normally would also have included negotiations with the players. This did not happen, perhaps due to the need for discretion as Lucas hid the affair from his UA partners until the deal was completed. What he thought he was also getting was the assistance of the Cleveland management to arrange matters with the players. They had little love for Lucas, whom they saw as the author of their financial woes. When Brooklyn offered its own financial inducement, reportedly $4,000, the Cleveland management was ready to lend its aid in that direction. Lucas, upon discovering what they had done, complained of their "bad faith," which was rather rich under the circumstances. Lucas refused to pay the outstanding $2,000, resulting in a lawsuit and eventual judgment against him, the interest owed bringing the debt up to $2,255.[32]

The second loose end was the detail that the NL's action in admitting Lucas's club was in flagrant violation of the National Agreement's protection of territorial rights. Chris Von der Ahe, owner of the AA St. Louis club, was not happy. By rights, the NL's action should have marked the reopening of the NL-AA war that the National Agreement had ended. Would either side really do this, coming on the heels of the UA war? The NL either would, or it made a good bluff of it. The National League stared down the American Association, asking the rest of the AA owners if they would really go to war for Von der Ahe. It turned out they would not. After a few tense weeks, Von der Ahe conceded. The terms, if any, were not put out for publication, allowing Von der Ahe to save face via rumors of concessions by Lucas. The NL owners took note of the AA's disunity. This would set the tone for relations between the two leagues in later years.[33]

The final loose end was the status of the players who had been expelled. Lucas needed a team, after all, and the NL needed him to have one. With the Cleveland players signed by Brooklyn, this left the expelled players. They fell into two classes: those who had abandoned signed contracts and those who had merely broken the reserve. The latter group was not a major issue. The Day resolution expelling such players was not part of the National Agreement, but rather than been adopted separately by both major leagues, making the players' reinstatement a league matter.

The contract jumpers, however, had been expelled under the National Agreement. The AA would have to agree to their reinstatement. The AA, whether out of genuine principle or lingering ire over the St. Louis affair, was not in a conciliatory mood. The NL simply acted unilaterally, reinstating the players at a special meeting just after the lucrative spring exhibition season had ended and before the opening of the regular season. The AA was outraged at this second breech of the National Agreement in three months and withdrew from it. The NL and AA were technically at war. Come the fall, however, when it was time to sign players for the next season, the AA again blinked. Its owners were unwilling to get into bidding wars for players and instead negotiated a new National Agreement. The war of 1885 was a phony war, so little disturbing the apparent baseball tranquility as to go unnoticed in baseball history.[34]

Lucas's experience as a National League owner was brief and unsatisfying. He turned out to be very bad at running a baseball club. He could buy his way to the UA pennant, but he could not build a winning team within the constraints of the reserve system. The team went 36–72 in 1885, finishing last in the NL, before improving to 43–79 for a sixth-place finish in 1886.

Lucas sold out his interest in the club that August, after less than two seasons in the National League. Between the UA and NL, he claimed to have lost $70,000 on baseball. Reports following the collapse of the UA had placed his losses at $40,000, between his own club and subsidizing others. There is no way to confirm either number, but both are plausible. Losing money to field a losing team turned out not to be fun, so he abandoned the project. The franchise was transferred to Indianapolis.[35]

Lucas was not merely bad at running a baseball club. He was bad at business in general. By 1890, he had to get a job. It is tempting to ascribe his financial woes to his baseball losses, but the Lucas family fortune was much larger than that. His lack of acumen ran deep. Persons with connections like his are rarely allowed to fall too far. He was appointed the head of the Chicago passenger department of the Baltimore & Ohio Railroad, despite the absence of any obvious qualifications for the job. A year later, he was a manager at a life insurance company in Chicago. His losing ways continued and in 1902 he filed for bankruptcy with $40,000 debt. The next year, his wife divorced him, citing desertion and non-support. He spent the last three years of his life as a St. Louis city street inspector, earning $75 a month.[36]

WHAT WERE THEY THINKING?

The Union Association was, from the modern perspective, obviously doomed. So what were they thinking? Was this merely a vanity project?

That interpretation works with respect to Lucas. He wanted to own a major-league baseball team. He succeeded, though in the end it brought him no joy. But what about the backers of the other teams? Were they seduced by Lucas's riches, or was there something more going on?

The key to unlocking the mystery of what were they thinking is how little was understood in 1884 about the business of baseball. The UA was an attempt to overlay a major league atop the existing major leagues—in other words, to double up teams in the various cities. The discussion about overturning the reserve system is a red herring. The American Association had used similar rhetoric before joining with the NL in the National Agreement. The American League would do the same thing in the early twentieth century.

An upstart league is by its nature opposed to the reserve. The whole point of the reserve is for the established leagues to secure control over players. In the ordinary course, this is to prevent bidding wars within organized baseball, but the reserve also blocked any outside leagues. The only options for the new league would be to accept that they would be restricted to players that none of the established leagues—major or minor—wanted, or to reject the legitimacy of the reserve. This did not mean, however, that the new league would continue to reject the reserve, should it succeed in establishing itself. At that point, the logic behind the system would prove compelling. The end game is membership within the establishment, which means the reserve system.[37]

The real issue was territorial rights. Could the UA cause the NL and AA so much financial pain that they would accept sharing their markets? This was not a ridiculous ambition. The American League would have a similar ambition and would succeed, in many cases in the same cities. The Federal League would take its unsuccessful shot a decade after that.

The UA's failure resulted from two miscalculations. The first was that it was underfunded for the impending fight, and with the bulk of its capital concentrated in the person of Henry Lucas, the entire enterprise was subject to his whims. The second miscalculation was how the fans would support a lesser team in the various markets.

Later experience would show this to be a tough sell. A team with an established fan base can keep it through hard times. A century of futility didn't turn Cubs fans to the White Sox. But putting a weak team in a city that already had a major-league team simply did not work.[38] This was not at all obvious at the time, or indeed for some years after. Minor leagues would repeatedly try the experiment, as in 1892, when the Pennsylvania State League included a team in Pittsburgh, using the same ballpark as the National League club, scheduled for when the big club was on the road. The experiment lasted two weeks.[39]

The Union Association's strategy was doomed, but this was not obvious, given the state of knowledge at the time. The backers were making, from their perspective, a high-risk, high-reward bid to force their way into organized baseball. They failed, but they were not irrational. ■

Notes

1. Richard Hershberger, "The First Baseball War: The American Association and the National League," *Baseball Research Journal* 49, no. 2 (Fall 2020).

2. "The New Association," *Sporting Life*, October 1, 1883; "The Union League," *Philadelphia Sunday Item*, January 6, 1884.

3. "Another New Association Movement," *Sporting Life*, September 2, 1883; "New Associations," *Sporting Life*, September 16, 1883.

4. "The League Convention," *New York Clipper*, December 18, 1880.

5. A major reason was the club's persistence in selling alcohol. At the same time, the New York club maintained a bar on its grounds. The claim was made that when the New York club joined the NL in 1883 it had an existing contract with the bar's proprietor. By 1886, people were wondering how long this contract extended. "Sports and Pastimes" *Brooklyn Eagle*, January 31, 1886.

6. "A Dish of 'Crow,'" *Cincinnati Enquirer*, January 6, 1884; "The Union League," *Philadelphia Sunday Item*, January 6, 1884; O.P. Caylor, "The National Agreement," *Sporting Life*, February 27, 1884.

7. Jeff Kittel, "The Lucas Family, Part One," This Game of Games, October 20, 2010; Kittel, "The Lucas Family, Part Two," This Game of Games, October 21, 2010. Both posts can be found via the Internet Archive Wayback Machine at https://bit.ly/3HFTTfH. Kittel cites James Neal Primm, *Lion of the Valley*, and Howard Conrad, *The Encyclopedia of the History of St. Louis*.

8. Kittel, "Chris Von der Ahe and the Creation of Modern Baseball: A Hall of Fame Argument," This Game of Games, http://www.thisgameofgames.com/chris-von-der-ahe-and-the-creation-of-modern-baseball.html, accessed February 1, 2024).

9. "The New Club," *St. Louis Republican*, October 26, 1883; "Regarding the New Club," *St. Louis Republican*, October 28, 1883.

10. The exception to the principle of local ownership was the NL Hartford club, which in 1877 played its games on Brooklyn's Union Ground. This was a special case. The Brooklyn ground had been vacated when the Mutual club disbanded the previous year, and William Cammeyer, its proprietor, sought a tenant and took on the role of local connection.

11. "Notes and Comments," *Sporting Life*, January 16, 1884; "Allegheny News," *Sporting Life*, September 24, 1883.

12. "From St. Louis," *Sporting Life*, November 3, 1886.

13. 1886 Missouri Pacific Railway timetable in the David Rumsey Map Center at Stanford University.

14. "The Change Effected," *St. Louis Republican*, June 3, 1884.

15. "A Reserve Schedule," *St. Louis Post-Dispatch*, March 13, 1884; "Reserve Schedule," *St. Louis Post-Dispatch*, March 18, 1884; "The Sporting World," *Cincinnati Enquirer*, October 26, 1884.

16. "The New Base-Ball Association," *Cincinnati Enquirer*, September 13, 1883.

17. *Constitution and Playing Rules of the National League of Professional Base Ball Clubs*, 1884, 47. For the American Association, see "The Reserve Rule," *St. Louis Post-Dispatch*, December 13, 1883.

18. "Base-Ball," Cincinnati Enquirer, January 20, 1884, quoting the *Pittsburgh Leader*.

19. "Our National Game," *Philadelphia Sunday Item*, January 13, 1884; "Sporting," *Missouri Republican* (St. Louis), July 11, 1884; "Big Pay For Ball Playing," *Philadelphia Times*, July 30, 1884.

20. "Base Ball," *Sporting Life* July 22, 1883

21. "Sporting World," *Cincinnati Enquirer*, December 23, 1883.

22. "Tom Pratt's Team," *Sporting Life*, March 26, 1884.

23. "The Union Association," *Sporting Life*, August 13, 1884; "Base Ball Players Desert," *Sporting Life*, August 13, 1884.

24. "The Chicago Unions Transferred," *Cincinnati Enquirer*, August 20, 1884.

25. "A Base Ball Sensation," *Sporting Life*, November 21, 1883; "Base-Ball," *Cincinnati Enquirer*, October 28, 1884.

26. "The Sporting World," *Cincinnati Enquirer*, January 14, 1884, quoting the *Mirror of American Sports*; "Diamond Chips," *St. Louis Post-Dispatch*, May 6, 1884.

27. "The Financial Part of It," *Sporting Life*, October 22, 1884; "From Washington," *Sporting Life*, August 13, 1884; "The American Association," *Sporting Life*, August 13, 1884.

28. "The Sporting World," *Cincinnati Enquirer*, December 9, 1884; "The Pennant Awarded," *St. Louis Post-Dispatch*, December 18, 1884. The connection between UA Washington of 1884 and NL Washington of 1886–89 is not recognized by the standard sources. For the move to the Eastern League, see "Local Base Ball," *Washington National Republican*, December 15, 1884. For the move to the National League, see "The Nationals' Chance," *Washington Critic*, January 13, 1886; "Eight Clubs," *Sporting Life*, January 20, 1886.

29. "Sporting," *Cincinnati Enquirer*, December 19, 1884; "A Sporting Budget," *St. Louis Post-Dispatch*, January 3, 1885.

30. "Sporting," *Cincinnati Enquirer*, January 9, 1885; "The League-Union Deal," *Cincinnati Enquirer*, January 11, 1885; "Base Ball," *Cincinnati Enquirer*, December 21, 1884.

31. "The Sporting World," *Cincinnati Enquirer*, January 16, 1885; "Sporting," *St. Louis Republican*, January 16, 1885. The report names the replacement organization the Western Association but it came to fruition as the Western League.

32. "The Sporting World," *Cincinnati Enquirer*, January 19, 1885; "The League-Union Deal," *Cincinnati Enquirer*, January 11, 1885; "The Brooklyn-Cleveland Deal," *Sporting Life*, January 21, 1885; "On The Ragged Edge," *Sporting Life*, January 28, 1885; "Passing Comments," *Sporting Life*, January 21, 1885; "Cleveland Beats Henry V. Lucas at Law," *Sporting Life*, April 20, 1887.

33. "Peace Once More," *Sporting Life*, February 4, 1885.

34. "The League's Flop," *Sporting Life*, April 22, 1885; "Another Speck of War," *Sporting Life*, April 29, 1885; "The Great Meeting," *Sporting Life*, October 21, 1885.

35. "Lucas Quits," *Sporting Life*, August 25, 1886; "The Sporting World," *Cincinnati Enquirer*, February 1, 1885.

36. "New Notes and Comments," *Sporting Life*, August 2, 1890; "St. Louis Siftings," *Sporting Life*, September 5, 1891; Joan M. Thomas, "Henry V. Lucas," SABR, https://sabr.org/bioproj/person/henry-v-lucas/.

37. The Players' League of 1890 is the possible exception. It sought not to join the established leagues, but to overturn them. On the other hand, had it succeeded, it seems unlikely that it could have found a different solution to the logic of bidding wars for players resulting in unsustainable salaries.

38. This is less true today than in earlier decades. Minor-league ball is no longer marketed as the home team competing to win a pennant. Not even the most callow 10-year-old lives and dies with the fortunes of the Lansing Lugnuts. Modern marketing is more as affordable family-friendly entertainment and a chance to see the stars of the future. This can differentiate the product enough to create a distinct audience.

39. "A State League Club," *Pittsburg Dispatch*, May 1, 1892; "Pittsburg Pencillings," *Sporting Life*, June 18, 1892.

An Infield Hit Model from the 2023 MLB Season

"Hit 'em where they ain't"

Donald Slavik

INTRODUCTION

Major league baseball teams routinely use analytics to position infielders based on hitter tendencies, but these data do not always provide a complete story. If a hitter always pulls the ball, it is difficult to use that data to assess *quantitatively* the benefits of balls hit into zones that exploit defensive alignment gaps. The purpose of this research was to develop a model that predicted hit trends impacted by infielder positioning. Baseball Savant data were used to establish hit probabilities from 53,075 groundballs, 29,398 line drives, and 8,509 popups from the 2023 season. The model inputs were batter handedness, batted ball type, spray angle, launch speed, and infield defensive alignment.

The model determined hit probabilities for each batted ball and summed them to predict hit totals for individual players and teams. Hit simulations were performed to highlight the quantitative impact of launch speed, batted ball type, and spray angle. These results were then used to define how hit outcomes could be improved for hitters. This study honors the instincts of the great hitter Wee Willie Keeler to "hit 'em where they ain't."

RESEARCH MOTIVATION

From 1892 to 1910, Wee Willie Keeler played for four teams in the American and National Leagues. He was inducted into the National Baseball Hall of Fame in 1939, and according to his plaque, he was "baseball's greatest place-hitter; best bunter."[1] Despite the 5-foot-4 frame that inspired his nickname, Keeler could really hit. In 1897, he had a 44-game hit streak and led baseball with a .424 batting average. In 1899, he struck out only twice in 633 plate appearances. Although he played in an era of higher batting averages and lower strikeout rates, Keeler was still an outlier. According to FanGraphs, his .341 career batting average was 24% higher than the league average for the time, making it the 15th-highest league-adjusted mark in AL/NL history among players with at least 600 plate appearances.[2] Willie outlined his legendary hitting philosophy to reporter Abe Yager of the *Brooklyn Daily Eagle* during a rain delay on August 7, 1901: "I have already written a treatise and it reads like this: 'Keep your eye clear and hit 'em where they ain't; that's all.'"[3]

How does that advice apply to baseball today? Hitters have focused on launch angle and launch speed for home run production. "If you're 10 years old and your coach says to get on top of the ball, tell them no," said Josh Donaldson in 2017. "Because in the big leagues these things that they call groundballs are outs. They don't pay you for groundballs. They pay you for doubles. They pay you for homers."[4] The infield shift further increased the focus on launch angle.

"Batters saw hit probability on grounders reduced by the shift, so they tried to hit over defensive alignments," wrote Tom Verducci. "From 2015 to '22, the shift helped take 2,065 ground-ball hits out of the game."[5] So in 2023 MLB banned the infield shift. According to MLB.com's Anthony Castrovince, "These restrictions are intended to increase the batting averages on balls in play, and to restore more traditional outcomes on batted balls."[6]

Every hitter would like to hit home runs or hard line drives into the gap in every at-bat. Since this is not possible, understanding the benefit of different hitting approaches in unique game situations is important. This study developed a model that predicted hit totals for players from the 2023 season. The model was then used for quantitative predictions of additional hits with different sensitivity study assumptions. How many extra hits are expected with increased launch speed? How many extra hits are expected with fewer popups, or more groundballs? And how many extra hits are expected from more favorable spray angles—from hitting 'em where they ain't?

PREVIOUS WORK

Using hit probabilities from the 2017 season, Jim Albert established a novel iterative approach to determine hit probabilities based on spray angle and launch speed.[7] That work did not take defensive alignment into account. More recent work has specifically focused on how infield alignment affects offensive performance.

In 2022, Russell Carleton broke down the effect of infield alignment on several offensive statistics for both left-handed and right-handed batters during the 2021 season.[8] The shift impacted the rates of strikeouts, walks, balls in play, singles, and other metrics, but no metric saw an increase or decrease of more than four percentage points. Carleton's study briefly highlighted spray angle as an important parameter, but it did not establish hit probabilities for different spray angles or hit types.

DATA

The goal of this work was to develop a predictive infield hit model. The baseline data were obtained using Baseball Savant's search feature.[9] For each batted ball type, a CSV file was downloaded containing 81 populated data parameters.[10] For reference, Figure 2 shows examples of infield alignments, as well as an example of the spray angle (phi). The shade infield alignment tag was introduced in 2023 to denote alignments in which a fielder is positioned outside of his traditional area of responsibility, such as a shortstop playing close to second base or in the hole over by the third baseman. Strategic infield alignment is a catch-all for other alignments, such as an infielder playing in or guarding the line. In Figure 2, the black dots show standard alignment, and the white dots show the infielders shaded toward the pull side. The strategic alignment and spray angle will be discussed more in upcoming sections.

A data scorecard of total at-bats by hit type is provided in Table 1. At-bats with incomplete information, labeled Null At-Bats, were excluded from the model.

Table 1. Counted At-Bats and Null At-Bats for Each Batted Ball Type

Hit Type	At-Bats	Null At-Bats	Null%
Groundball	53,075	496	0.93
Line Drive	29,398	106	0.36
Popup	8,509	19	0.22
Fly Ball	31,593	135	0.43
Total	**122,575**	**756**	**0.62**

MODEL METHOD AND ASSUMPTIONS

Batted Ball Types: The model focused on balls in play impacted by infield alignment. In the first three columns of Table 2, field outs are separated by batted ball type and broken down by whether they were hit to an infielder or an outfielder.[11] The batting averages of different batted ball types are broken down in the last four columns of Table 2. The columns on the left were used to understand trends, while the columns on the right were used for model development. Nearly all groundball and popup outs were fielded by infielders, so the infield hit probability model included all groundballs and popups. Most fly ball outs were fielded by outfielders, so fly balls were excluded from the probability model.

Line drives were more complicated. Infielders caught 29.7% of line drive outs and outfielders caught the other 70.3%. Line drive outs as a function of launch speed and launch angle are shown in Figure 3. If an infielder was in the right position, he made the play on all line drives below 60 mph, as well as harder-hit line drives at launch angles below 12 degrees. The infield line-drive envelope is shown with

Figure 2. Infield Alignments and Spray Angle

 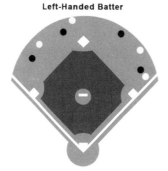 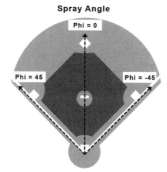

Table 2. Ball in Play Data Broken Down by Batted Ball Type

Hit Type	Outs Infield	Outs Outfield		Hit Type	At-Bat	Hit	Hits/At-Bat
Groundball	39,534	1		Groundball	52,579	13,042	.248
Line Drive	3,088	7,321		Line Drive	11,233	8,133	.724
Popup	8,370	6		Popup	8,490	115	.014
Fly Ball	838	22,072		Fly Ball	N/A	N/A	N/A
Total	**51,830**	**29,400**		**Total**	**72,302**	**21,290**	**.294**

Infield Hit Data for Model Development

solid line fits in Figure 3. All line drives within the darker envelope are defined as infield line drives and included in this study.[12]

Please note that for the purposes of this study, the term "infield balls" does not refer to balls that stay in the infield. It refers to balls that could be fielded by an infielder, were they in position to make the play. Specific model input parameters will be discussed in detail next.

Spray Angle: A ball hit right back to the pitcher would have a phi of 0 degrees, while a ball hit down the third base line would have a phi of 45 and a ball hit down the first base line would have a phi of -45. Unfortunately, spray angle was not directly provided in Baseball Savant. It was calculated using the location where the ball was fielded (variables hc_x and hc_y), according to an equation produced by Jeff and Darrell Zimmerman and published by Bill Petti:[13]

Equation 1. Spray Angle

$$\text{Spray Angle} = -0.75(180/\pi)\,\text{atan}\,[(hc\_x - 125.42)/(198.27 - hc\_y)]$$

The adjusted spray angle from Equation 1 is defined as a positive number for pulled balls, and it is calculated by multiplying the spray angle of left-handed batters by -1.

Reference Launch Speed: As the work evolved, it became apparent there was no simple step or equation that could predict hits directly from the adjusted spray angle. But it was possible to break the problem into easily understood steps that gradually led toward the desired result. The first major step focused on hit trends for the most common launch speed, known as the reference launch speed. This was established from the baseline datasets for each batted ball type. Infield line drives were hit hardest, with only a slight decrease for groundballs and a larger decrease for popups. Launch speeds were reasonably uniform between adjusted spray angles of 40 degrees and -30 degrees, with a drop-off at the extremes.[14]

Reference Hit Probabilities: Reference hit probability, or ref hit prob, is the batting average for each batted ball type within 5 mph of its reference launch speed. The reference hit probabilities of groundballs for left-handed hitters are shown for standard/strategic alignments and shade alignment in Figure 5. For zones with fewer than

Figure 3. 2023 Line-Drive Outs

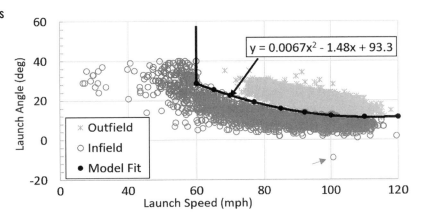

Figure 4. Median/Reference Launch Speeds

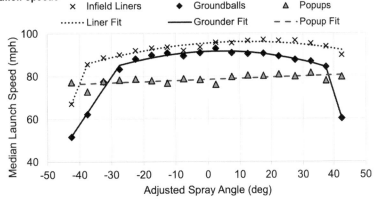

10 at-bats, batted balls were grouped across adjoining zones to produce reasonable statistics. These are indicated by an x in subsequent graphs. Reference hit probabilities for standard and strategic infield alignments were similar, so these categories were grouped together. The solid black lines are model input curves, and infielder representative positions are marked by circles on the x-axis. Hit probabilities vary dramatically based on spray angle and infielder positioning, with probability minimums at angles where fielders are positioned. Peaks and minimums differ slightly for shaded and non-shaded alignments. Adjusted spray angles near 2.5 degrees and below -30 degrees were great places for lefties to hit the ball.

Reference hit probabilities of groundballs for right-handed hitters are provided in Figure 6. Between the middle infielders, around 2.5 degrees, was a great place to hit the ball for righties.

Reference hit probabilities for line drives are shown in Figure 7. Line drives have local minimums where infielders are stationed. A right-handed shade hit probability could be considered in the future if larger sample size becomes available. It was not surprising that hit probabilities were good for infield line drives, but it was surprising to the author that the hit probabilities were above .500 for almost all spray angles.

Finally, hit probabilities for popups are provided in Figure 8. Popups resulted in very poor hit outcomes, with no significant correlation with launch speed.

Launch Speed Factors: The author evaluated a number of different approaches to include launch speed effects in the hit model. After a significant amount of trial and error, a relatively simple equation was developed that captured hit trends.

Hit probability, or hit_prob, was calculated using the launch speed, the reference launch speed, the reference hit probability, and the launch speed factor, or m. If the launch speed constant m was zero, launch speed had no impact on hit probabilities. For large m, increased launch speeds increased hit probabilities. The launch speed constants were determined with an iteration algorithm that minimized the difference between observed and predicted total hits in each spray angle zone for high and low launch speeds. Hit probabilities were constrained to physically possible values between 0% and 100%. This check was required at very high and very low launch speeds during the optimization routine and/or for hit predictions.

Groundball launch speed factors at low hit speeds (launch speeds below the reference launch speed) and high hit speeds (launch speeds above the reference

Figure 5. Hit Probabilities for Groundballs at Reference Launch Speeds for Left-Handed Hitters

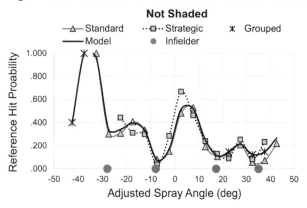
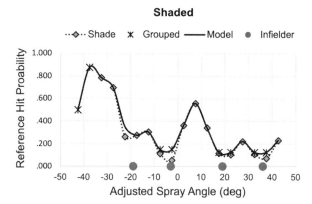

Figure 6. Hit Probabilities for Groundballs at Reference Launch Speeds for Right-Handed Batters[15]

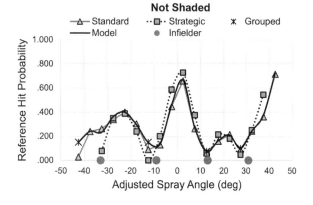
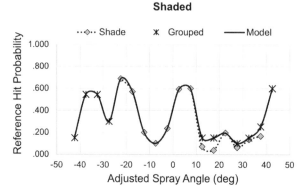

Equation 2. Hit Probability

$$hit\_prob = (ref\_hit\_prob) \times [1 + m \times (launch\_speed - ref\_launch\_speed)/100]$$

Figure 7. Hit Probabilities for Line Drives at Reference Launch Speeds[16]

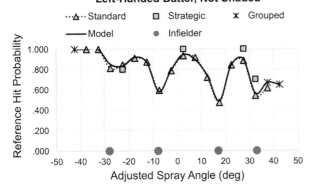

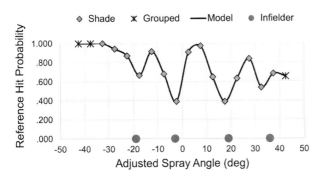

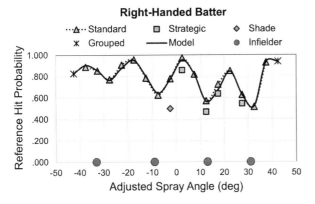

Figure 8. Hit Probabilities for Popups

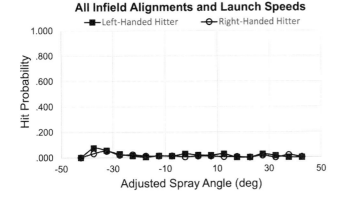

launch speed) are shown in Figure 9. Balls hit with high and low launch speeds exhibited different behavior. The launch speed impact on hits was less at low launch speeds, with m typically between 0 and 5. It was more pronounced at high launch speeds, with m up to 11. This was incorporated into the model with a high- and low-speed fit constant. The optimizer initially produced large swings in m for zones with very low reference hit probabilities below .150. These zones were generally found to have much higher hit probabilities at both low and high launch speeds. A modest increase in the very low reference hit probability led to convergence with consistent values across adjacent spray angles for these cases. This was the main step where user judgement was required; it can be thought of as a data-grouping beyond +/-5 mph launch speeds for these special cases. These adjustments are identified with x symbols at the intermediate angles in Figures 5 and 6.

Note that the launch speed constants were negative at some spray angle extremes, indicating a benefit from a reduced launch speed. This would be on poorly hit balls down the line that are a difficult play for the pitcher or corner infielder playing at typical depths.

Speed factors for infield line drives are shown in Figure 10. Launch speed did not have much effect on hit probability.

Finally, there were no hit speed factors for popups in the model. Popup hit probabilities were so low that no attempt was made to further quantify popups. Hitters should simply minimize popups as best they can.

Infield Hit Model: Model constants were the infield line drive envelope (Figure 3), the reference launch speed (Figure 4), the reference hit probabilities (Figures 5 through 8), and the launch speed factors (Figures 9 and 10). Since reference batted ball type probabilities and launch speed curves were highly non-linear, no attempt was made to fit equations across spray angles for these terms. Values for each zone were instead put in lookup tables that were accessed for each at-bat.

The launch angle was not directly included as a model input, but it was indirectly accounted for through unique hit probability fits for each batted ball type. The handedness of the pitcher was not included in the model, as it was shown not to impact hit probabilities early in model development. The pitcher impacts whether and where the ball is put in play, but not whether it will turn into a hit. Model constants with all adjustments are provided in Appendix II, available online at SABR.org.

Figure 9. Groundball Launch Speeds for High and Low Launch Speed Factors[17]

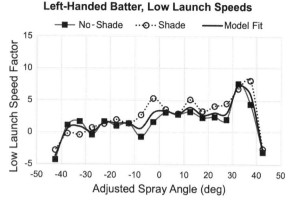

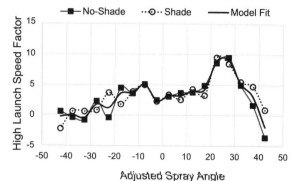

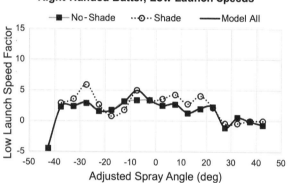

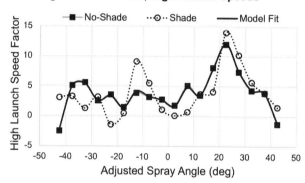

Figure 10. Line Drive Launch Speeds for High and Low Launch Speed Factors

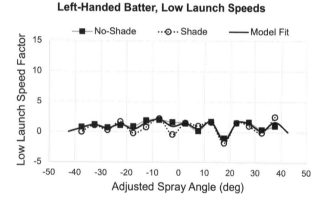

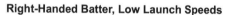

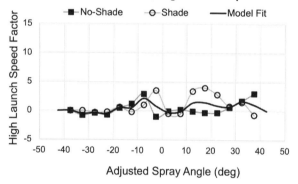

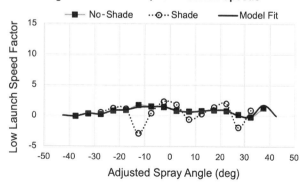

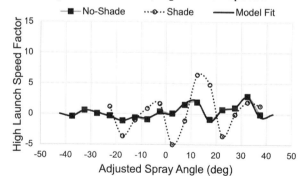

MODEL RESULTS

Model equations and constants were first confirmed from hits for subgroups into each hit zone. Python code was written to count observed hits and to predict hits in each spray angle zone. Total predicted hits were determined by adding hit probabilities for each at-bat using Equation 3.

Hit probability for each at-bat was determined using Equation 3, ref hit prob were the hit probabilities established from values in Figures 5 through 8, and hit adder was a hit probability term that reflected launch speed effects. The observed and predicted hits in each zone for each batted ball type are shown in Figure 11. Each symbol represents the total hits in each subgroup and each zone. A solid line is a perfect correlation. The model accurately predicts overall hit behavior in all spray angle zones for all batted ball types.

Hit probabilities were next determined for each player, using Equations 2 and 3. Figure 12 shows predicted and observed hits for each MLB player and each MLB team. On the left, each symbol represents the hit totals for 645 MLB players with 72,302 at-bats. The solid line represents a perfect correlation. Overall, the model works quite well for all players. Luis Arráez, who led MLB in batting average, and Ronald Acuña Jr., who led in total hits, are highlighted. The total number of predicted infield hits, 21,252, was just 0.18% below the observed hits of 21,290.

Equation 3. Predicted Hits

hits = ΣAt-Bats(hit_prob) = ΣAt-Bats(ref_hit_prob) + ΣAt-Bats(hit_adder)

Figure 11. Model Check of Hits in Each Spray Angle Zone for All Batted Ball Types

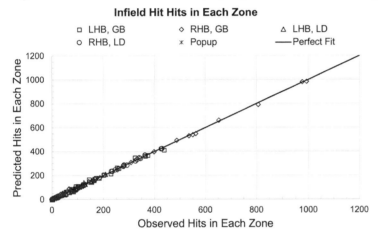

Figure 12. Hit Predictions for the 2023 MLB Season

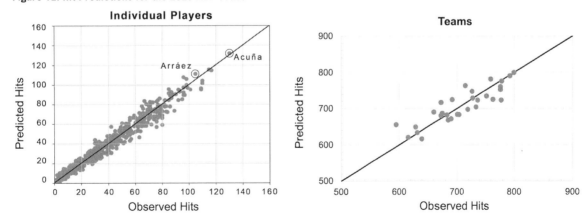

On the right, each symbol represents the infield hits for one of the 30 teams. Predicted and observed hits with each team name are also provided in Figure 13. The model was representative of the total hits of all MLB teams.

SENSITIVITY STUDIES AND DISCUSSION

The model was next used for sensitivity studies to understand how players and teams can best improve hit outcomes. How many additional hits can be expected with: a) 10 mph increase in launch speed for popups (PU); b) 10 mph increase in launch speeds for groundballs (GB); c) slightly reduced launch angle contact, converting popups into line drives (PU to LD); d) slightly increased launch angle contact, converting groundballs into line drives (GB to LD); or e) groundballs hit at more favorable spray angles (GB Spray Angle)? Sensitivity studies assumed 10% of baseline

events would be converted to the new hitter-friendly condition. Sensitivity study results are summarized as extra predicted hits in Figure 14 and the Table 3.

Increase in Popup Launch Speed: Popups hit harder just go up higher before they are caught. No attempt was made to model small changes in hit probabilities for popups at different launch speed, so the model predicts no extra hits for popups. In reality, launch speed could be a small benefit for a few popups that turn from popups to fly ball bloop singles.

Increase in Groundball Launch Speed: Groundballs hit harder were more likely to reach the outfield as hits. Figure 15 shows the hit probabilities for groundballs hit both 10 mph harder and 10 softer when the infield is not shaded. An increase of 10 mph raises hit probabilities in a few spray angle zones. If 10% of groundballs were hit

Figure 13. Predicted and Observed Hits by Team

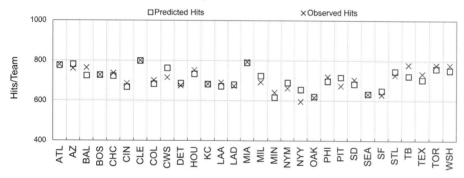

Figure 14. Extra Predicted Hit Sensitivity Study

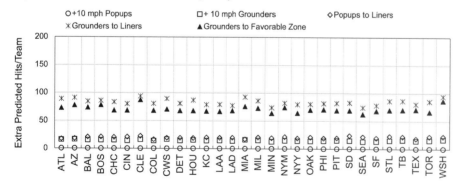

Table 3. Extra Predicted Hit Sensitivity Study Summary

Favorable Condition	Extra Hits LHB	Extra Hits RHB	Total	Per Team	AVG LHB	AVG RHB
+10 mph PU	0.0	0.0	0.0	0.0	.247	.249
+10 mph GB	180.6	262.5	443.1	14.8	.250	.252
PU to LD	225.8	355.4	581.3	19.4	.251	.253
GB to LD	967.8	1438.9	2,406.8	80.2	.262	.264
GB Spray Angle	1,046.0	992.6	2,038.6	68.0	.263	.259

10 mph harder, this would lead to 443 extra hits per season, or 14.8 per team. This was only the second-best strategy to achieve extra hits, according to the sensitivity studies.

Popups Converted to Groundballs: Popups have the worst hit probability of all batted ball types (Table 2). Any reduction of the worst thing is a good thing. Converting 10% of the 8,490 popups, which have an average hit probability of .014, to infield line-drives which have an average hit probability of .724, would lead to 581 extra hits per season.

Groundballs Converted to Infield Line Drives: Since the vast majority of infield balls in play were ground balls—72.7%, as shown in Table 2—this option produced a significant jump in extra hits. The model predicted 2,407 extra hits per season. Line drives are a lovely path toward getting on base.

Groundballs Hit at More Favorable Spray Angles: We have finally come around to the "hit 'em where they ain't" option. This option assumes the groundballs were hit at the median speed. The assumed favorable hit probability

was .759 for left-handed hitters (balls hit at spray angles below -30 degrees), and .579 for right-handed hitters (balls hit at a spray angle zone of 2.5 degrees, between the middle infielders). The model predicted 2,039 extra hits per season. But is this path possible for MLB hitters today? Hit probabilities and groundball counts in each hit zone are provided in Figure 16. Lefties in particular pull most balls to spray angles greater than 15 degrees, where hit probabilities are terrible (the dashed box in Figure 16). Lefties hit relatively few balls the other way at spray angles below -30 degrees, where hit probabilities are great. For left-handers, the 6x benefit of hitting balls the other way comes not from hitting the ball exceptionally hard or into a precise zone, but hitting it to the left side avoiding only the lonely third baseman covering that side of the infield. The benefit for right-handed hitters is less obvious, but shifting any balls out of the poor hitting zone between 10 degrees and 35 degrees would produce more hits. The author knows hitting the ball the other way is difficult. But is it more difficult than hitting balls harder or turning popups and grounders into line drives? I expect Wee Willie would have a clear and concise answer to this question.

Figure 15. Launch Speed Impact on Groundball Hit Probabilities

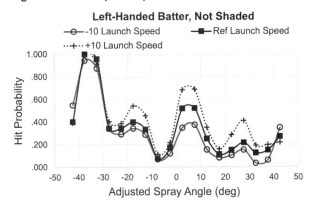

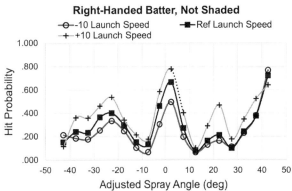

Figure 16. Hit Probabilities for Groundballs

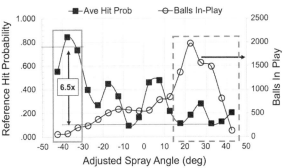

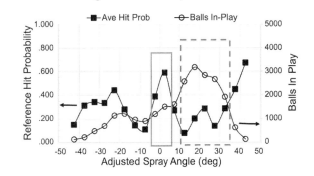

CASE STUDIES FOR ELITE MLB LEFT-HANDED HITTERS

Given a quantitative understanding of how batted ball type influences infield hit probabilities, the study now turns to individual hitters to assess how batted ball type and spray angle impact their predicted hits. I chose four elite left-handed hitters, but the study can be easily applied to other players, including right-handers. In 2023, Luis Arráez won the National League batting title with a .354 batting average, Freddie Freeman set a Dodgers record with 59 doubles, Matt Olson led all of MLB with 54 home runs, and Kyle Schwarber hit the longest home run of any player in the NL at 483 feet. Standard batting statistics and a breakdown of infield batted ball types are provided in Table 4.

Groundball distribution for different spray angle zones is provided in Figure 17. All hitters put a similar number of balls into the poor hitting zone above 15 degrees. Arráez was best at sending grounders up the middle and the other way.

A summary of groundball hits and groundballs in play for each batter is shown in Table 5. Grounders hit to the opposite field had a batting average of .407, compared to .310 for grounders up the middle and .141 for pulled grounders. This confirms again the benefit of hitting the ball toward favorable zones. The far-right column focuses only on grounders hit at a spray angle below -30 degrees, which have a batting average of .824. Though this is a small sample size and not an easy spot to put the ball, the rewards are considerable.

CONCLUSION

The obvious challenge is to hit line drives or grounders to more favorable spray angles without a significant reduction in power or an increase in strikeouts or

Table 4. Batter Statistics and Batted Ball Type Breakdown

Player	AB	AVG	K	Hits	HR	GB	IF LD	PU
Luis Arráez	574	.354	34	203	10	232	62	10
Freddie Freeman	637	.331	121	211	29	185	58	19
Matt Olson	608	.283	167	172	54	171	27	26
Kyle Schwarber	585	.197	215	115	47	128	20	43
					Infield Hits	716	167	98
					Hits/AB	.232	.737	.020

Figure 17. Groundball Distribution

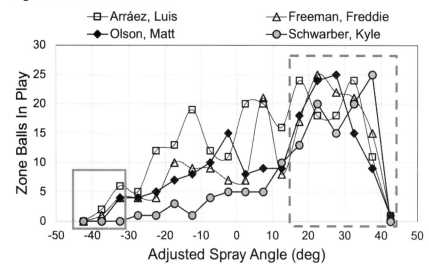

Table 5. Groundballs by Spray Angle (Hits/At-Bats)

Player	-45 to -15	-15 to 15	15 to 45	Total	-45 to -30
Luis Arráez	13/38	32/98	14/96	59/232	7/8
Freddie Freeman	13/23	16/61	10/101	39/185	4/5
Matt Olson	9/20	23/59	15/92	47/171	¾
Kyle Schwarber	0/5	6/30	15/93	21/128	0/0
Total	35/86	77/248	54/382	166/716	14/17
Hits/At-Bats	0.407	.310	.141	.232	.824

popups. The author does not expect that any of these adjustments will be easy. Infielders will react to balls placed more frequently into favorable zones. So the hitter approach will need to evolve continually. But if a hitter better understands his own tendencies, how infielders defend against his tendencies, and the quantitative benefits of balls hit into favorable zones, he could end up with more hits. Even for exceptional hitters, directing more balls toward the most favorable hitting zones would be a path to extra hits; a strategy Wee Willie Keeler would have embraced. ■

Acknowledgments

The author thanks reviewers Cindy Slavik, Jay Kelly, and the anonymous peer reviewers for invaluable feedback that made this a much better paper. The author also appreciates the helpful edits suggested by the *BRJ* editors. The author is also grateful to Professor Mehdi Norouzi's class at the University of Cincinnati, Intro to Programing Python and R.

Notes

1. "Willie Keeler," National Baseball Hall of Fame, accessed January 29, 2024, https://baseballhall.org/hall-of-famers/keeler-willie.

2. "Major League Leaders," FanGraphs, accessed January 29, 2024, https://www.fangraphs.com/leaders/major-league?pos=all&stats=bat&lg=al%2Cnl&type=23&season=2023&month=0&season1=1871&ind=0&team=0&rost=0&players=0&sortcol=5&sortdir=default&qual=1000&pageitems=50.

3. "Good Advice by Willie Keeler," *Pittsburgh Press*, March 25, 1904, 24, https://news.google.com/newspapers?id=7ggbAAAAIBAJ&sjid=rkgEAAAAIBAJ&pg=4433%2C1761576&dq=keep+your+eye+clear+hit+em+where+they+that%27s+all.

4. Dave Sheinin, "These days in baseball, every batter is trying to find an angle," *Washington Post*, June 1, 2017, https://www.washingtonpost.com/graphics/sports/mlb-launch-angles-story/.

5. Tom Verducci, "How Banning Infield Shifts Will Change MLB," *Sports Illustrated*, November 21, 2022, https://www.si.com/mlb/2022/11/21/banning-infield-shifts-impact.

6. Anthony Castrovince, "Pitch timer, shift restrictions among the announced rule changes for 2023," MLB.com, February 1, 2023, https://www.mlb.com/news/mlb-2023-rule-changes-pitch-timer-larger-bases-shifts.

7. Jim Albert, "Chance of Hit as Function of Launch Angle, Exit Velocity, and Spray Angle," Exploring Baseball Data with R, Jan 15, 2018, https://baseballwithr.wordpress.com/2018/01/15/chance-of-hit-as-function-of-launch-angle-exit-velocity-and-spray-angle/.

8. Russell A. Carleton, "So You've Decided to Ban the Shift," *Baseball Prospectus*, March 9, 2022, https://www.baseballprospectus.com/news/article/73029/baseball-therapy-so-youve-decided-to-ban-the-shift/.

9. The search selections were: A) Player Type = Batter; B) IF Alignment = Standard, Strategic, and Shade; C) Season = 2023 Regular Season; and D) PA Result = Base Hit and all balls in-play except for sacrifices. This study focused on balls in play directly impacted by the infield alignment: hits, errors, and outs in the field. Although walks, strikeouts, and sacrifice outs could be indirectly impacted a small amount by the defensive alignment, they were not considered.

10. Baseball Savant limits output files to approximately 25,000 rows. Files were downloaded for each hit type to keep each file below the maximum limit. Individual files were then concatenated with Python code written by the author.

11. In this case the pitcher and catcher are considered infielders.

12. Figure 3 includes a single line drive out at 100.6 mph and -9 degrees. This was a groundball incorrectly tagged as a line drive. It was difficult to fully assess all points for data quality, but a total of one poorly tagged point out of 10,409 line-drive outs was representative of a very good system with few data errors.

13. Bill Petti, "Research Notebook: New Format for Statcast Data Export at Baseball Savant," *The Hardball Times*, April 28, 2017, https://tht.fangraphs.com/research-notebook-new-format-for-statcast-data-export-at-baseball-savant/

14. Separate median launch speeds were considered for left-handed and right-handed hitters, but this was a small effect and therefore not included in this evaluation.

15. Since the shade infield alignment was employed infrequently for righties, the approximate infielder position was not included in that plot.

16. Given there were very few line drives hit into the shade infield alignment for right-handed batters, a single model fit was derived for all infield configurations.

17. The infield alignment was a minor factor on the launch speed constant, so a single model fit line was developed for each case. The variation for right-handed hitters on grounders (Figure 9) and line drives (Figure 10) with the shade alignment is due to a small sample size.

Plummeting Batting Averages Are Due to Far More than Infield Shifting

Part One: Fielding and Batting Strategy

Charlie Pavitt

In 2022, the Lords of Baseball decreed that the full infield shift, which had become commonplace in baseball, would be banned. Since the 2023 season, all four infielders must be within the outer boundary of the dirt, with two on each side of second base and no switching sides. After a violation, the wronged team can either accept the outcome of the play or continue the previous at-bat with a ball added to the count. In a press release, Major League Baseball claimed that "these restrictions will return the game to a more traditional aesthetic by governing defensive shifts, with the goals of encouraging more balls in play, giving players more opportunities to showcase their athleticism, and offsetting the growing trend of alignments that feature four outfielders."[1] Partial shifts, with one of the middle infielders just to their side of second base, are still allowed.

In contrast with two other rule changes announced at that time—the pitch timer and larger bases—MLB provided no factual rationale for these restrictions. However, some commentators provided one: a significant drop in batting averages over time. For example, Matt Snyder noted that the composite .243 batting average for 2022 was the lowest since 1968, the Year of the Pitcher, when the two major leagues batted .237.[2] In fact, the league also batted .245 in 2020 and .244 in 2021, for a combined .243 average from 2020 to 2022. That's the fourth-lowest three-year average since 1901, trailing the spans that ended in 1968, 1909, and 1969 by less than one-thousandth of a percentage point. Snyder and others implied that the motivation for the ban was a desire for more base hits, additional baserunners, and a more attractive product that would draw more fan interest.[3]

Figure 1 shows the ebbs and flows of batting average in the American and National Leagues since the start of the live ball era in 1920.[4] Note the sharp drop starting in 2007. From 2007 to 2022, the league batting average fell 25 points from .268 to .243. This essay will focus on this period of time.

If the goal is returning the batting average to the level of 2007, banning the shift will not be enough to accomplish it alone. This drop was the result of several factors, of which the infield shift was just one. Shifting among outfielders has probably been more consequential. Intentional revisions in batting strategy, favoring fly balls over grounders, have also had a discernible impact. These three factors were likely responsible for most of a 13-point decrease in batting average on balls in play (BABIP) over this time period. But looming over all of this is the much-discussed rise in strikeouts, which probably accounts for the bulk of the remaining 12 points. The rule change will have no effect on the last three factors, and there is no reason to believe that their impact will change dramatically in the coming years without either further rule changes or revisions in strategy.

Figure 1. Batting Average, 1920–2022

The goal of this essay is an in-depth examination of the effect of the first three of these factors. The infield shift has garnered the most attention and is the object of the rule change, so it will receive the bulk of the discussion here. A second essay on factors impacting strikeout rate will appear in the future.

CHANGES IN BASIC BATTING METRICS FROM 2007 TO 2022

I begin this examination with two graphs, Figures 2 and 3. The first shows counting stats in each year up to 2022, the last season of the full infield shift.[5] In order to keep the scale consistent, I have used the ratio between each season's totals and the totals in 2007 rather than the raw numbers.[6]

Walks have generally bounced between 3.0 and 3.5 per game starting in the 1950s, so any trends implied here may be an illusion. Homers, at 1.02 per game per team in 2007, increased starting in 2016 and reached a peak at 1.39 in 2019, but appear to be returning to

their previous level ever since. In contrast, hits have dropped steadily, from 9.25 per team per game in 2007 to 8.04 in 2020. Singles, doubles, and triples have generally followed the same path. Strikeouts have changed the most conspicuously, rising from 6.62 per team per game in 2007 to 8.81 in 2019, though they fell to 8.40 in 2022.

Turning to averages, batting average fell from .268 in 2007 to .243 in 2022 as discussed earlier. On-base average fell a similar amount, 24 points from .336 to .312. Slugging average was a roller-coaster ride, down from .423 in 2007 to .386 in 2014 as doubles and triples fell, then up to .435 in 2019 as homers increased, but back to .395 in 2022 as homers and triples dropped (and doubles were up only a bit). The shift ban is specifically targeted at BABIP. To add some historical context, BABIP stayed in the .280s from 1973 to 1992. It jumped to .294 in 1993 and stayed in the mid .290s through low .300s until 2020. The 2007 figure of .303 was the high-water mark. The drop in this decade brought BABIP down to levels not seen since the early 1990s.

The following three sections cover the three factors behind the drop in BABIP: infield shifting, outfield shifting, and changes in batting strategy.

INFIELD SHIFTING

Philadelphia's Cy Williams is generally considered the first batter to regularly fall victim to defensive shifts back in 1923.[7] But there is evidence of infield shifts being used as early as 1877.[8] Another Williams, Ted, at least occasionally faced both infield and outfield shifts beginning in 1946. Thereafter, shifts were applied from time to time against lefty pull hitters, including Willie McCovey, Boog Powell, and David Ortiz. The value of the shift was intuitive. An early study from the Elias Sports Bureau revealed that, even with fielders generally shading in that direction, when there was no shift, batters had higher batting averages on balls hit to their pull side than to the opposite side (with hits up the middle ignored). Of 84 players with at least 400 balls in play in 1990 (excluding switch-hitters, unless they accumulated 400 from one side of the plate), 71, or 84.5%, hit for a higher average on their pull side.[9]

Figure 2. Basic Offensive Metrics Compared to 2007

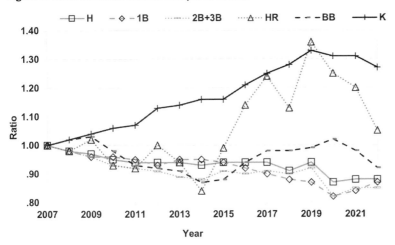

Figure 3. Offensive Averages Compared to 2007

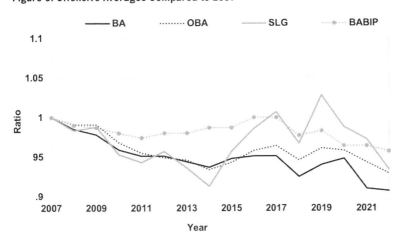

By the end of the aughts, the Rays had begun the final era of the infield shift. As spray angle data became more widespread, other teams quickly followed their lead. From 2011 to 2015, full shifts increased from 1,389 per year to 11,524, while partial shifts increased from 968 to 6,214.[10] The distinction between full and partial is critical; Rosales and Spratt noted that between 2010 and 2015, batting averages on grounders and short line drives were actually higher with partial shifts (.265) than with no shift at all (.258). Sports Information Services' Mark Simon came to a similar conclusion for the 2017 season, with weighted batting averages of .271 with no shift and .269 with a partial shift.[11]

According to Baseball Savant, by 2022 the full shift was used 60,779 times.[12] There is no question that it was successful in reducing batting averages. Figure 4 includes batting averages and BABIPs for batters facing either a full shift or no shift between 2015 and 2022.

Over those eight seasons, the league batted .240 with a full shift and .252 with none. The difference between the two widened to 19 points by 2022 (.229 and .248). Without strikeouts to mask the effect, the divergence in BABIP was even greater: .279 with a full shift and .300 with no shift. In 2022, the difference was 26 points: .273 with a full shift and .298 with no shift. However, these metrics mask significant differences based on batter handedness across a wide range of metrics. Figure 5 breaks down the results during full shifts by batter handedness.

All told, right-handed batters consistently had higher batting averages and BABIP against the shift than left-handed batters. In fact, the righty advantage went beyond batting average. Table 1, offered by Russell Carleton, compares performance at the level of the individual batter with and without shifts for batters with more than 50 non-shifted PAs between 2015 and 2019; these tendencies remained in place through 2021 and the first half of 2022.[13]

First, when the defense was shifted, walk rates increased enough to make up for at least part of the decrease in singles. Going into more detail, pitch-tracking data revealed that when the defense was shifted,

pitchers threw inside more often to take advantage of the infield being stacked to the pull side and to discourage hitting to the opposite field, resulting in more inside pitches that were called balls.[14] Pitchers were also more likely to throw balls above the strike zone. The major takeaway is that whereas left-handed batters were hurt by shifts, right-handed batters were

Figure 4. Batting Average and BABIP With and Without Shifts, 2015–2022

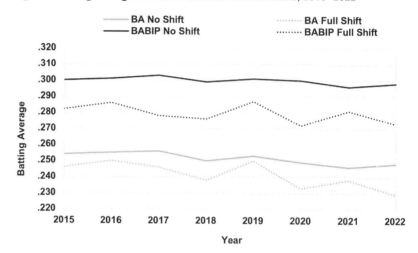

Figure 5. Performance Against Full Shift By Batter Handedness 2015–2022

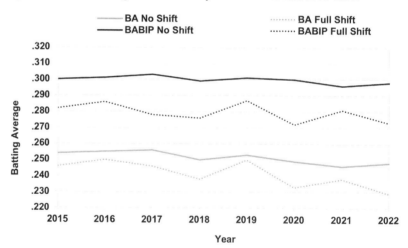

Table 1. Batter Performance When Shifted, 2015–2019

Metric	LHB	RHB
Strikeout	+2.2%	-4.7%
Walk	+1.1%	+0.9%
HBP	-0.0%	+0.0%
Single	-2.0%	+0.2%
Double/Triple	-0.0%	+0.3%
Home Run	+0.0%	+0.4%
Out in Play	-1.3%	+2.8%
On Base Event	-0.9%	+2.0%
BABIP	-.016	-.006
Linear Weight Runs (per PA)	-.007	+.018

helped by them. As Carleton observed, part of the reason for this discrepancy was the difference in fielder positioning. Against left-handed batters, the left side of the infield was patrolled by the infielder with the greatest range, the shortstop. Against right-handed batters, the right side of the infield was covered by the infielder with the worst range, the first baseman, who had to stay close enough to the base to take throws from the other infielders. Righties were able to take advantage of the large hole on the right side of the infield. Carleton concluded that they essentially faced only partial shifts, which were hardly better for the defense than no shift at all.[15]

Table 2, once again courtesy of Carleton, shows the difference in BABIP broken down by whether the ball was pulled.[16]

Table 2. BABIP and Groundball Location, 2016–20

Direction	No Shift		Shift		Difference	
	RHB	LHB	RHB	LHB	RHB	LHB
Pull	.211	.168	.175	.122	-.036	-.046
Straight/Oppo	.285	.300	.324	.325	+.039	+.025

Because of the longer throw from the left side of the infield, right-handed batters fared better than left-handed batters when they pulled the ball, whether into a standard defensive alignment or a shift. But the real kicker is that because shifts against right-handed batters were partial, their loss of 36 points of batting average on pulled grounders was counterbalanced by their gain of 39 points on non-pulled grounders. On the other hand, not only did left-handed batters lose out when they pulled the ball due to the shorter throw to first, they also lost out when they went the other way, because they faced an optimally placed shortstop rather than a first baseman who was tethered to the bag.

Right-handed batters also fared better on line drives when the defense was shifted. On line drives hit at a spray angle of between 20 and 35 degrees (roughly the area between the first and second basemen in a standard alignment), right-handed batters were more successful to the tune of 27 points of BABIP.[17] All told, from 2015 to 2022, left-handed batters had a .315 wOBA with no shift, better than the .312 wOBA of right-handed batters. But against a full shift, lefty wOBA was .319, far below the righty wOBA of .341. As a result, Sports Info Solutions recommended that teams not shift against right-handed batters who didn't pull at least 80% of their batted balls to the infield. By 2021, teams seemed to notice. Carleton noted that while overall shifting against lefties increased slightly from 50.2% in 2020 to 51.5% in 2021, it dropped

markedly against righties, from 23.0% to 16.8%.[18]

In conclusion, the shift had little impact on offense, as the resulting benefits for right-handed batters more than made up for any detriment to lefties. Repurposing the wOBA figures from the previous paragraph, wOBAs against the shift were higher for both right-handed and left-handed batters. However, these overall wOBAs are biased in that shifts were employed against better batters. Carleton's calculations in Table 1 account for that bias and show that while the full shift did hurt lefty hitters a bit, it helped righties get more hits and increased walks for everyone. As will be covered later, it also sparked a strategic decision to beat shifts by hitting more homers.

In addition to the shift, Robert Arthur noted a general tendency for fielders to play more deeply that started by 2015 (if not earlier, as that was the first year Statcast's defensive positioning data became publicly available). Despite their lack of positional flexibility given their need to be close to the base, first basemen had moved back a foot or so on average by 2017. Shortstops had shifted backward about two feet by 2019. Second basemen were back about four feet by the first month of 2021. The most significant drop was by third basemen, about nine feet by 2020. Of course, some of this was an artifact of general infielder shifting given that infielders were often placed in the outfield, and in fact there was little or no impact on BABIP for most of the infield. However, third basemen had actually moved back even more, about 10 feet, on plays in which there was no shift. As a consequence, the BABIP on balls hit to third dropped an incredible 40 points between 2017 and the beginning of 2021.[19] In a follow-up, Arthur noted that balls hit up to 175 feet away from home plate were less likely to become hits over that period, with BABIP down over 100 points for those between 120 and 150 feet.[20] Next, we turn to a type of shift that worked far better for the defense.

OUTFIELD SHIFTING

It is more difficult to measure the impact of shifting in the outfield. Infield shifting can be measured by the location of the fielders in relation to second base. In a presentation at the 2019 SABR Analytics Conference, Sports Info Solutions' Brian Reiff pointed out that to define an outfield as shifted, one must consider how many outfielders have moved, what constitutes their starting point, and the distance from it that would count as a shift, all while keeping in mind issues such as batter handedness and ballpark dimensions.[21] According to Sports Info Solutions (SIS), in 2017, left, center, and right fielders respectively stood an average of 296, 318, and 294 feet from home plate. Left fielders were stationed at an average spray angle of 26.9 degrees toward left field, right fielders were stationed an average of 27 degrees toward right, and center fielders were very nearly dead center. Those measurements constitute the average starting point for each outfielder, but there was significant variance. On the average play, the starting positions of the three outfielders were a combined 40 feet from those locations. SIS defined an outfield as shifted if the total distance, adjusted for all of these factors, was greater than 110 feet. As with infield shifts, the number rose in the late 2010s. Mark Simon reported 2,814 such shifts in 2018, a 28% increase over 2017, and an astounding 89% increase from 2016.[22] Overall, the greater the deviation from average, the more effective the outfield positioning. According to Reiff's paper, OPS was at or above .750 for deviations of 30 feet or less, dipped below .700 at 70 feet, below .600 at 90 feet, and was just over .500 for 120 feet. The more extreme the batter's spray angle tendencies, the more likely they were to face a shift.

As I write this in 2023, the publicly available data on the effectiveness of outfield shifts are sparse and indirect, but they still suggest that outfield positioning has probably had a bigger impact than infield shifts on offensive performance. Using Baseball Savant positioning data, Robert Arthur was able to compare seven teams that were not adjusting their outfield positioning in 2016 but had implemented shifts by 2020.[23] Relevant BABIP dropped 10 points as a result.[24] Arthur also uncovered evidence that outfielders were being positioned deeper starting in 2015 or earlier. Although BABIP on balls hit to them was roughly the same, right fielders were positioned four feet deeper in 2019 than they were in 2015, and left fielders were positioned seven feet deeper. In contrast, center fielders were positioned 12 feet deeper in 2020 than in 2015, and BABIP on balls hit into their territory dropped by an astounding 40 points.[25]

Overall, from 2015 to 2022, BABIP on fly balls and line drives hit to the outfield fell from .412 to .400, according to data from Baseball Savant. This was part of a larger decline since the beginning of the pitch-tracking era. Over the same period, BABIP on groundballs fell from .249 to .241. This smaller drop brought groundball BABIP in line with the first several years of the pitch-tracking era. See Figure 6 for the entire 2008–23 era.

CHANGES IN BATTING STRATEGY

In the face of increased shifts, many batters responded by attempting to hit the ball over them. There is no doubt that such a strategy increased the home run rate. According to FanGraphs, from 2015 to 2023, the MLB groundball rate fell from 45.3% to 42.9% while the fly ball rate rose from 33.8% to 37.2%, as demonstrated in Figure 7.

Those fly balls were also more productive, as their isolated power rose from .391 to .573. The increase was particularly pronounced when batters faced shifts. Against strategic and full shifts, batters had an average launch angle of 11.7 degrees in 2015. That launch angle rose to 12.7 degrees in 2016 and 13.4 in 2017. From 2018 to 2022, it fell below 14 degrees in just one season. When the defense was in a standard alignment,

Figure 6. BABIP on Groundballs and Outfield Fly Balls and Line Drives

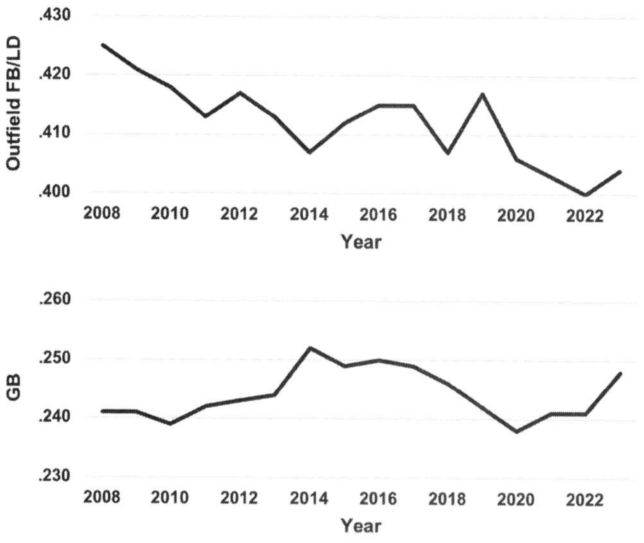

Figure 7. Batted Ball Types Compared to 2007

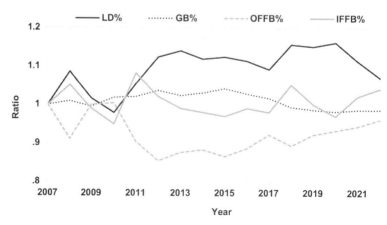

the average launch angle rose above 12 degrees just once, in 2023. In addition to lifting the ball more often when shifted, both left-handed and right-handed batters did more damage on balls in the air. The rate of home runs per fly ball, which never exceeded 11.4% between 2007 and 2014, rose as high as 15.3% in 2019, as demonstrated in Figure 8.

To demonstrate the benefits of lifting the ball more, Rob Mains looked at the 185 batters who made at least 350 plate appearances in both 2015 and 2016. He split them into deciles based on the year-over-year change in their groundball rate. Using Baseball Prospectus's True Average (TAv) metric, which places all offensive production on a scale analogous to batting average, he found that players who lowered their groundball rate in 2016 performed better overall and those who hit more groundballs performed worse, although the difference was small.[26]

Batters adopted two tactics that led to the increased home run rate. The first tactic was pulling the ball more often, as seen in Figure 9.

Between 2013 and 2020, the pull rate of fly balls rose from 22.7% to 24.5%. It's no secret that pulled fly balls are more dangerous. From 2008 to 2022, pulled fly balls and line drives ran a slash line of .612/.603/1.356, whereas fly balls and line drives hit to center and to the opposite field had a slash line of .388/.379/.640. Using the same method described earlier, Rob Mains discovered that players who pulled the ball more also improved their overall performance.[27]

The second tactic for increasing the home run rate was improving the quality of contact. The distinction between hard, medium, and soft contact shown in Figure 9 is based on Sports Info Solutions data. SIS uses a proprietary method to classify batted balls based on the type of batted ball, time in the air, and landing location combined.[28]

The rate of hard-hit balls topped 30% just once between 2007 and 2015, but it has done so in every year since 2016, as demonstrated in Figure 10 (page 92).

However, the topic at hand is batting average, rather than overall offensive performance. Because fly balls and popups have had a lower combined batting average than groundballs, the league's shift away from groundballs and toward fly balls has depressed batting averages overall.

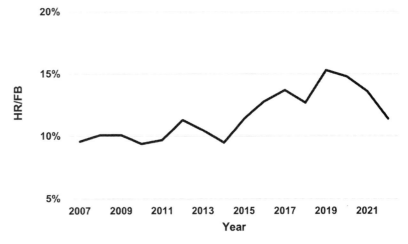

Figure 8. Home Runs Per Fly Ball

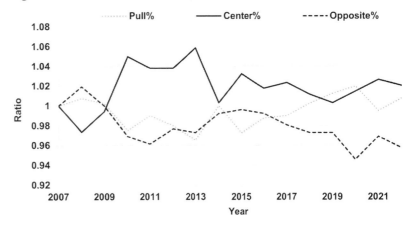

Figure 9. Batted Ball Distribution Compared to 2007

Table 3. Effect of Change in Groundball Rate, 2015 to 2016

Decile	1	2	3	4	5	6	7	8	9	10
Change in GB%	+6.5	+3.2	+1.7	+0.6	-0.7	-1.7	-3.2	-4.4	-5.7	-8.3
Change in TAv	-.006	-.014	-.005	-.007	+.003	-.003	+.011	+.010	+.015	+.002

Table 4. Effect of Change in Pull Rate, 2015 to 2016

Decile	1	2	3	4	5	6	7	8	9	10
Change in Pull%	-10.7	-6	-3.2	+1.5	+0.2	+2	+3.8	+5.8	+8.7	+14.1
Change in TAv	-.001	-.009	-.001	+.001	-.006	+.005	+.003	+.002	+.010	+.001

Figure 10. Batted Ball Quality Compared to 2007

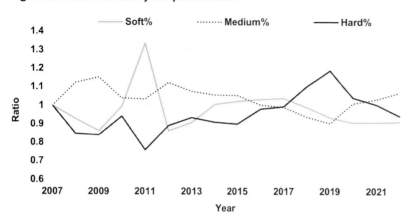

CONCLUSION

Given its immediate aftermath, the infield shift ban must be considered a qualified success. The 2023 MLB batting average increased by five points to .248. BABIP rose seven points to .297, and all four hit types increased in frequency. Right-handed hitters saw no decrease in batting average or BABIP, and left-handed hitters improved both their average and BABIP by 10 points. The 2023 figures were right in line with what would be expected if full shifts were replaced by partial ones. Indeed, Russell Carleton calculated a correlation coefficient of .775 between the percentage of full shifts a left-handed batter faced in 2022 and the percentage of "strategic" shifts they faced in the first half of 2023. The corresponding figure for right-handed batters was 0.542.[29] Carleton also noted that the overall performance of batters facing strategic shifts was similar to those reported in Table 1.

In 2023, both batting average and BABIP reached their highest marks since 2019, but BABIP saw a larger increase. The league's .248 batting average was still the fifth-lowest mark of this century. If the Lords of Baseball want more drastic changes, they will probably need to consider other options. Restricting outfield positioning could have a real effect on both BABIP and batting average, but to the best of my knowledge there has been no serious consideration of this possibility. Any further changes would need to move beyond defensive positioning and address the effects of the strikeout epidemic. A discussion of these changes and what they might accomplish will come in the second half of this two-part study.[30] ■

Acknowledgments

Thanks to Dick Cramer for writing suggestions, Pete Palmer for always reading what I write, Davy Andrews for supplying me with the Baseball Savant data used here, and Cliff Blau both for being a superb volunteer copy editor and fact checker and for informing me of Peter Morris's reference to nineteenth-century shifting.

Notes

1. "MLB announces rule changes for 2023 season," MLB.com, September 9, 2022, https://www.mlb.com/press-release/press-release-mlb-announces-rule-changes-for-2023-season.
2. Matt Snyder, "MLB rule changes: What to know about the extreme shift ban, what defensive tricks are sill allowed," CBS Sports, March 2, 2023, https://www.cbssports.com/mlb/news/mlb-rule-changes-what-to-know-about-the-extreme-shift-ban-what-defensive-tricks-are-still-allowed/.
3. Kevin Skiver, "MLB infield shift rules, explained: How new restrictions, minimums & violations will impact 2023 games," *The Sporting News*, March 30, 2023, https://www.sportingnews.com/us/mlb/news/mlb-infield-shift-rules-violation-2023/j5euqqru11cghxrgtayvzpdl.
4. FanGraphs, https://www.fangraphs.com/leaders/major-league?pos=all&stats=bat&lg=al&lg=nl&qual=y&type=0&month=0&ind=0&team=0%2Css&startdate=&enddate=&pageitems=200&season1=1920&season=2022. This information is for 1920 through 2022.
5. Based on data mostly from Baseball Reference (https://www.baseball-reference.com/leagues/majors/bat.shtml) but with batting average on balls in play (BABIP) numbers from FanGraphs.
6. Despite the oddity of the season, I have included 2020 as it was similar to the two after it.
7. See https://commons.wikimedia.org/wiki/File:Cy_Williams_defensive_shift.jpg for a newspaper account from May 24 of that year.
8. Peter Morris, *A Game of Inches,* Vol. 1 (Chicago, Ivan R. Dee, 2006), 222. Thanks to Cliff Blau for informing me of this.
9. Seymour Siwoff, Steve Hirdt, Tom Hirdt, and Peter Hirdt, *The 1991 Elias Baseball Analyst* (New York: Simon and Schuster, 1991), 79–80.
10. Joe Rosales and Scott Spratt, "The Effectiveness of Full vs. Partial Shifts," in *The Hardball Times Baseball Annual 2016*, prod. Paul Swydan (Fangraphs, 2016), 307–315.
11. Mark Simon, "Has the Shift Seen its Day?" Presented at the 2018 SABR Analytic Conference.
12. https://baseballsavant.mlb.com/visuals/team-positioning?teamId=111&venue=home&firstBase=0&shift=0&batSide=&season=2022
13. Russell A. Carleton, "The Mirror Told Me I Was Backward." Baseball Prospectus, https://www.baseballprospectus.com/news/article/61566/baseball-therapy-the-mirror-told-me-i-was-backward/; Carleton, "The Shift that Happened in 2021," Baseball Prospectus, https://www.baseballprospectus.com/news/article/71913/baseball-therapy-the-shift-that-happened-in-2021/; Carleton, "Shifting to the Right," Baseball Prospectus, https://www.baseballprospectus.com/news/article/76073/shifting-to-the-right/.
14. Russell A. Carleton, "The Walk Penalty and the Death of the Shift." Baseball Prospectus, https://www.baseballprospectus.com/news/article/61143/walk-penalty-infield-kill-the-shift-mlb-defense/.
15. Carleton, "The Mirror Told Me I was Backward."
16. Carleton, "Why the Shift Works (Sometimes)," Baseball Prospectus, https://www.baseballprospectus.com/news/article/65133/baseball-therapy-why-the-shift-works-sometimes/.
17. Carleton, "New Year, New Rules–Part 1," Baseball Prospectus, https://www.baseballprospectus.com/news/article/65496/baseball-therapy-new-year-new-rules/.
18. Carleton, "The Shift that Happened in 2021."
19. Robert Arthur, "The League's Defensive Positioning has Changed," Baseball Prospectus, https://www.baseballprospectus.com/news/article/67237/moonshot-the-leagues-defensive-positioning-has-changed/.

20. Arthur, "Better Defense is Costing MLB Thousands of Hits," Baseball Prospectus, https://www.baseballprospectus.com/news/article/67362/moonshot-better-defense-is-costing-mlb-thousands-of-hits/.

21. Brian Reiff, "The Effectiveness of Strategic Outfield Positioning," Presented at 2019 SABR Analytics Conference.

22. Simon, "The Rise of Outfield Shifts," Bill James Online, https://www.billjamesonline.com/the_rise_of_outfield_shifts/.

23. The Reds, Pirates, Marlins, Nationals, Rangers, Orioles, and Tigers.

24. Arthur, "Outfield Shifts are Shockingly Effective," Baseball Prospectus, https://www.baseballprospectus.com/news/article/65713/moonshot-outfield-shifts-are-shockingly-effective/.

25. Arthur, "The League's Defensive Positioning has Changed."

26. Mains, "New Year's Resolutions: Ground-Ball Hitters, Baseball Prospectus, https://www.baseballprospectus.com/news/article/30932/flu-like-symptoms-new-years-resolutions-ground-ball-hitters/.

27. Mains, "New Year's Resolutions: Going the Other Way," Baseball Prospectus, https://www.baseballprospectus.com/news/article/30914/flu-like-symptoms-new-years-resolutions-going-the-other-way/.

28. Neil Weinberg, "Quality of Contact Stats," FanGraphs, https://library.fangraphs.com/offense/quality-of-contact-stats/.

29. Carleton, "The Afterlife of the Shift, Baseball Prospectus, https://www.baseballprospectus.com/news/article/83984/baseball-therapy-the-afterlife-of-the-shift/.

Going Beyond the Baseball Adage "One Game at a Time"

A Geek's Peek at Streaks

Ed Denta

Professional baseball players and coaches shrug off questions from reporters about the future with responses such as "all our focus is on winning today's game" or "we'll worry about the next series when we get there." The media and fans, however, are mesmerized by historical statistics and records, with particular attention paid to streak records on the verge of falling, such as "the Atlanta Braves have now homered in 26 consecutive games and are threatening the all-time mark of 31 set by the 2019 New York Yankees," as reported by MLB network during the 2023 All-Star break. The Braves eventually got to 28 games but were held homerless by the Chicago White Sox in an 8–1 defeat on July 16.

As a lifelong baseball aficionado, my interest in baseball history, trivia, and statistics has grown with each passing season. After the Baltimore Orioles started the 1988 season with 21 consecutive losses, the 2002 Oakland A's ran off 20 consecutive wins, and the 2017 Cleveland Indians coupled streaks of 22 and five games to win 27 of 28 late in the season, I became fascinated with baseball's winning and losing streaks. How often and when do they occur? Do they follow patterns? Are they predictable?

My aspiration is to combine a) my passion for baseball statistics and numbers, b) my experience as an engineer using database programs and Excel, and c) my extreme attention to detail, to contribute something unique to the annals of baseball analysis.

This research paper represents an in-depth analysis of all winning and losing streaks in the American and National Leagues since 1901. A reader with only limited knowledge of probability theory should still be able to understand the concepts and appreciate the results of this never-before-seen analytical picture of streaks.

RESEARCH PROCEDURES

The research set begins in 1901 with the advent of the American League (AL) as a major league. In 1901, the American League and National League (NL) each had eight teams, with teams from both leagues in Boston, Chicago, and Philadelphia, and by 1903 in the

New York metro area. As of 2024, MLB has 30 active franchises playing from coast to coast. Through 2023, 206,711 games have been played.

Obtaining and Formatting Game Results. Game results (win, loss, tie) for all games and all teams in sequence came from Baseball Reference and Retrosheet. I then developed and applied a proprietary conversion scheme using Excel, to replace each win, loss, and tie with an encoded numerical value. This new dataset facilitates all filtering and parsing necessary to extract and analyze winning and losing streaks.[1]

Identifying Analysis Objectives. After encoding all win-loss-tie data, I next had to decide what streak attributes to research and extract. The results had to be both innovative and appealing to baseball fans, and particularly a baseball audience primarily of SABR members. In the end, my analysis produced two papers. This paper explains the mathematical theory behind winning and losing streaks and develops predictive equations, then compares the prognostications to actual streak results. The second paper, not presented here, explores streak data from a historical perspective.

STREAKS DEFINED

Winning streaks consist of sequences of consecutive wins or ties. Losing streaks consist of sequences of consecutive losses or ties. For purposes of this paper, *ties are considered a neutral result*. Ties neither terminate a streak nor extend the length of the streak. As a result, the nine-game sequence WWWTWWTWW is considered a seven-game win streak. Likewise, LLTTLLL is a five-game losing streak.

Of the 206,711 games played, 777 resulted in a tie with no winner determined. Ties were quite common in the first half of the twentieth century, with 82.5% of the tie games occurring by 1950. The last tie game occurred on September 29, 2016, between the Chicago Cubs and the Pittsburgh Pirates, when play was halted due to rain in the top of the sixth inning with the score tied, 1–1. The game was called and not suspended since it was late in the season and the result would have had no effect on the National League standings. Table 1 depicts the number of tie games by decade.

Going forward, all references to the number of games or decisions played denote only non-tie results, i.e. wins or losses. Games are played. Decisions are the team results of the game. Each team gets one result per game played and each game played produces two decisions for the league. The number of games and the number of decisions is the same (and interchangeable) when referring to a single team.

Preference for Seasonal Streaks. Streaks are characterized as either seasonal or wraparound. Seasonal streaks are confined to a single season, while wraparound streaks extend from one season to the next if the final non-tie result (either W or L) of Season **n** matches the first non-tie result of Season **n** + 1. Only seasonal streaks are considered in this paper.

Measure of Streakiness. Streakiness is defined as the state or condition of being streaky. Streaky can be described as having streaks. To evaluate the positive and negative streakiness of a team during a given season, consider these new metrics and definitions:

- **Streak Wins (SW)** is the number of wins during a season that are part of winning streaks of five or more games.

- **Streak Losses (SL)** is the number of losses during a season that are part of losing streaks of five or more games.

Table 1. Tie Games By Decade

Decade	Ties	Cumulative Ties	Cumulative Tie %
1901-1910	215	215	27.7%
1911-1920	167	382	49.2%
1921-1930	62	444	57.1%
1931-1940	98	542	69.8%
1941-1950	99	641	82.5%
1951-1960	55	696	89.6%
1961-1970	36	732	94.2%
1971-1980	14	746	96.0%
1981-1990	18	764	98.3%
1991-2000	8	772	99.4%
2001-2010	4	776	99.9%
2011-2023	1	777	100.0%
Total	**777**		

- **Win Streak Quotient (WSQ)** is defined as Streak Wins (SW) divided by total wins (TW).

- **Loss Streak Quotient (LSQ)** is defined as Streak Losses (SL) divided by total losses (TL).

- **Total Streak Quotient (TSQ)** is defined as Streak Wins (SW) plus Streak Losses (SL) divided by Total Decisions (D).

WSQ=SW/TW   (Equation 1)
LSQ=SL/TL   (Equation 2)
TSQ=(SW+SL)/D   (Equation 3)

Example: A team with a 97–64–1 record, with win streaks of 6, 9, 5, 5, 13, and 12 and loss streaks of 5, 7, and 5 has a WSQ of .515, an LSQ of 0.266, and a TSQ of 0.416.

WSQ=(6+9+5+5+13+12)/97=50/97=.515
LSQ=(5+7+5)/64=17/64=.266
TSQ=(50+17)/161=67/161=.416

MATHEMATICAL THEORY

Derivation and Calculations of Expected Streaks (50–50 scenario). To gain a mathematical understanding of how often winning and losing streaks occur, let's review some elementary probability theory. The chance of tossing a single coin and getting a specific result (either heads or tails) is 1 out of 2, or 0.5. The chance of getting a specific sequential result when tossing two coins (either HH, HT, TH, or TT) is 0.5 times 0.5, or 1 out of 4, or 0.25. Three coins yields 1 out of 8, or 0.125, and so on. To generalize, tossing a coin K times yields 1 of 2^K sequential results. The probability, **PK**, of getting any one specific result is ½ times ½…times ½ a total of K times, which is the value ½ raised to the power of **K**. Equation 4 shows this expression algebraically, where **K** is the number of independent coin tosses:

$$PK=(1/2)^K=1/2K=2^{-K} \qquad \text{(Equation 4)}$$

The probability of a baseball team getting all wins in K consecutive games against another team is equivalent to tossing a coin K times and getting all heads, assuming each team has a one in two chance of winning each game.

Every win streak has a defined beginning and end. For a five-game win streak at the beginning of the season the game sequence is WWWWWL, during the season it is LWWWWWL, and at the end of the season it is LWWWWW. Note that except for the beginning and end of the season, the required decision sequence has an L before and an L after the string of five W's. This seven-game decision string is the test sequence (TS) for a five-game win streak. A six-game win streak requires an eight-game test sequence. To generalize, an S-game streak (either winning or losing) requires an S + 2 length test sequence. Therefore, TS = S + 2.

Let's determine how many times a win streak of five games (S = 5) can be expected in a game sequence of 162 games (N = 162) for a single team. The appropriate test sequence to identify a five-game win streak is LWWWWWL. The length of this test sequence (TS) is 7. Figure 1 depicts a WL game sequence of 162 games. To detect all five-game win streaks, the seven-game test sequence must be slid sequentially left to right across all 162 games.

Test 1 aligns the first W of the test sequence (its second entry) with Game 1. Note that only four of the necessary six entries for this first test location are a match, shaded test sequence entries 2, 4, 5, and 6. The first entry for Test 1 is given a match, since there is no corresponding decision in the game sequence, therefore, a five-game win streak is not detected in the first five games by Test 1.

Test 2 slides the test sequence one game to the right. Again, four entries match: 3, 4, 5, and 6.

Test 3 slides the test sequence another game to the right. In this case all seven entries in the test sequence match the game sequence, thereby detecting the first five-game win streak. This slide right process continues until the five wins in the test sequence align with the final five games in the game sequence as indicated by Test 158. Note that Test 155 detected a second five-game win streak near the end of the game sequence (Game No. 154 through Game No. 160).

Since a streak can occur at either the beginning or the end of a game sequence, the number of required tests (T) for an N-game sequence is T = N-S + 1, where S is the streak length. From Figure 1, 158 tests are required to detect all five-game win streaks in 162 decisions, T = 162-5 + 1 = 158.

To generalize, for a .500 team the expected number of S-game win streaks, EWS, in a decision sequence length of N is calculated by multiplying the required number of tests, T, by the probability of the test sequence, TS, matching the game sequence.

$$EWS=T(2^{-TS})=(N-S+1)/(2^{TS}) \qquad \text{(Equation 5)}$$

For very large values of N compared to S, Equation 5 simplifies to

$$EWS=N/(2^{TS}) \qquad \text{(Equation 6)}$$

For the case shown in Figure 1, S = 5, TS = 7, and N = 162, therefore EWS = (162-5 + 1)/(2^7) = 158/128 = 1.234. One way to interpret an EWS of 1.234, is to say that there are 5-to-4 odds that a .500 team will have a single five-game win streak in a 162-decision sequence. This special case corresponds to a decision sequence of a team with equal probability of winning and losing (50–50), Therefore, expected loss streaks ELS equals EWS, 1.234 for a five-game losing streak.

The expected number of total S-game streaks, ETS, is given by Equation 7 where ELS = EWS for a .500 team.

$$ETS=EWS+ELS=2N/(2^{TS}) \qquad \text{(Equation 7)}$$

In the example above, the .500 team can be expected to have 1.234 five-game winning streaks and 1.234 five-game losing streaks for a total of just under 2.5 five-game streaks in the 162-game season. Obviously

Figure 1. Test Sequence Action for Determining a Five-Game Win Streak

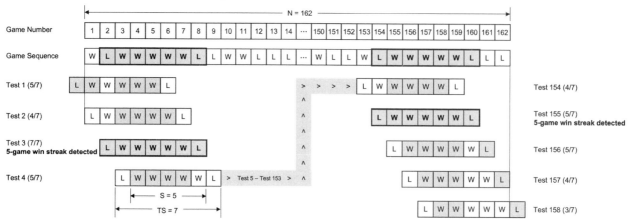

fractional (non-whole) numbers of streaks are not possible. This concept is established in the short run so it can be understood and applicable in long runs of thousands of games.

Table 2 evaluates Equation 7 and shows the expected combined number of total streaks, ETS, by streak length (S) for various sizes of game sequences for a team with a 50–50 chance to win each game.

Calculation of Expected Streaks (Non 50–50 scenarios). Equation 7 shows the Expected Number of total streaks (ETS) for a team having a 50–50 chance of winning each game. Expected win streaks (EWS) and loss streaks (ELS) each make up half the total (ETS). Let's examine the changes when the team is better than a .500 club.

Let PW be the probability of a win and PL the probability of a loss. PW and PL are both greater than 0 and less than 1 and sum to 1. Let's generalize Equation 6, $EWS = N/(2^{TS})$. The value two in this equation is the number 1 divided by the probability of a win, PW, or $1/PW$, which equals two for a .500 team.

$$EWS=N/(2^{TS})=N/(1/PW)^{TS}=N/[(1/PW)(1/PW...(1/PW)(1/PW)]$$

PW is the probability of a win and $(1/PW)$ is multiplied TS times (the required length of the test sequence) in the denominator.

An S-game winning streak must have a loss right before and a loss right after the win streak in the test sequence. EWS now becomes

$$EWS=N/[(1/PL)(1/PW)...(1/PW)(1/PL)]$$

where $1/PL$ appears twice in the denominator and $1/PW$ appears S times (the streak length).

The generalized expected number of S-game winning streaks in N games for a team with a PW win probability and PL loss probability is as follows:

$$EWSG=N/(1/PW)^S(1/PL)^2$$
$$EWSG=N(PW)^S(PL)^2 \qquad \text{(Equation 8)}$$

The generalized expected number of S-game losing streaks in N games for a team with a PW win probability and a PL loss probability is as follows:

$$ELSG=N/(1/PL)^S(1/PW)^2$$
$$ELSG=N(PL)^S(PW)^2 \qquad \text{(Equation 9)}$$

The generalized total expected number of S-game streaks in N games for a team with a PW win probability and a PL loss probability is as follows:

$$ETSG=EWSG+ELSG \qquad \text{(Equation 10)}$$
$$ETSG=N(PW)^S(PL)^2 +N(PL)^S(PW)^2$$
$$ETSG=N(PW)^2(PL)^2[(PW)^{S-2} +(PL)^{S-2}]$$

Table 3 (page 98) evaluates Equations 8, 9, and 10 to show the expected number of streaks in 100,000 games by streak length S, for Teams A, B, and C with win probabilities (PW) equal to .400, .500. and .550, respectively.

Table 2. Expected Total Streaks (ETS) by Streak Length (S) for a Team Playing (N) Games

For 50-50 win percentages		Games (N)						
Streak (S)	Test Sequence (TS)	162	1000	5000	10000	50000	100000	500000
5	7	2.5	15.6	78.1	156.3	781.3	1562.5	7812.5
6	8	1.3	7.8	39.1	78.1	390.6	781.3	3906.3
7	9	0.6	3.9	19.5	39.1	195.3	390.6	1953.1
8	10	0.3	2.0	9.8	19.5	97.7	195.3	976.6
9	11	0.2	1.0	4.9	9.8	48.8	97.7	488.3
10	12	0.1	0.5	2.4	4.9	24.4	48.8	244.1
11	13	0.0	0.2	1.2	2.4	12.2	24.4	122.1
12	14	0.0	0.1	0.6	1.2	6.1	12.2	61.0
13	15	0.0	0.1	0.3	0.6	3.1	6.1	30.5
14	16	0.0	0.0	0.2	0.3	1.5	3.1	15.3
15	17	0.0	0.0	0.1	0.2	0.8	1.5	7.6
16	18	0.0	0.0	0.0	0.1	0.4	0.8	3.8
17	19	0.0	0.0	0.0	0.0	0.2	0.4	1.9
18	20	0.0	0.0	0.0	0.0	0.1	0.2	1.0
19	21	0.0	0.0	0.0	0.0	0.0	0.1	0.5
20	22	0.0	0.0	0.0	0.0	0.0	0.0	0.2
	Total Streaks >>	5.1	31.2	156.2	312.5	1562.5	3125.0	15624.8

Team B's (PW = .500) total winning streaks are equal to its losing streaks, 1,562. Not surprisingly, Team A's (PW = .400) total losing streaks exceed its winning streaks, 3,110 to 614. While Team C's (PW = .550) total winning streaks exceed its losing streaks, 2,265 to 1,015. The more a team's PW deviates from .500 the greater the number of expected total streaks, ETSG. Streak totals of 3125, 3280, 3725 for Team B, C, and A, with deviations of .000, .050. and .100 independent of direction. The greater the performance diversity from .500, the more total streaks.

Equation 8 expresses the expected number of win streaks for only one streak length, S, to occur in N games. To calculate the expected number of total win streaks, EWSGS in N games, Equation 8 must be summed for all streak lengths of interest. This research paper is focused on all streaks from five to 26. Expected streaks of greater than 26 games are minuscule for less than 500,000 games.

Therefore, the Expected Number of Total Win Streaks for all streak lengths S, EWSGS, is expressed as

$$EWSGS = \sum_{S=5}^{26} N(PW)^S(PL)^2, \text{ where } PL=1-PW \qquad \text{(Equation 8a)}$$

Similarly, the Expected Number of Total Loss Streaks for all streak lengths S, ELSGS, is expressed as

$$ELSGS = \sum_{S=5}^{26} N(PL)^S(PW)^2, \text{ where } PW=1-PL \qquad \text{(Equation 9a)}$$

The expected number of total streaks, both winning and losing for all streak lengths S, ETSGS, is:

$$ETSGS=EWSGS+ELSGS \qquad \text{(Equation 10a)}$$

The previous discussion applies to the evaluation of streaks for a single team. Since there are two decisions for each game played, the number of games, N, must be replaced by the number of decisions, D, when evaluating league-wide streaks. Therefore, when considering league-wide results, equations 8a, 9a, and 10a become equations 8b, 9b, and 10b respectively.

$$EWSGSL = \sum_{S=5}^{26} D(PW)^S (PL)^2, \text{ where } PL=1-PW \qquad \text{(Equation 8b)}$$

$$ELSGSL = \sum_{S=5}^{26} D(PL)^S (PW)^2, \text{ where } PW=1-PL \qquad \text{(Equation 9b)}$$

$$ETSGSL=EWSGSL+ELSGSL \qquad \text{(Equation 10b)}$$

Equations 8b, 9b, and 10b are called the *expected streak equations*.

Table 3. Streaks by Length (S) and Probability of a Win (PW) for 100,000 Games (N)

N = 100000 games

	Team A			Team B			Team C		
PW, PL >>	.400	.600		.500	.500		.550	.450	
Streak (S)	EWSG	ELSG	ETSG	EWSG	ELSG	ETSG	EWSG	ELSG	ETSG
5	368.6	1244.2	1612.8	781.3	781.3	1562.5	1019.2	558.2	1577.3
6	147.5	746.5	894.0	390.6	390.6	781.3	560.5	251.2	811.7
7	59.0	447.9	506.9	195.3	195.3	390.6	308.3	113.0	421.3
8	23.6	268.7	292.3	97.7	97.7	195.3	169.6	50.9	220.4
9	9.4	161.2	170.7	48.8	48.8	97.7	93.3	22.9	116.1
10	3.8	96.7	100.5	24.4	24.4	48.8	51.3	10.3	61.6
11	1.5	58.0	59.6	12.2	12.2	24.4	28.2	4.6	32.8
12	0.6	34.8	35.4	6.1	6.1	12.2	15.5	2.1	17.6
13	0.2	20.9	21.1	3.1	3.1	6.1	8.5	0.9	9.5
14	0.1	12.5	12.6	1.5	1.5	3.1	4.7	0.4	5.1
15	0.0	7.5	7.6	0.8	0.8	1.5	2.6	0.2	2.8
16	0.0	4.5	4.5	0.4	0.4	0.8	1.4	0.1	1.5
17	0.0	2.7	2.7	0.2	0.2	0.4	0.8	0.0	0.8
18	0.0	1.6	1.6	0.1	0.1	0.2	0.4	0.0	0.4
19	0.0	1.0	1.0	0.0	0.0	0.1	0.2	0.0	0.2
20	0.0	0.6	0.6	0.0	0.0	0.0	0.1	0.0	0.1
21	0.0	0.4	0.4	0.0	0.0	0.0	0.1	0.0	0.1
22	0.0	0.2	0.2	0.0	0.0	0.0	0.0	0.0	0.0
23	0.0	0.1	0.1	0.0	0.0	0.0	0.0	0.0	0.0
24	0.0	0.1	0.1	0.0	0.0	0.0	0.0	0.0	0.0
25	0.0	0.0	0.0	0.0	0.0	0.0	0.0	0.0	0.0
Totals	614	3110	3725	1562	1562	3125	2265	1015	3280

Through this point in the paper, we have developed a lot of equations. Figure 2 clarifies equation nomenclature.

Figure 2. Expected Streak Equations Nomenclature

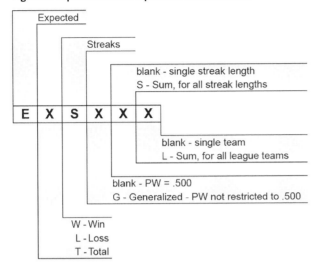

A consolidated listing of all expected streak equations is shown below.

For a .500 team (PW=.500) and single streak length

Equation 5: $EWS = T(2^{-TS}) = (N-S+1)/(2^{TS})$

Equation 6: $EWS = N/(2^{TS})$, for $N \gg S$

Equation 7: $ETS = EWS + ELS = 2N/(2^{TS})$,
    since $ELS = EWS$ for a .500 team

For a generalized team (PW does not have to equal .500) and a single streak length

Equation 8: $EWSG = N(PW)^S(PL)^2$

Equation 9: $ELSG = N(PL)^S(PW)^2$

Equation 10: $ETSG = EWSG + ELSG = N(PW)^2(PL)^2[(PW)^{S-2} + (PL)^{S-2}]$

For a generalized team (PW does not have to equal .500) and all streak lengths

Equation 8a: $EWSGS = \sum_{5}^{26} N(PW)^S(PL)^2$, where $PL = 1-PW$

Equation 9a: $ELSGS = \sum_{5}^{26} N(PL)^S(PW)^2$, where $PW = 1-PL$

Equation 10a: $ETSGS = EWSGS + ELSGS$

For multiple teams and all streak lengths, N games replaced by D decisions

Equation 8b: $EWSGSL = \sum_{5}^{26} D(PW)^S(PL)^2$, where $PL = 1-PW$

Equation 9b: $ELSGSL = \sum_{5}^{26} D(PL)^S(PW)^2$, where $PW = 1-PL$

Equation 10b: $ETSGSL = EWSGSL + ELSGSL$

Simulations. There have been 411,868 non-tie decisions in the AL and NL from 1901 through 2023. The 206,711 games played, minus 777 ties, equals 205,934, times two decisions per game, equals 411,868 decisions.

To verify the derived Expected Streak calculations in Equations 8b and 9b, multiple game simulations were run (and averaged) using Microsoft Excel 365. Ten columns of 411,870 random numbers evenly distributed between zero and one were populated using the RAND() function to create 10 independent simulations of 411,870 decisions. The RAND() function uses the Mersenne Twister algorithm (MT19937) to generate random numbers. Decision thresholds were imposed on each cell to render a win or a loss. To simulate streaks for a team with a .550 win probability, all random numbers between 0 and .450 were deemed a loss and all random numbers from greater than .450 to 1.000 were deemed a win. The sequence of wins and losses were evaluated and counted for streaks of various lengths. Simulation results were compared to results obtained by evaluating Equations 8b and 9b for various win probabilities for 411,870 decisions. The logarithmic chart in Figure 3 (page 100) displays the results for two different win probabilities, .500 (50_50 case) and .600 (60_40 case).

Note that the simulation and predictive curves are nearly exact through the 16-game streak for the 50_50 case and through 21 games for the 60_40 case. The deviation beyond these points is due to limited simulation data. Evaluating more decisions and/or running and averaging more simulations would drive the simulation to converge with the prediction at the longer streak lengths. Despite this slight deviation, the simulations confirm the validity and accuracy of the predictive analysis.

STREAKINESS AND PERFORMANCE DIVERSITY

Streakiness. Previous analysis and simulations have demonstrated that higher win probabilities produce more total streaks (and increased streakiness). Let's test this hypothesis against actual data by examining the 123 years of historical win-loss records in our dataset. Higher win probabilities are manifested in the real world by greater performance diversity among the competing teams.

Expanding upon Table 3, Figure 4 (page 100) summarizes the results of Equations 8a, 9a, and 10a for the Expected Number of Summed Win Streaks, EWSGS, Expected Number of Summed Loss Streaks, ELSGS, and the Expected Number of Summed Total Streaks, ETSGS, in 100,000 games, N, for a team's Winning Averages, PW, from .500 to .660.

Note that EWSGS = ELSGS = 3,125 for PW = .500. As PW increases, EWSGS and ETSGS increase while ELSGS decreases. This is as expected: the better the team, the better the chances for additional win streaks and fewer loss streaks. For a good team, win streaks increase at a higher rate than loss streaks decrease, resulting in more total streaks. A team with a .600 winning average will have 99% more win streaks (3,110 to 1,562), 61% fewer loss streaks (614 to 1,562), and

Figure 3. Simulated Vs. Predicted Results

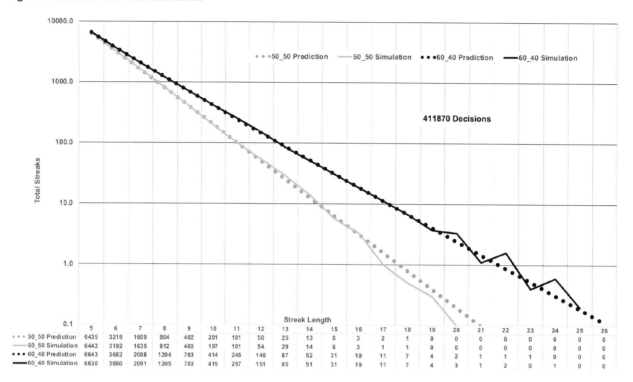

	5	6	7	8	9	10	11	12	13	14	15	16	17	18	19	20	21	22	23	24	25	26
50_50 Prediction	6435	3218	1609	804	402	201	101	50	25	13	6	3	2	1	0	0	0	0	0	0	0	0
50_50 Simulation	6443	3192	1635	812	402	197	101	54	29	14	6	3	1	1	0	0	0	0	0	0	0	0
60_40 Prediction	6643	3682	2088	1204	703	414	245	146	87	52	31	19	11	7	4	2	1	1	1	0	0	0
60_40 Simulation	6630	3660	2091	1205	703	415	257	151	85	51	31	19	11	7	4	3	1	2	0	1	0	0

Figure 4. Expected Number of Total Streaks in 100,000 Decisions by Winning Average (PW)

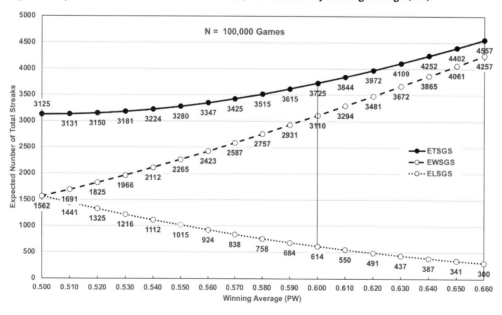

19.2% more totals streaks (3,725 to 3,125) of five or more games in 100,000 decisions than a .500 team.

Based on this analysis and backed by simulations, expect more total streaks of five or more games (and more streakiness) in seasons when teams have greater talent and performance diversity than when there is more parity. Let's determine if this has been the case for 1901–2023.

Total Streak Quotient (TSQ, see Equation 3) is used to assess the seasonal streakiness of past results. TSQ is a normalized metric that scales streak results by the number of decisions in the space being analyzed. This allows for direct comparison between teams and seasons, independent of the number of games played or teams in the league.

Streak Wins (SW) is the number of wins during a season that are part of winning streaks of five or more games. Streak Losses (SL) is the number of losses during a season that are part of losing streaks of five or more games. Each game played by a single team results in one decision for that team. Equation 3 still applies when evaluating TSQ for the entire league, since each game played results in two decisions, a win to one team and a loss to the other.

Figure 5 displays the seasonal Total Streak Quotient (TSQ) for all of baseball.

The seasons with the highest TSQ, 1906, 1908, 1927, 1930, 1939, and 1953, all exceed .275. The lowest TSQs, all below .175, occurred in 1934, 1959, 1983, and 2014.

Figure 5 shows a large spike in streakiness since 2014. This could be due in part to "tanking." According to *Forbes*, "tanking refers to the practice of a team deliberately fielding a lesser line-up for an entire season in order to extract a better position in the next amateur draft." It might also involve trading or selling off high-priced aging veterans to depress payroll and better position the organization for future spending. These management practices can result in miserably deficient teams becoming league leaders in just a handful of seasons, as with the Houston Astros. The Astros lost 324 games from 2011 to 2013, but starting in 2015 made the playoffs in eight of nine years, won more than 100 games four times, appeared in four World Series, and won two (2017 and 2022). The Chicago Cubs had a similar turnaround. They lost 377 games from 2011 to 2014, but beginning in 2015, made the playoffs five of six ensuing years and won the World Series in 2016.

The three biggest losers in 2021, the Baltimore Orioles (110 losses), Arizona Diamondbacks (110), and Texas Rangers (102) all had considerable success in 2023. The Orioles had the best record in the American League, winning 101 games, while the Diamondbacks and Rangers both made the playoffs as wild-card teams and then faced each other in the World Series. Although lower than 2022, TSQ for 2023 (0.214) was still well above the linear trendline.

Performance Diversity. AVGDEV is used to quantify performance diversity. AVGDEV, Average Deviation, is defined as the average of the absolute deviations (DEV) of the winning average for all teams in the league from the mean for a given season. Since all times in both leagues are considered, the mean is .500 (i.e., total wins for the season equals total losses). To determine the deviation for each team, its winning

Figure 5. Seasonal Total Streak Quotient (TSQ)

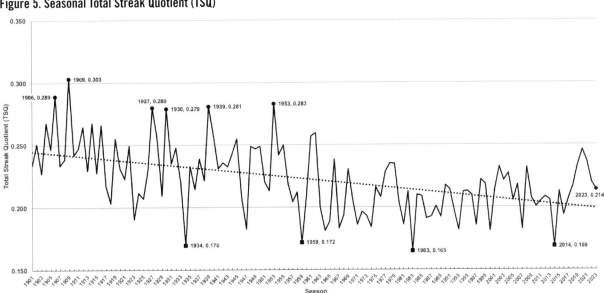

average (PW) is subtracted from .500 and the result taken as a positive number (i.e., greater than 0). The positive deviation for all teams is then averaged, to produce AVGDEV for the season. The greater the performance diversity, the greater the AVGDEV. Figure 6 depicts the seasonal AVGDEV.

The seasons with the greatest team performance diversity mostly occurred early in the twentieth century: 1904, 1906, 1909, and 1954. The seasons with the most parity have all occurred since the late 1950s: 1958 and 1984.

Since the big leagues expanded to 30 teams in 1998 (ignoring the COVID-19 shortened 2020 season), there have been 84 instances of a team either winning or losing 100 games. Here is the breakdown by nine-year increments: 1998–2006: 29 times, 2007–15: 14 times,

and 2016–23 (only eight years): 41 times. This indicates significantly more performance diversity 2016–23 than 2007–15.

Streakiness Vs. Performance Diversity. Figure 7 merges analyses of streakiness, TSQ, and performance diversity, AVGDEV, from Figures 5 and 6 to graphically demonstrate the correlation.

Note the obvious correlation between the two plots. More performance diversity, higher AVGDEV, begets more streakiness, higher TSQ. Also note the similarity between the two five-season moving average trendlines. It is apparent that there is less performance diversity and less streakiness (i.e., lower TSQs) in baseball beginning in the mid-1950s continuing through 2014, with an uptick beginning in 2015.

Figure 6. Seasonal AVGDEV

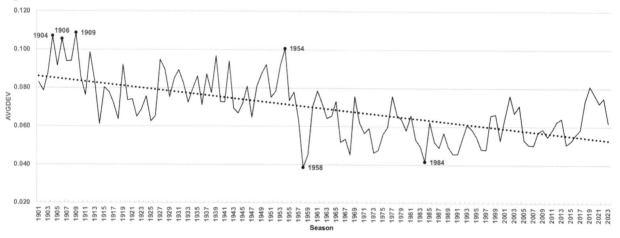

Figure 7. Seasonal Performance Diversity (AVGDEV) and Streakiness (TSQ)

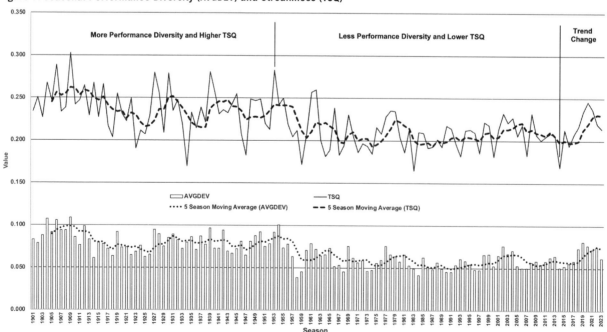

Another way to visualize the correlation between performance diversity, AVGDEV, and streakiness, TSQ, is with a scatterplot (AVGDEV on horizontal axis and TSQ on vertical axis) as shown in Figure 8, where the upward dashed linear trendline clearly demonstrates that more performance diversity leads to more streakiness.

The two most significant outliers were 1914 and 1934 (highlighted by perpendicular lines to the trendline). 1914 had middle diversity (AVGDEV of .061 against a mean of .069) and high streakiness (TSQ of .268 in contrast to a mean .219). At the other extreme, 1934 had high diversity (AVGDEV of .080 against a mean of .069) and low streakiness (TSQ of .170 against a mean of .219). These results are somewhat noteworthy as outliers, but not totally unexpected due to the relatively small sample size of only about 2,450 decisions per season.

The 1909 season clearly stands out as the prime season that validates the hypothesis that greater performance diversity (manifested by higher winning averages) produces more total streaks (and increased streakiness). This season has both the highest all-time performance diversity (AVGDEV) and Total Streak Quotient (TSQ), .109 and .303, respectively. At the opposite end of the spectrum is 1959, with very low values for AVGDEV (.045 in 1959 against a minimum .039 in 1958) and TSQ (.172 in 1959 against a minimum .165 in 1983).

Table 4 lists the seasonal values of the performance diversity measure, AVGDEV, and the streakiness metric, TSQ, for both the pre- and post-expansion eras (data plotted in Figure 8).

The down and up arrow icons highlight the bottom and top 20 percentile (i.e., 25 seasons) for each measure. Note the correlation between AVGDEV and TSQ. There are 14 instances in the 123 seasons where both measures are in the top 20% and eight instances for both in the bottom 20%. Even more glaring is the discrepancy between pre- and post-expansion values. All 25 of the highest performance diversity seasons and 23 of the 25 highest streakiness seasons (only exceptions being the early expansion years of 1961 and 1962) occurred prior to 1956. All 25 of the lowest performance diversity seasons and 22 of the 25 lowest streakiness seasons (exceptions 1923, 1934, and 1947) occurred after 1957.

Figure 8. Performance Diversity (AVGDEV) and Total Streak Quotient (TSQ) Scatterplot

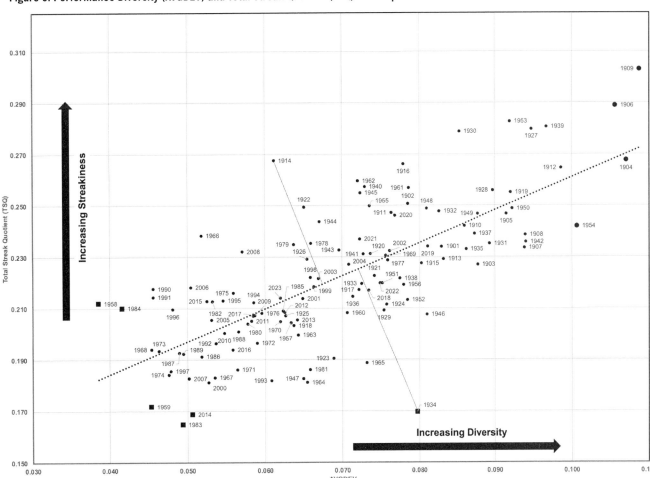

Table 4. Seasonal Performance Diversity and Streakiness Measures

Pre-Expansion

Season	Teams		AVGDEV		TSQ
1901	16	▲	0.083		0.234
1902	16		0.078	▲	0.251
1903	16	▲	0.088		0.227
1904	16	▲	0.107	▲	0.268
1905	16	▲	0.091	▲	0.247
1906	16	▲	0.106	▲	0.289
1907	16	▲	0.094		0.234
1908	16	▲	0.094		0.239
1909	16	▲	0.109	▲	0.303
1910	16	▲	0.086		0.242
1911	16		0.076	▲	0.247
1912	16	▲	0.099	▲	0.265
1913	16	▲	0.083		0.229
1914	16		0.061	▲	0.268
1915	16		0.080		0.227
1916	16		0.078	▲	0.266
1917	16		0.072		0.217
1918	16		0.064		0.203
1919	16	▲	0.092	▲	0.255
1920	16		0.074		0.231
1921	16		0.074		0.223
1922	16		0.065	▲	0.249
1923	16		0.069	▽	0.190
1924	16		0.076		0.212
1925	16		0.063		0.207
1926	16		0.065		0.229
1927	16	▲	0.095	▲	0.280
1928	16	▲	0.090	▲	0.256
1929	16		0.075		0.209
1930	16	▲	0.085	▲	0.279
1931	16	▲	0.089		0.235
1932	16	▲	0.083	▲	0.248
1933	16		0.072		0.220
1934	16		0.080	▽	0.170
1935	16	▲	0.086		0.233
1936	16		0.071		0.215
1937	16	▲	0.087		0.239
1938	16		0.077		0.222
1939	16	▲	0.097	▲	0.281
1940	16		0.073	▲	0.257
1941	16		0.073		0.231
1942	16	▲	0.094		0.236
1943	16		0.070		0.233
1944	16		0.067		0.244
1945	16		0.072	▲	0.255
1946	16		0.081		0.208
1947	16		0.065	▽	0.183
1948	16		0.081	▲	0.249
1949	16	▲	0.088	▲	0.247
1950	16	▲	0.092	▲	0.249
1951	16		0.075		0.220
1952	16		0.078		0.213
1953	16	▲	0.092	▲	0.283
1954	16	▲	0.101		0.242
1955	16		0.074	▲	0.250
1956	16		0.078		0.219
1957	16		0.063		0.204
1958	16	▽	0.039		0.212
1959	16	▽	0.045	▽	0.172
1960	16		0.071		0.208
Seasons in Top 20%		▲	25	▲	23
Seasons in Bottom 20%		▽	2	▽	4
Seasons Both in Top 20%		▲			14
Seasons Both in Bottom 20%		▽			1

Post-Expansion

Season	Teams		AVGDEV		TSQ
1961	18		0.079	▲	0.257
1962	20		0.072	▲	0.260
1963	20		0.064	▽	0.200
1964	20		0.065	▽	0.181
1965	20		0.073	▽	0.189
1966	20	▽	0.052		0.238
1967	20	▽	0.054	▽	0.183
1968	20	▽	0.045	▽	0.194
1969	24		0.076		0.231
1970	24		0.062		0.205
1971	24		0.056	▽	0.186
1972	24		0.059	▽	0.196
1973	24	▽	0.046	▽	0.193
1974	24	▽	0.048	▽	0.184
1975	24		0.056		0.216
1976	24		0.060		0.208
1977	26		0.076		0.229
1978	26		0.066		0.235
1979	26		0.064		0.235
1980	26		0.058		0.204
1981	26		0.066	▽	0.186
1982	26	▽	0.053		0.213
1983	26	▽	0.049	▽	0.165
1984	26	▽	0.042		0.210
1985	26		0.062		0.209
1986	26	▽	0.052	▽	0.191
1987	26	▽	0.049	▽	0.193
1988	26		0.057		0.201
1989	26	▽	0.049	▽	0.192
1990	26	▽	0.046		0.218
1991	26	▽	0.046		0.214
1992	26	▽	0.054	▽	0.196
1993	28		0.061	▽	0.182
1994	28		0.059		0.212
1995	28	▽	0.055		0.213
1996	28	▽	0.048		0.210
1997	28	▽	0.048	▽	0.186
1998	30		0.066		0.222
1999	30		0.066		0.218
2000	30	▽	0.053	▽	0.181
2001	30		0.065		0.214
2002	30		0.076		0.232
2003	30		0.067		0.221
2004	30		0.071		0.227
2005	30	▽	0.053		0.206
2006	30	▽	0.050		0.218
2007	30	▽	0.050	▽	0.183
2008	30		0.057		0.232
2009	30		0.059		0.207
2010	30		0.055		0.200
2011	30		0.058		0.205
2012	30		0.063		0.208
2013	30		0.064		0.205
2014	30	▽	0.051	▽	0.169
2015	30	▽	0.052		0.213
2016	30		0.056	▽	0.194
2017	30		0.058		0.207
2018	30		0.073		0.217
2019	30		0.081		0.234
2020	30		0.077		0.246
2021	30		0.072		0.237
2022	30		0.075		0.220
2023	30		0.062		0.214
Seasons in Top 20%		▲	0	▲	2
Seasons in Bottom 20%		▽	23	▽	21
Seasons Both in Top 20%		▲			0
Seasons Both in Bottom 20%		▽			8

Table 5 depicts a statistical summary of the seasonal values of AVGDEV and TSQ from Table 4.

Table 5. Seasonal Performance Diversity and Streakiness Metrics

	Average Deviation AVGDEV	Streakiness TSQ
Maximum	.109 (1909)	.303 (1909)
Minimum	.039 (1958)	.165 (1983)
Median	.069	.218
Average	.069	.222
Range	.070	.138

COMPARATIVE ANALYSIS: PREDICTIONS VS. ACTUALS

Seasonal streaks are constrained to a single season for a single team. The number of teams has ranged from a low of 16 in 1901–60 to the current high of 30. Each current franchise that existed in 1901 has played 123 seasons through 2023. Each season constitutes one of their 123 team-seasons. The 1998 expansion Tampa Bay Rays and Arizona Diamondbacks have played 26 team-seasons. There has been a total of 2,646 team-seasons since 1901.

Predicting Seasonal Streaks. It has been shown that higher performance diversities lead to more total streaks. Performance Diversity (PD) measures the absolute difference between a team's winning average (PW), expressed as a three digit decimal number between .000 and 1.000, and .500. The more a team's winning average deviates from .500 the greater the team's performance diversity, as demonstrated back in Figure 4. Figure 9 is a snapshot of two Excel tables (aka Model) that implement the expected streak equations to calculate total streaks by streak length. Values for PW (or PD) and the number of games (or decisions) are entered into the cells highlighted in black. PL need not be entered; it is calculated from PW.

Two views of the Model are shown: one used for Team-Season streaks and the other for Global Streaks. The calculations implemented by each version are identical. Both versions are shown to illustrate that winning, losing streaks, and total streaks are predicted by the Team-Season approach when winning average, PW, and Games Played are the inputs. A PW less than .500 will result in more expected loss streaks than win streaks. The example shown is the 1919 Philadelphia Athletics, the team with the single highest actual LSQ, who finished with a record of 36–104, PW = .257. The Model predicts eight losing streaks and an LSQ of .457. Results were streakier than predicted with 12 losing streaks (5, 6, 5, 6, 6, 6, 8, 6, 9, 5, 8, 5) and an LSQ of .721 (75/104). As will be revealed later, the summation of all 2646 team-seasonal predictions is highly accurate.

Figure 9. Excel Models that Calculate Expected Streaks

Model for Team-Season Streaks

Example: 1919 Philadelphia Athletics 36-104, 0.2571, 140 Games

	Entry 1	Entry 2	
	PW	Games	PL=1-PW
	.2571	**140**	.7429
Streak Length	Win Streaks	Loss Streaks	Total Streaks
5	0.1	2.1	2.2
6	0.0	1.6	1.6
7	0.0	1.2	1.2
8	0.0	0.9	0.9
9	0.0	0.6	0.6
10	0.0	0.5	0.5
11	0.0	0.4	0.4
12	0.0	0.3	0.3
13	0.0	0.2	0.2
14	0.0	0.1	0.1
15	0.0	0.1	0.1
16	0.0	0.1	0.1
17	0.0	0.1	0.1
18	0.0	0.0	0.0
19	0.0	0.0	0.0
20	0.0	0.0	0.0
21	0.0	0.0	0.0
22	0.0	0.0	0.0
23	0.0	0.0	0.0
24	0.0	0.0	0.0
25	0.0	0.0	0.0
26	0.0	0.0	0.0
	EWSGS 0.1	ELSGS 8.1	ETSGS 8.2
	WSQ 0.0045	LSQ 0.4565	TSQ 0.4609

(Win Streaks column labeled EWSG; Loss Streaks column labeled ELSG; Total Streaks column labeled ETSG)

Model for Global Streaks

Average PD for all thirty 2023 Team-Seasons is 0.5617

	Entry 1	Entry 2	
	PD	Decisions	
	.5617	**4860**	
Streak Length	Win Streaks	Loss Streaks	Total Streaks
5			77.0
6			40.2
7			21.2
8			11.3
9			6.1
10			3.3
11			1.8
12			1.0
13			0.6
14			0.3
15			0.2
16			0.1
17			0.1
18			0.0
19			0.0
20			0.0
21			0.0
22			0.0
23			0.0
24			0.0
25			0.0
26			0.0
	EWSGSL	ELSGSL	ETSGSL 163
	WSQ	LSQ	TSQ 0.2065

(Win Streaks column labeled EWSG; Loss Streaks column labeled ELSG; Total Streaks column labeled ETSG)

The Global approach is used to evaluate streaks for an aggregate of team-seasons, using an averaged PD and the total number of decisions for the appropriate team-seasons. Win and loss streaks are not applicable, only the total streak parameters ETSG and ETSGSL are relevant. Figure 9 shows that 163 total streaks were expected in 2023 based on a seasonal PD of 0.562. Actual streaks totaled 159, with 80 winning and 79 losing streaks of at least five games.

Let's predict the expected total number of seasonal streaks, by streak length, since 1901, using three distinct approaches: Global, Seasonal, and Team-Seasonal. Figure 10 outlines the methodology for each approach.

Global Prediction. The Global Prediction method calculates the average of the 2,646 team-seasonal PDs. The Model predicts 14,002 total expected streaks, Table 6, using a PD value of .5669 and 411,868 global decisions. Streaks are rounded to the nearest whole number.

Seasonal Prediction. The Seasonal Prediction method parses the 2,646 team-seasons into the 123 seasons. The average PD is calculated, and the total number of decisions summed for each season. The average PD and

the number total decisions for each season is input to an instance of the Model yielding the predicted number of streaks for each season by streak length. To efficiently process 123 seasonal data pairs, an Excel macro to implement the expected streak Model was developed. The power of the macro was crucial to this prediction and even more important when evaluating the Model 2,646 times during the Team-Season approach.

The number of streaks for each streak length is summed for the 123 seasons to yield 14,042 total expected streaks, Table 7.

Table 8 (opposite) shows the results of the seasonal streak prediction season by season.

Team-Season Prediction. The Team-Season Prediction method is similar to the Seasonal method. The most critical difference is that it uses the winning average, and not the performance diversity, for each team and each season. This allows both winning and losing streaks to be calculated for each team-season. The PW and decisions for each team-season is input to an instance of the Model yielding the predicted number of both winning and losing streaks for each team-season by streak length.

Figure 10. Streak Prediction Methodologies

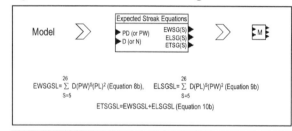

$$EWSGSL = \sum_{S=5}^{26} D(PW)^S(PL)^2 \text{ (Equation 8b)}, \quad ELSGSL = \sum_{S=5}^{26} D(PL)^S(PW)^2 \text{ (Equation 9b)}$$

$$ETSGSL = EWSGSL + ELSGSL \text{ (Equation 10b)}$$

Acronyms
AVG	Average
D	Decisions
ELSG(S)	Expected Losing Streaks Generalized (by Streak Length)
ETSG(S)	Expected Total Streaks Generalized (by Streak Length)
EWSG(S)	Expected Wining Streaks Generalized (by Streak Length)
M	Model
N	Number of Games
PD	Performance Diversity
PL	Probability of a Loss
PW	Probability of a Win
S	Streak Length
TS	Team-Season

Table 6. Expected Streaks by Streak Length Using the Global Prediction Method

										Streak Length												
5	6	7	8	9	10	11	12	13	14	15	16	17	18	19	20	21	22	23	24	25	26	Total
6540	3438	1832	988	538	296	163	91	51	28	16	9	5	3	2	1	1	0	0	0	0	0	**14002**

Number of Streaks

Table 7. Expected Streaks by Streak Length Using the Seasonal Prediction Method

										Streak Length												
5	6	7	8	9	10	11	12	13	14	15	16	17	18	19	20	21	22	23	24	25	26	Total
6542	3444	1839	994	543	300	166	93	52	29	17	9	5	3	2	1	1	0	0	0	0	0	**14042**

Number of Streaks

Table 8. Predicted Seasonal Streaks Vs. Actuals

Pre-Expansion						Post-Expansion				
Season	PD	Decisions	Predicted (ETSGSL)	Actual		Season	PD	Decisions	Predicted (ETSGSL)	Actual
1901	.583	2190	77.5	80		1961	.579	2846	99.6	109
1902	.578	2190	76.7	84		1962	.572	3236	111.4	134
1903	.588	2198	78.9	77		1963	.564	3236	109.3	100
1904	.607	2440	92.9	100		1964	.565	3240	109.8	99
1905	.591	2436	88.4	94		1965	.573	3238	111.8	94
1906	.606	2416	91.6	101		**1966**	**.552**	**3226**	**106.2**	**131**
1907	.594	2406	88.0	87		1967	.554	3234	106.8	98
1908	.594	2456	89.8	91		1968	.545	3238	105.3	104
1909	.609	2436	93.3	110		1969	.576	3886	135.0	137
1910	.586	2446	87.4	90		1970	.562	3886	130.6	129
1911	.576	2436	84.8	92		1971	.556	3874	128.7	121
1912	.599	2438	90.4	99		1972	.559	3716	124.1	119
1913	.583	2426	86.0	90		1973	.546	3884	126.5	120
1914	**.561**	**2456**	**82.4**	**103**		1974	.548	3882	126.8	120
1915	.580	2444	86.0	87		1975	.556	3866	128.3	141
1916	.578	2454	85.8	95		1976	.560	3878	129.7	132
1917	.572	2450	84.4	88		1977	.576	4206	146.2	151
1918	.564	2012	67.9	66		1978	.566	4204	142.6	155
1919	.592	2226	80.9	89		1979	.564	4194	141.5	164
1920	.574	2456	84.9	88		1980	.558	4202	140.0	134
1921	.574	2452	84.9	85		1981	.566	2778	94.2	83
1922	.565	2462	83.3	99		1982	.553	4212	139.0	138
1923	.569	2452	83.8	76		1983	.549	4212	138.0	116
1924	.576	2448	85.1	82		1984	.542	4208	136.0	149
1925	.563	2448	82.4	82		1985	.562	4202	141.4	144
1926	.565	2444	82.8	87		1986	.552	4204	138.4	135
1927	.595	2456	90.0	102		1987	.549	4210	137.8	133
1928	.590	2454	88.6	98		1988	.557	4196	139.4	138
1929	.575	2442	84.8	82		1989	.549	4206	137.8	132
1930	.585	2464	87.9	108		1990	.546	4210	137.0	155
1931	.589	2454	88.5	88		1991	.546	4208	136.9	145
1932	.583	2456	87.0	97		1992	.554	4212	139.1	135
1933	.572	2432	83.8	87		1993	.561	4536	152.1	133
1934	**.580**	**2430**	**85.3**	**69**		1994	.559	3198	106.7	108
1935	.586	2438	87.2	84		1995	.555	4032	133.4	143
1936	.571	2456	84.4	81		1996	.548	4532	148.1	156
1937	.587	2452	87.9	89		1997	.548	4532	148.1	141
1938	.577	2414	84.3	84		1998	.566	4860	164.8	168
1939	.597	2442	90.1	105		1999	.566	4854	164.8	171
1940	.573	2456	84.7	102		2000	.553	4856	160.1	143
1941	.573	2462	84.9	89		2001	.565	4856	164.3	169
1942	.594	2430	88.9	90		2002	.576	4850	168.7	178
1943	.570	2454	84.0	89		2003	.567	4858	165.2	176
1944	.567	2462	83.7	93		2004	.571	4856	166.7	176
1945	.572	2436	83.9	100		2005	.553	4860	160.3	160
1946	.581	2466	86.9	84		2006	.550	4858	159.5	169
1947	.565	2464	83.4	71		2007	.550	4862	159.5	149
1948	.581	2460	86.7	98		2008	.557	4856	161.5	183
1949	.588	2464	88.5	97		2009	.559	4860	162.2	165
1950	.592	2460	89.5	99		2010	.555	4860	160.9	159
1951	.575	2470	85.7	81		2011	.558	4858	162.0	161
1952	.578	2462	86.2	86		2012	.563	4860	163.6	167
1953	.592	2458	89.4	108		2013	.564	4862	164.2	161
1954	.601	2464	92.0	87		**2014**	**.551**	**4860**	**159.6**	**136**
1955	.574	2462	85.1	98		2015	.552	4858	160.1	169
1956	.578	2464	86.1	88		2016	.556	4854	161.0	154
1957	.563	2460	82.9	83		2017	.558	4860	162.1	164
1958	.539	2462	79.2	85		2018	.573	4862	168.0	173
1959	.545	2468	80.3	69		2019	.581	4858	171.3	187
1960	.571	2464	84.5	84		2020	.577	1796	62.6	72
						2021	.572	4858	167.3	177
						2022	.575	4860	168.5	167
						2023	.562	4860	163.3	159
						Totals	**.569**	**411868**	**14042**	**14366**

Outliers in scatterplot, Figure 8

Largest difference between predicted and actual number of streaks

107

The number of streaks for each streak length and decision type is then summed for the 2,646 team-seasons to yield the expected streak totals as shown in Table 9.

Note that there are more losing streaks than winning streaks for all streak lengths from eight through 22 with only two exceptions (where they are equal), streak

Table 9. Expected Streaks by Streak Length Using the Team-Season Prediction Method

Streak Length

	5	6	7	8	9	10	11	12	13	14	15	16	17	18	19	20	21	22	23	24	25	26	Total
Winning Streaks	3286	1757	956	529	297	169	98	57	34	20	12	7	5	3	2	1	1	0	0	0	0	0	7236
Losing Streaks	3263	1745	953	531	301	174	102	61	37	23	14	9	6	4	2	2	1	1	0	0	0	0	7229
Total Streaks	6549	3502	1910	1060	599	343	200	118	71	43	26	16	10	6	4	3	2	1	1	0	0	0	14465

Number of Streaks

Table 10. Team-Season Prediction Results

Current Franchise	Team	Season	PW	Non-Tie Decisions	Win Streaks	Loss Streaks	Total Streaks
Atlanta Braves	Boston Doves	1909	.294	153	0.2	7.9	8.1
Baltimore Orioles	St. Louis Browns	1909	.407	150	1.0	4.5	5.5
Boston Red Sox	Boston Red Sox	1909	.583	151	4.2	1.1	5.3
Chicago White Sox	Chicago White Sox	1909	.513	152	2.6	2.1	4.8
Chicago Cubs	Chicago Cubs	1909	.680	153	7.1	0.4	7.5
Cincinnati Reds	Cincinnati Reds	1909	.503	153	2.5	2.3	4.8
Cleveland Guardians	Cleveland Naps	1909	.464	153	1.8	3.1	4.9
Detroit Tigers	Detroit Tigers	1909	.645	152	6.0	0.6	6.6
Los Angeles Dodgers	Brooklyn Superbas	1909	.359	153	0.6	5.9	6.5
Minnesota Twins	Washington Nationals(1)	1909	.276	152	0.2	8.3	8.5
New York Yankees	New York Highlanders	1909	.490	151	2.2	2.6	4.7
Oakland Athletics	Philadelphia Athletics	1909	.621	153	5.4	0.7	6.1
Philadelphia Phillies	Philadelphia Phillies	1909	.484	153	2.1	2.7	4.8
Pittsburgh Pirates	Pittsburgh Pirates	1909	.724	152	8.3	0.2	8.5
San Francisco Giants	New York Giants	1909	.601	153	4.8	0.9	5.7
St. Louis Cardinals	St. Louis Cardinals	1909	.355	152	0.6	6.0	6.6
Atlanta Braves	Boston Bees	1939	.417	151	1.1	4.2	5.3
Baltimore Orioles	St. Louis Browns	1939	.279	154	0.2	8.4	8.6
Boston Red Sox	Boston Red Sox	1939	.589	151	4.4	1.0	5.4
Chicago White Sox	Chicago White Sox	1939	.552	154	3.6	1.5	5.1
Chicago Cubs	Chicago Cubs	1939	.545	154	3.4	1.6	5.0
Cincinnati Reds	Cincinnati Reds	1939	.630	154	5.7	0.7	6.3
Cleveland Guardians	Cleveland Indians	1939	.565	154	3.9	1.4	5.2
Detroit Tigers	Detroit Tigers	1939	.526	154	2.9	1.9	4.9
Los Angeles Dodgers	Brooklyn Dodgers	1939	.549	153	3.4	1.6	5.0
Minnesota Twins	Washington Nationals(1)	1939	.428	152	1.2	4.1	5.3
New York Yankees	New York Yankees	1939	.702	151	7.7	0.2	7.9
Oakland Athletics	Philadelphia Athletics	1939	.362	152	0.6	5.8	6.4
Philadelphia Phillies	Philadelphia Phillies	1939	.298	151	0.2	7.7	7.9
Pittsburgh Pirates	Pittsburgh Pirates	1939	.444	153	1.5	3.6	5.1
San Francisco Giants	New York Giants	1939	.510	151	2.6	2.2	4.7
St. Louis Cardinals	St. Louis Cardinals	1939	.601	153	4.8	0.9	5.7
Arizona Diamondbacks	Arizona Diamondbacks	2023	.519	162	2.9	2.2	5.1
Atlanta Braves	Atlanta Braves	2023	.642	162	6.3	0.6	6.9
Baltimore Orioles	Baltimore Orioles	2023	.623	162	5.7	0.8	6.5
Boston Red Sox	Boston Red Sox	2023	.481	162	2.2	2.9	5.1
Chicago Cubs	Chicago Cubs	2023	.512	162	2.8	2.3	5.1
Chicago White Sox	Chicago White Sox	2023	.377	162	0.8	5.7	6.5
Cincinnati Reds	Cincinnati Reds	2023	.506	162	2.7	2.4	5.1
Cleveland Guardians	Cleveland Guardians	2023	.469	162	2.0	3.2	5.2
Colorado Rockies	Colorado Rockies	2023	.364	162	0.7	6.1	6.8
Detroit Tigers	Detroit Tigers	2023	.481	162	2.2	2.9	5.1
Houston Astros(A)	Houston Astros(A)	2023	.556	162	3.8	1.6	5.4
Kansas City Royals	Kansas City Royals	2023	.346	162	0.5	6.7	7.2
Los Angeles Angels	Los Angeles Angels	2023	.451	162	1.7	3.7	5.3
Los Angeles Dodgers	Los Angeles Dodgers	2023	.617	162	5.6	0.8	6.4
Miami Marlins	Miami Marlins	2023	.519	162	2.9	2.2	5.1
Milwaukee Brewers(N)	Milwaukee Brewers(N)	2023	.568	162	4.1	1.4	5.5
Minnesota Twins	Minnesota Twins	2023	.537	162	3.4	1.9	5.2
New York Mets	New York Mets	2023	.463	162	1.9	3.4	5.2
New York Yankees	New York Yankees	2023	.506	162	2.7	2.4	5.1
Oakland Athletics	Oakland Athletics	2023	.309	162	0.3	7.9	8.2
Philadelphia Phillies	Philadelphia Phillies	2023	.556	162	3.8	1.6	5.4
Pittsburgh Pirates	Pittsburgh Pirates	2023	.469	162	2.0	3.2	5.2
San Diego Padres	San Diego Padres	2023	.506	162	2.7	2.4	5.1
Seattle Mariners	Seattle Mariners	2023	.543	162	3.5	1.8	5.3
San Francisco Giants	San Francisco Giants	2023	.488	162	2.3	2.8	5.1
St. Louis Cardinals	St. Louis Cardinals	2023	.438	162	1.5	4.0	5.4
Tampa Bay Rays	Tampa Bay Rays	2023	.611	162	5.4	0.9	6.3
Texas Rangers	Texas Rangers	2023	.556	162	3.8	1.6	5.4
Toronto Blue Jays	Toronto Blue Jays	2023	.549	162	3.7	1.7	5.3
Washington Nationals	Washington Nationals	2023	.438	162	1.5	4.0	5.4
All-Season Totals			.500	411868	7236	7229	14465

lengths 19 and 21. However, winning streaks exceed losing streaks for streak lengths from five through seven. This will become more noteworthy when we compare predictions to actuals and seek to understand the underlying mathematics. Stay tuned.

Table 10 displays a few selected season results from the team-season prediction. Highlighted entries represent high winning averages resulting in more streak wins than losses during each season and the reverse for low winning averages.

Actual Seasonal Streaks. Actual seasonal streaks are deduced from the encoded data set using filters and functions in Excel. Table 11 breaks down 14,366 actual

Table 11. Actual Seasonal Streaks

Franchise	Seasonal Win Streaks	Seasonal Loss Streaks	Total Seasonal Streaks	Streak Length	Seasonal Streaks by Streak Length
Atlanta Braves	307	359	666	5	6506
Arizona Diamonbacks	63	77	140	6	3565
Baltimore Orioles	279	423	702	7	1868
Boston Red Sox	383	287	670	8	1055
Chicago Cubs	333	293	626	9	570
Chicago White Sox	322	321	643	10	342
Cincinnati Reds	312	342	654	11	197
Cleveland Guardians	362	310	672	12	90
Colorado Rockies	62	111	173	13	65
Detroit Tigers	340	313	653	14	45
Houston Astros	168	177	345	15	22
Kansas City Royals	125	166	291	16	9
Los Angeles Angels	156	162	318	17	10
Los Angeles Dodgers	396	259	655	18	5
Miami Marlins	55	101	156	19	7
Milwaukee Brewers	107	169	276	20	5
Minnesota Twins	275	370	645	21	2
New York Mets	143	195	338	22	1
New York Yankees	507	190	697	23	1
Oakland Athletics	316	418	734	24	0
Philadelphia Phillies	289	428	717	25	0
Pittsburgh Pirates	350	355	705	26	1
San Diego Padres	107	179	286		14366
Seattle Mariners	92	140	232		
San Francisco Giants	435	260	695		
St. Louis Cardinals	396	267	663		
Tampa Bay Rays	73	79	152		TSQ
Texas Rangers	132	182	314		0.2180
Toronto Blue Jays	111	124	235		
Washington Nationals	138	164	302		
Baltimore Orioles (Defunct)	2	9	11		
Totals	7136	7230	14366		

Table 12. Actual Streaks Vs. Predictions

Streak Length	Total Actual Streaks	Global Streak Prediction	Seasonal Prediction	Team-Season Prediction
5	6506	6540	6542	6549
6	3565	3438	3444	3502
7	1868	1832	1839	1910
8	1055	988	994	1060
9	570	538	543	599
10	342	296	300	343
11	197	163	166	200
12	90	91	93	118
13	65	51	52	71
14	45	28	29	43
15	22	16	17	26
16	9	9	9	16
17	10	5	5	10
18	5	3	3	6
19	7	2	2	4
20	5	1	1	3
21	2	1	1	2
22	1	0	0	1
23	1	0	0	1
24	0	0	0	0
25	0	0	0	0
26	1	0	0	0
Total Streaks	14366	14002	14042	14465

Figure 11. Actual Streaks Versus Predictions

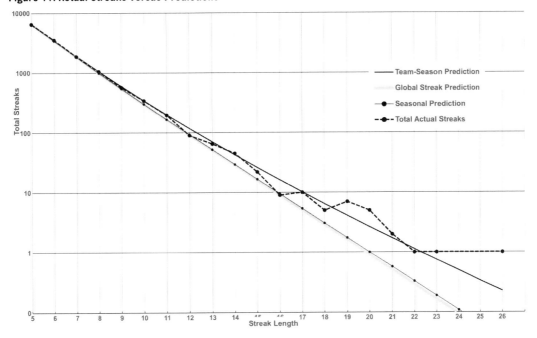

seasonal winning and losing streaks by franchise and total streaks by streak length.

For those curious to know more, in the Appendix on SABR.org, Tables Appendix 1 and Appendix 2 enumerate franchise seasonal streaks by streak length.

Global Comparison of Streak Predictions to Actuals. Figure 11 plots the predicted number of seasonal streaks for all three prediction methods along with the actual streaks by streak length for all 411,868 decisions. This is a logarithmic plot. Each horizontal line represents a 10 times difference. The separation between 1 and 10 are all single-digit number of streaks.

Global and Seasonal predictions are virtually indistinguishable. The Team-Seasonal prediction is very accurate. Actual streaks, 14,366, differ from the Team-Season prediction, 14,465, by only 99 (0.68%). Note that the Team-Season prediction has a slight upward curve.

Figure 12 plots actual win and loss streaks by streak length against the Team-Season predictions.

It is clear that there are more loss streaks (dashed line) than win streaks (solid line), both actual (dark lines) and prediction (gray lines), for streak lengths beginning at 11.

Understanding the Difference Between the Team-Season and Seasonal Analysis. On Figure 11, the Seasonal Prediction appears to be linear, but the Team-Season Prediction has a slight upward bend that more accurately matches the actual number of total streaks. Figure 10 shows that both these prediction methods utilize the Model multiple times and then sum the output expected streaks by streak length. The Seasonal method utilizes 123 instances of the Model (one per season). The Team-Seasonal method utilizes 2,646 instances of the Model (one per team-season).

When the PDs of the individual teams are averaged to derive the seasonal PD, higher and lower individual team PDs get suppressed. Example, in 2010, the Tigers and the Athletics each had a PD of .500 (lowest) and the Pirates and Mariners had PDs of .648 and .623 (the highest two), respectively. The seasonal PD for 2010 is .555 (the average). The Seasonal PDs range from a low of .539 (1958) to a high of .609 (1909). Team-Season PDs range from a low of .500 to a high of .765 (by the 1916 Philadelphia A's).

Figure 13 (opposite), shows the distribution of the PD values input to the Model for the two prediction methods. This is a bin plot; values are counted and placed in bins. The data point 269 on the Team-Season

Figure 12. Actual Win and Loss Streaks Vs. Predictions

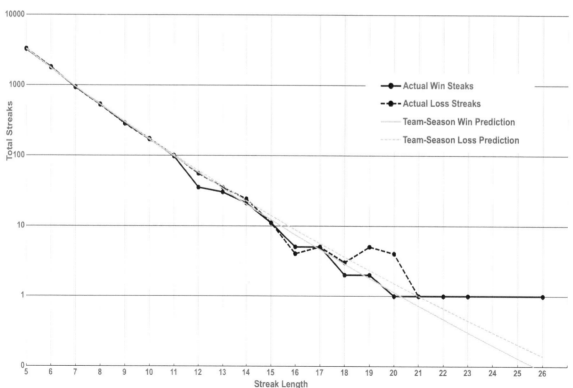

plot at .625 indicates that 269 of the 2,646 PDs are in the range from .601 to .625.

The shaded area of Figure 13 shows that 484 of the 2,646 PD instances (18.1%) for the Team-Season pre-diction exceed the maximum PD input to the Model for the Seasonal prediction of .609.

Figure 14 displays the expected number of streaks (between lengths 7 and 15) in 1,000 decisions for several

Figure 13. PD Bins for Seasonal and Team-Seasonal Analysis

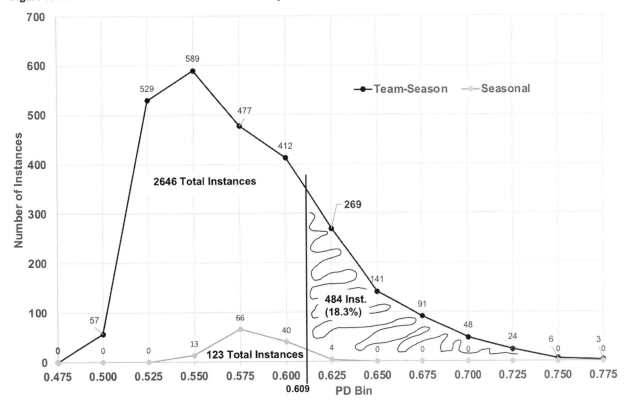

Figure 14. Streaks per 1000 Decisions by Streak Length and PD

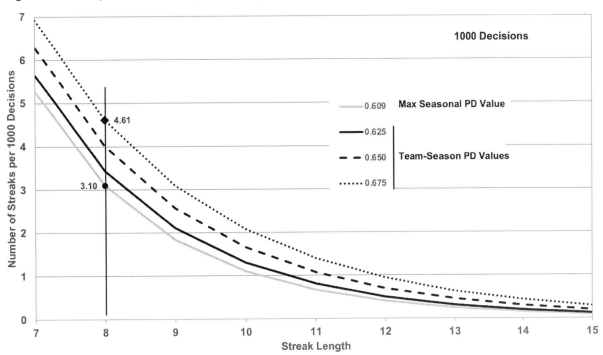

PDs used in the Team-Seasonal Prediction (.625, .650, and .675) and .609 the highest PD in the Seasonal Prediction.

Figure 15 plots the streak differences (per 1,000 decisions) between PD Team-Seasonal values 0.625 and .650) and the highest PD value (.609) used in the Seasonal Analysis. Clearly the Team-Seasonal prediction yields more long length streaks. Hence, the greater the number of long streaks in the Team-Seasonal prediction in Figure 11.

Seasonal Comparison of Streak Predictions to Actuals. Figure 16 plots the predicted number of seasonal streaks against actuals taken from Table 8. Very good correlation can be seen in spite of the relatively small seasonal decision space, less than or equal to 4,860 decisions, 30 teams playing 162 games.

Actual streaks in 1966 exceeded predictions by the largest amount, 131 to 108.3. Actual streaks lagged predictions by the greatest amount in 2014, 136 to 161.9.[2]

Figure 17 (page 114) provides a more rigorous view of the accuracy of the seasonal streak predictions. It plots the ratio of Actual Streaks to Predicted Streaks, ETSGSL. Actuals differed from predictions by more than 15% in only nine of the 123 seasons (7.3%). Only three seasons deviated by more than 20%: 1914 and 1966 by +21% and 1934 by -22%. As expected, 1914 and 1934 are the noteworthy outliers on the scatterplot in Figure 8.

Figure 15. Difference in Streaks per 1,000 Decisions by Streak Length and PD

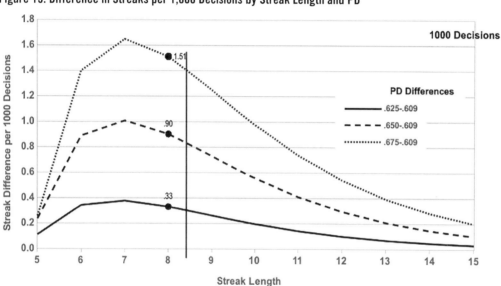

Figure 16. Actual Seasonal Streaks Vs. Streak Predictions

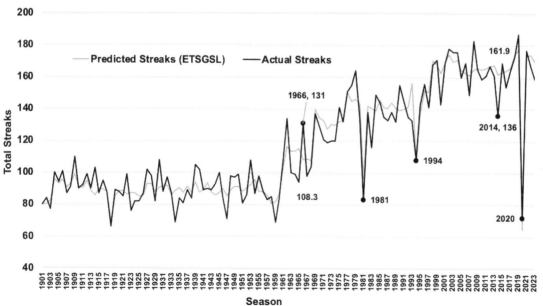

Figure 17. Seasonal Ratio of Actual to Predicted Streaks

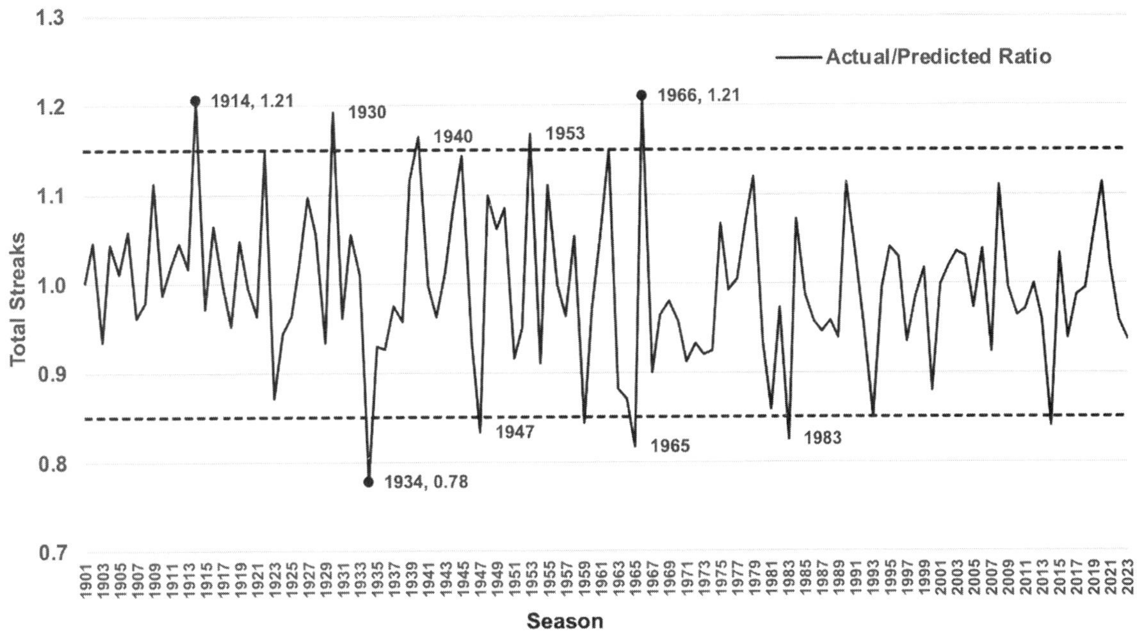

CONCLUSIONS

The primary goals in writing this research paper were to:

- explore an area of baseball's recorded history using a novel analysis technique;

- satisfy my curiosity and fascination about baseball winning and losing streaks;

- present results that would be easily understood by an average, interested baseball fan.

I grouped my analysis into three main areas:

- Mathematical theory and equations to predict streaks verified by simulations;

- Analysis of the correlation between streakiness and performance diversity;

- Comparative analysis between streak predictions and actual results.

I posed two questions: How often and when do streaks occur? Do they follow any predictable patterns?

Streak Prediction. Streak prediction in the long run is embodied by algebraic expressions based on streak length (S), winning average (PW), performance diversity (PD), and the number of the games (N)/decisions (D)

being analyzed. (See equations 8b, 9b, and 10b which were confirmed by simulations, Figure 3).

This analysis cannot predict, however, when a streak is likely to start or end, only how often they are likely to occur, given a team's winning average (PW).

Correlation of Streakiness and Performance Diversity. A new metric, Total Streak Quotient (TSQ), was defined to measure and quantify seasonal streakiness. TSQ is defined as Streak Wins (SW) plus Streak Losses (SL) divided by Decisions (D). SW (or SL) is number of wins (or losses) during a season that are part of winning (or losing) streaks of five or more games. Seasonal performance diversity was quantified by Average Deviation (AVGDEV) which is defined as the average of the absolute deviations of the winning average of all teams in the league from the mean for a given season (which is always .500).

Season by season comparison of TSQ and AVGDEV shows noteworthy correlation as evidenced by the scatterplot of Figure 8. Greater performance diversity (higher AVGDEV) leads to greater streakiness (higher TSQ) and more total streaks.

Comparison of Streak Actuals and Predictions. The total number of streaks by streak length in the global sense is quite predictable, as evidenced by Figure 11 and 12. The following critical components were developed to investigate winning and losing streaks:

113

- A proprietary conversion scheme to replace each win, loss, and tie in baseball history since 1901 with an encoded numerical value that facilitates streak data extraction;

- An easily understood test sequence slide model used to develop the expected streak equations (8b, 9b, and 10b);

- An Excel Macro Model to repeatedly evaluate the expected streak equations and predict streaks on a team-season and seasonal basis;

- A detailed visualization of the mathematical relationship between performance diversity and streaks.

The total number of streaks for the league in shorter seasonal runs is still predictable within slight margins, as evidenced by Figures 16 and 17. The specific teams that own the streaks during a given season are not necessarily predictable. However, it is obvious that better teams have more winning streaks than losing streaks, and poorer teams more losing streaks than winning streaks.

Although there are many factors that can give one team an edge, the outcome of any specific baseball game is uncertain. Winners are determined on the field and outcomes can exhilarate and surprise. Some things, however, are undeniable.

- Every (non-tie) game played to completion has only a winner and a loser.

- There are an equal number of wins and losses in the league each season.

- More than 206,000 games have been played.

- Some teams are better than others.

These certainties and the degree to which teams are better or worse than .500 form the basis for the predictability of streaks.

I trust my research has fostered a new understanding of modern baseball's winning and losing streaks. ■

Notes

1. Baseball Reference and other sites owned by Sports Reference LLC allow the general public to share, export, and use their data as long as they are credited. Game results are also found at Retrosheet.org.
2. Seasons 1981 and 1994 were shortened seasons due to work stoppages. 2020 was a 60-game season because of COVID-19 mitigation measures.

Jews and Baseball

Part One: History and Demographics

Peter Dreier

American Jews have long had a love affair with baseball. They have played baseball since the game was developed in the mid-1800s. Some have made it to the professional ranks and a few have climbed to the very top—the major leagues. Jews have also become coaches and managers at all levels of the sport, from Little League to the majors, in addition to being sportswriters, umpires, owners, and executives. But even Jewish baseball fans may be surprised to learn that the 19 Jews who played on major league rosters in 2023 represented the highest number for a season in history. Although 19 is the peak in the *number* of Jewish players, it is only 1.3% of all players on the 30 current teams. The highest *proportion* of Jews occurred in 1937, 1938, and 1951, when Jews represented 2% of all players, and the big leagues had only 16 teams. Yet even that 2% figure is somewhat misleading, as we'll discuss.

To put these and other facts in context, this article examines the history of Jews and baseball. The topic is so large that we have split the article into two parts. In Part One we will review—for the first time—year-by-year and decade-by-decade levels of participation since 1901, and discuss the ways in which Jewish participation in baseball does, and sometimes does not, reflect the changes in demographics throughout the United States. In Part Two, which will appear in the next issue of the *Baseball Research Journal*, we will tackle topics including anti-Semitism and the contributions of several significant individuals, including not only record-breaking players but also sportswriters, umpires, and others.

The primary sources of data on Jewish ballplayers are *Jewish Baseball News* (*JBN*) and the Jewish Baseball Museum (JBM), in addition to books that include profiles of Jewish players, biographies and autobiographies of players, newspaper and magazine articles, and the biographies published by the Society for American Baseball Research.[1] *JBN* considers a player to be Jewish if he has a Jewish parent or converted to Judaism, does not practice another faith, and is willing to be identified as a Jew. But that definition can be difficult to apply, especially to players from earlier periods who were not asked or did not clarify how they identified in religious or ethnic terms. For example, some players have Jewish ancestry but were not raised as Jews, some were the offspring of intermarried parents and their religious identity is unclear, some married Jewish women but did not convert, some converted to Judaism after they ended their baseball careers, and some changed their names to avoid anti-Semitism.[2]

JEWISH IMMIGRATION TO THE UNITED STATES

Historians and sociologists look at American immigration in terms of being a "melting pot" or a "salad bowl." In the former, immigrants seek to assimilate into the mainstream culture and, in the process of doing so, change that culture to incorporate different ideas, languages, and customs. In the latter, immigrants do not forge together into a common culture, but seek to maintain their distinct identities and cultures. The country's history of racism, of course, conforms to neither model. Baseball has reflected these tensions. During the nineteenth and early twentieth centuries, immigrants from Europe—first Germans and Irish, then Italians, Slavs, Czechs, Poles, and Jews—were not immediately attracted to baseball, since their primary concern was gaining an economic foothold in the new society. They also lacked the time or money to attend professional or semiprofessional games. But their children—and then subsequent generations—took to baseball. The rosters of minor and major league teams reflected the nation's evolving demographics—with the exception of African Americans, who were excluded from the late 1800s until 1947.[3]

The first Jews arrived in what is now the United States during colonial times. They were mostly of Spanish and Portuguese descent, primarily from Brazil, Amsterdam, and England. By 1840, the American Jewish community had grown to about 15,000 people. The next wave of Jews arrived from Germany and Austria starting in the middle 1800s. By 1880, the Jewish population reached about 250,000. Between 1880 and 1920, more than 2 million Jews came to the US, primarily from Eastern Europe (Russia, Poland,

Lithuania, Belarus, Ukraine, and Moldova), seeking to escape violent anti-Jewish riots called pogroms. Most American Jews today are descendants of the third wave of immigration.[4]

Lipman Pike was one of the first group of players—and the only Jew among them—to accept payment in 1866 for playing baseball, putting them among the first "professional" ballplayers.[5] Pike was born in New York in 1845 to Dutch Jewish parents. Pike began playing baseball as a teenager and in 1866, at 21, he agreed to play for the Philadelphia Athletics for $20 a week. That year he belted five home runs in one game, establishing his reputation as America's first great slugger. Pike played for several professional teams until he retired in 1881. Upon his retirement, Pike took over his father's Brooklyn haberdashery shop and ran it until he died of heart disease at the age of 48 in 1893.

When Jewish immigrants arrived from Eastern Europe, baseball was as foreign to them as ham. In 1903, the *Jewish Daily Forward*, a widely read Yiddish newspaper, published a letter from a Russian Jewish immigrant. "What is the point of a crazy game like baseball?" the reader wanted to know. "I want my boy to grow up to be a mensch, not a wild American runner." "Let your boys play baseball and play it well," *Forward* editor Abraham Cahan responded in the letters-to-the-editor column. "Let us not raise the children that they grow up foreigners in their own birthplace."[6]

Baseball became a way for Jews to show that they wanted to be full-fledged Americans, even as they also sought to maintain their group identity.

The overcrowded Jewish immigrant neighborhoods of the early 1900s provided few parks or playgrounds for Jews to play baseball. In New York, young Jews learned to play versions of baseball—using broom handles for bats and manhole covers for bases—on the streets. Athletic-oriented children of early Jewish immigrants were more likely to focus on boxing, basketball, and track-and-field, sports where Jews rose to prominence in amateur and professional ranks.[7]

As Jewish families moved from the tenement ghettoes to working class areas like the Bronx, with more spacious playgrounds and ballfields, and as public schools and Jewish settlement houses (such as the Young Men's Hebrew Association) fielded baseball teams, the sons of immigrants had more opportunities to play baseball. After World War II, like many other white Americans, many Jews moved to the suburbs, with more ballfields and public school teams. Starting in the 1950s, many Jews also played on Little League teams.

From 1920 through 1957, the Giants and Dodgers, but not the Yankees, tried to recruit Jewish players to attract Jewish fans, as New York City's population at the time about one-third Jewish. During those years, the Giants had 11 Jews on their rosters, the Dodgers had 10, while the Yankees had only three. Harry Danning, Sid Gordon, Phil Weintraub, Goody Rosen, and Harry Feldman played for at least five years for either the Giants or Dodgers.

In 1923, Mose Solomon led the Southwestern League with 49 homers and a .421 batting average. The Giants put him on their roster at the end of the season. Writers called him the "Rabbi of Swat." In two games, he had three hits in eight at-bats for a .375 average. But he got into a dispute with manager John McGraw and was sent back to the minors, where he played until 1929.

In 1926, the Giants added infielder Andy Cohen to their roster. He was born in Baltimore, grew up in El Paso, and played baseball at the University of Alabama. He became the next "Great Jewish Hope." Sent back to the minors for 1927, he returned to the Giants in 1928. An estimated 25,000 to 35,000 fans, many of them Jewish, came to the Opening Day game at the Polo Grounds. Cohen drove in two runs and scored two more in the Giants' 5–2 victory. In his three years with the Giants, he had a .281 batting average, but he returned to the minors after the 1929 season and never played in the majors again.

Like ballplayers in general, many Jewish players played for one season, or just a handful of games. For example, Robert Berman, born in New York City in 1899, graduated from high school, went to a Washington Nationals tryout, played in two games during the 1918 season, then spent a few years in the minors. He later played for barnstorming semipro teams, including an all-Jewish team, the South Philadelphia Hebrews, and the House of David team (which, despite its name, had few Jews). Then he returned to college and spent 43 years (1925–68) as a high school coach in New York.[8]

THE RISE, FALL, AND RISE OF JEWISH MAJOR LEAGUERS

Since 1871, 193 Jews have played in the major leagues, identified in Table 1 (opposite). Six, including Pike, played before 1901, when the American League (AL) joined the National League (NL) to form the two major leagues that are still active today. Since then, 187 identifiable Jews have played in the majors. Jews have thus composed about 1% of the roughly 19,000 big league players between 1901 and 2023. This is less than half of Jews' proportion of the American population (about 2.5%) during those years. Jewish representation on major league rosters has fluctuated, as revealed in Figures 1 and 2 (page 118).

Table 1. Chronological Listing of Jewish Major League Players, 1871–2023

Name	Years Active	Name	Years Active	Name	Years Active	Name	Years Active
Lipman Pike	1871–87	Fred Sington	1934–39	Richie Scheinblum	1965–74	Adam Stern	2005–10
Nate Berkenstock	1871	Syd Cohen*	1934–37	Ken Holtzman*	1965–79	Craig Breslow*	2005–17
Israel Pike	1877	Chick Starr	1935–36	Mike Epstein	1966–74	Scott Feldman*	2005–17
Jake Goodman	1878–82	Harry Eisenstat*	1935–42	Dave Roberts*	1969–81	Adam Greenberg	2005 and 2012
Sammy Samuels	1895	Morrie Arnovich	1936–46	Lloyd Allen*	1969–75	Jason Hirsh*	2006–08
Leo Fishel*	1899	Goody Rosen	1937–46	Ron Blomberg	1969–78	Ian Kinsler	2006–19
Bill Cristall*	1901	Harry Chozen	1937	Elliott Maddox	1970–80	Ryan Braun	2007–20
Harry Kane*	1902–06	Sam Nahem*	1938–48	Steve Stone*	1971–81	Sam Fuld	2007–15
Barney Pelty*	1903–12	Eddie Feinberg	1938–39	Skip Jutze	1972–77	Josh Whitesell	2008–09
Phil Cooney	1905	Dick Conger*	1940–43	Dick Sharon	1973–75	Brian Horwitz	2008
Moxie Manuel*	1905–08	Sid Gordon	1941–55	Jeff Newman	1976–84	Aaron Poreda*	2009–14
Erskine Mayer*	1912–19	Harry Feldman*	1941–46	Ross Baumgarten*	1978–82	Ryan Sadowski*	2009
Ed Mensor	1912–14	Moe Franklin	1941–42	Jim Gaudet	1978–79	Danny Valencia	2010–18
Fred Graf	1913	Harry Shuman*	1942–44	Steve Ratzer*	1980–81	Ike Davis	2010–16
Henry Bostick	1915	Cy Block	1942–46	Jeff Stember*	1980	Ryan Kalish	2010–16
Sam Mayer	1915	Eddie Turchin	1943	Bob Tufts*	1981–83	Ryan Lavarnway	2011–21
Sammy Bohne	1916–26	Hal Schacker*	1945	Mark Gilbert	1985	Josh Satin	2011–14
Jake Pitler	1917–18	Mike Schemer	1945–46	Steve Rosenberg*	1988–91	Michael Schwimer*	2011–12
Ed Corey*	1918	Herb Karpel*	1946	Jose J. Bautista*	1988–97	Kevin Pillar	2013–23
Bob Berman	1918	Al Rosen	1947–56	Steve Wapnick*	1990–91	Josh Zeid*	2013–14
Sam Fishburn	1919	Mickey Rutner	1947	Wayne Rosenthal*	1991–92	Nate Freiman	2013–14
Al Schacht*	1919–21	Bud Swartz*	1947	Eddie Zosky	1991–2000	Joc Pederson	2014–23
Lefty Weinert*	1919–31	Marv Rotblatt*	1948–51	Ruben Amaro Jr.	1991–98	Cody Decker	2015
Jesse Baker	1919	Joe Ginsberg	1948–62	Jesse Levis	1992–2001	Jon Moscot*	2015–16
Reuben Ewing	1921	Saul Rogovin*	1949–57	Brad Ausmus	1993–2010	Richard Bleier	2016–23
Heinie Scheer	1922–23	Cal Abrams	1949–56	Shawn Green	1993–2007	Alex Bregman	2016–23
Lou Rosenberg	1923	Sid Schacht*	1950–51	Eric Helfand	1993–95	Ty Kelly	2016–18
Mose Solomon	1923	Al Federoff	1951–52	Mike Lieberthal	1994–2007	Ryan Sherriff*	2017–23
Joe Bennett	1923	Lou Limmer	1951–54	Andrew Lorraine*	1994–2002	Harrison Bader	2017–22
Moe Berg	1923–39	Duke Markell*	1951	Brian Bark*	1995	Max Fried*	2017–23
Happy Foreman*	1924–26	Al Richter	1951–53	Brian Kowitz	1995	Brad Goldberg*	2017
Sy Rosenthal	1925–26	Herb Gorman	1952	Bill Hurst*	1996	Robert Stock*	2018–21
Andy Cohen	1926–29	Moe Savransky*	1954	Al Levine*	1996–2005	Jeremy Bleich*	2018
Ike Danning	1928	Sandy Koufax*	1955–66	Mike Milchin*	1996	Zack Weiss*	2018–23
Jonah Goldman	1928–31	Al Silvera	1955–56	Micah Franklin	1997	Rowdy Tellez	2018–22
Ed Wineapple*	1929	Hy Cohen*	1955	Mike Saipe*	1998	Garrett Stubbs	2019–23
Hank Greenberg	1930–47	Barry Latman*	1957–67	Keith Glauber *	1998–2000	Rob Kaminsky*	2020
Jim Levey	1930–33	Ed Mayer*	1957–58	Gabe Kapler	1998–2010	Dean Kremer*	2020–23
Jimmie Reese	1930–32	Larry Sherry*	1958–68	Scott Schoeneweis*	1999–2010	Scott Effross*	2021–23
Harry Rosenberg	1930	Don Taussig	1958–62	David Newhan	1999–2008	Eli Morgan*	2021–23
Max Rosenfeld	1931–33	Bob Davis	1958–60	Frank Charles	2000	Jake Bird*	2022–23
Louis Brower	1931	Norm Sherry	1959–63	Jason Marquis*	2000–15	Jake Fishman*	2022
Alta Cohen	1931–33	Alan Koch*	1963–64	Tony Cogan*	2001	Dalton Guthrie	2022–23
Izzy Goldstein*	1932	Larry Yellen*	1963–64	Mike Koplove*	2001–07	Kenny Rosenberg*	2022–23
Milt Galatzer	1933–39	Conrad Cardinal*	1963	Justin Wayne*	2002–04	Bubby Rossman	2022
Phil Weintraub	1933–45	Steve Hertz	1964	Matt Ford*	2003	Zack Gelof	2023
Harry Danning	1933–42	Norm Miller	1965–74	John Grabow*	2003–11	Spencer Horwitz	2023
Cy Malis*	1934	Art Shamsky	1965–72	Kevin Youkilis	2004–13	Matt Mervis	2023
						Jared Shuster*	2023

NOTE: Pitchers are identified with an asterisk

All but four of the 193 Jewish major leaguers were born in the US or Canada. Other than Jose J. Bautista, born in the Dominican Republic, the other three—William Cristall (born in 1875), Reuben Cohen (who played under the name Reuben Ewing and was born in 1899), and Isidore "Izzy" Goldstein (born in 1908)—were all, by coincidence, born in Odessa (then in the Russian empire, now in Ukraine).[9]

Only five Jews played on major league teams during the first decade (1901–1910) of the twentieth century and in most years, there were only one or two Jews on big league rosters. By the second decade (1911–1920), an average of 2.4 Jews wore major league uniforms each year, ranging from 0.2% to 0.8% of all players. The next decade saw an average of 3.5 Jews in uniform each year, ranging from 0.4% to 1.2% of all players. The 1930s saw a spurt of Jewish major

leaguers, averaging 8.1 a year and ranging from 1.2% to 2% of all players. In the peak years of that decade—1937 and 1938—10 Jews played each season. In the 1940s, the average number of big league Jews declined to 6.1, while the proportion ranged from 0.7% to 1.8%. In the 1950s, the number averaged 6.3 and the annual proportion from 0.9% to 2.0%.

In the 1960s, MLB began expanding the number of teams and increased the total number of players. In that decade, the average number of Jews in the big leagues was 7.4, ranging from 0.7% to 1.0% of the total. The 1970s saw an uptick, with an average of 8.4 Jews in big league uniforms, ranging from 0.8% to 1.3% of all players.

In the 1980s, the average fell significantly to 2.4 and the proportion ranged from 0% to 0.8%. In 1984 and 1985, only one Jew wore a major league uniform and in

Figure 1. Number of Jewish Players in the Major Leagues, 1901–2023

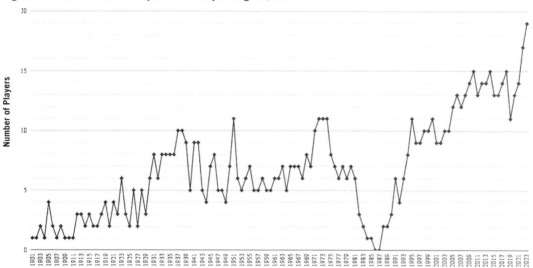

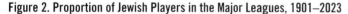

Figure 2. Proportion of Jewish Players in the Major Leagues, 1901–2023

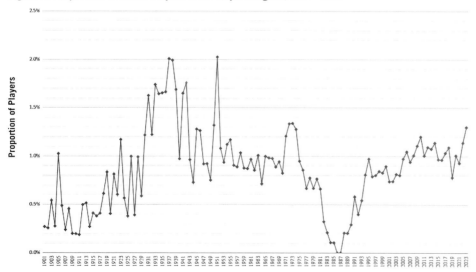

1986 and 1987, not a single Jew played in the majors. In the 1990s, an average of 7.6 Jews played in the majors, while the proportion ranged from 0.3% to 1.0%.

It is difficult to explain the low proportion of Jews in the majors during the 1980s and early 1990s. This was at the start of the influx of Latino players, but the increase was not yet sizable.[10] There is no evidence that it was the result of anti-Semitism by scouts or ballclubs. It may simply be a statistical fluke in light of the relatively low number of Jews in the overall US population rather than changes in young Jews' career aspirations or talents.

The number and proportion of major league Jews increased significantly in the twenty-first century. From 2000 to 2009, an average of 11.3 Jews were on rosters, ranging from 0.9% to 1.1%. Between 2010 and 2023, an average of 14 Jews played on major league teams each year, ranging from 0.8% to 1.3% of all players. The 19 Jewish players in 2023 matched the highest proportion (1.3%) since 1974.

Another way to look at Jews' participation in baseball is to compare their proportion of all players to their proportion of the American population. Because the Census does not ask about religion, demographers have periodically sought other ways to identify and calculate the number of Jewish Americans, although their methods may not be as rigorous as the Census.

Based on best estimates, Jews represented 3.7% of the U.S. population in 1937—the highest it has ever been. That year and the following one, Jews were 2% of all major league players—or 54% of their proportion in the overall population. In 1951, Jews' representation in the population had fallen to 3.5%, and Jews' proportion of major league players was once again 2%—or 57% of their proportion in the total population.[11] In 2023, Jews were 2.2% of the US population, and as previously mentioned, 1.3% of all major leaguers.[12] This represents 59% of their proportion of the nation's population—an all-time high.

CHANGING DEMOGRAPHICS

Several demographic and sociological factors explain the increase in Jewish ballplayers in this century. The proportion of Americans living in California increased from 6.6% in 1950 to 10.4% in 1980 to 12% in 2010, while the proportion living in Florida grew from 1.7% to 4.3% to 6.1% in those years. After World War II, Americans Jews were in the forefront of moving from the East Coast and Midwest to California and Florida and from cities to suburbs. The Sunbelt allows for longer baseball seasons, and suburban and private high schools have more athletic resources (both in facilities and coaching) than urban public schools. Moreover, recent Jewish ballplayers have been much more likely than their predecessors to attend college and have received athletic scholarships. More than the earlier generations of Jewish players who had immigrant parents, recent players have parents who are more likely to support their sons' pursuit of careers in sports.

Until the 1950s, most Jewish major leaguers were sons of immigrants. Many of their parents adhered to strict Jewish customs. Most of their offspring followed some, if not all, of those traditions. Interfaith marriages were almost taboo within the Jewish community. By the late twentieth century, most Jews were two or three generations removed from the immigrant generation. Interfaith marriages became more widely accepted. Like Jews in general, today's Jewish players are more likely to be offspring of interfaith parents.

Some Jewish players were the sons not only of interfaith but also interracial couples, such as Ruben Amaro Jr. (son of a Jewish mother and Mexican-Cuban Catholic father who played in the majors), Jose J. Bautista (who was born to a Dominican father and an Israeli mother, had his bar mitzvah in the Dominican Republic, married a Jew, and kept a kosher home), Micah Franklin (son of a Jewish mother and African-American father), Kevin Pillar (son of a Jewish mother and Christian father), and Rowdy Tellez (who has a Jewish mother and Mexican Catholic father).

In the first half of the 1900s, few American men attended college. Among those born between 1906 and 1915, only 9% attended college.[13] Few major leaguers born in that period did so. In fact, many dropped out of high school to join a minor league team, which was, in their minds, better than working on a farm or in a factory. Players and managers often called players with even one year of higher education "college boy," not always meant as a compliment.

In the early 1900s, Jewish ballplayers were more likely than their non-Jewish teammates to have finished high school and even gone to college. Among the Jewish players who were born before 1900, 20% attended college. Among those born between 1900 and 1919, 52% went to college, even if they didn't graduate. For example, Hank Greenberg, born in 1911, dropped out of New York University to play pro ball.

After World War II, more American men, and more pro ballplayers, attended college, thanks to the federal Serviceman's Readjustment Act ("GI Bill") and an increase in athletic scholarships. Among males born between 1930 and 1939, 29% attended college, but among Jewish major leaguers born in that period, 67% did. More than three-quarters of Jewish players born between 1940 and 1959 (76%) and 1960 and 1979 (79%) attended college.

By the twenty-first century, most male high school graduates had some college experience. Among those born between 1980 and 1989, 59% attended college.[14] Among Jewish major leaguers born during that decade, 93% attended college.

The 22 Jewish major leaguers who played in 2022 (17 players) and 2023 (19 players) provide a window into the transformation of Jewish and American life.

Sixteen of this group of 22 grew up in Southern, Southwestern, and Western states with post war population booms—13 in California, two in Florida, and one in New Mexico. Eighteen went to high schools in the suburbs. Nineteen (86%) have attended college. At least 11 have one non-Jewish parent, at least two of whom later converted to Judaism. Only nine had a bar mitzvah. Few claim to be religious but most of them feel an affinity with their Jewish identity. For example, 14 have played for Team Israel in the World Baseball Classic and several others have said they'd like to do so.[15]

Harrison Bader, born to a Catholic mother and Jewish father, grew up in the New York suburbs and attended Horace Mann high school. The family never attended synagogue and Bader didn't have a bar mitzvah. As his father explained in early 2023, while growing up, Bader didn't identify either as Jewish or Catholic, "but has talked to me recently about converting to Judaism. He's spoken to rabbis in New York about this. It is on his mind."[16] He attended the University of Florida on a baseball scholarship. He intended to play for Team Israel in 2023 but injuries kept him from doing so.

Jake Bird was raised in Valencia, California, to a Catholic mother and a half-Jewish father (giving him a Jewish grandmother and non-Jewish grandfather). The family didn't attend a synagogue or Passover seders and Jake did not attend Hebrew school or have a bar mitzvah. After pitching and playing outfield for West Ranch High School, he attended UCLA, where he pitched for the Bruins for four seasons, was an Academic All-American, and graduated in 2018 with a degree in economics and a 3.62 grade point average. He played for Team Israel in 2023.

Richard Bleier's father was born Jewish and his mother converted to Judaism. He grew up in South Florida, where he went to Hebrew school and had a bar mitzvah at Beth Am Israel, a Conservative synagogue in Cooper City. The family celebrated the High Holidays, had annual Passover seders, and lit Sabbath candles each week. Growing up, he played basketball and roller hockey at the local Jewish Community Center and said that "My dad would take me out of Hebrew school if I had baseball practice." He played for Florida Gulf Coast University. Bleier and his wife, who is Catholic, "try to respect both of our traditions."[17] They don't attend church or temple, but in 2022 they lit Hanukkah candles every night and also had a Christmas tree. They gave their daughter Murphy, now 3 years old, a Hebrew middle name—Adira. He played for Team Israel in 2013 and 2023.[18]

Alex Bregman's father is Jewish. His mother was born Catholic but converted to Judaism. He had his bar mitzvah at Temple Albert in Albuquerque, New Mexico. He played for Louisiana State University.

Scott Effross grew up as a member of Congregation Shir Shalom in Bainbridge, Ohio, where he celebrated his bar mitzvah in 2006. He wears a Star of David necklace when he pitches. He played for Indiana University. He announced he would play for Team Israel in the 2023 WBC, but changed his mind due to injuries.[19]

Jake Fishman is the son of Harris Fishman and Cindy Layton.[20] He attended Hebrew School and had his bar mitzvah at Congregation Klal Yisrael in Sharon, Massachusetts. He graduated from Union College, where he played baseball. Fishman played for the Israeli team in 2017 and 2023, and in the 2021 Olympics.[21]

Max Fried grew up in Santa Monica, California, with two Jewish parents. He attended synagogue on the High Holidays and had a bar mitzvah. In 2009, at age 14, he pitched for the US baseball team that won the gold medal in the Maccabiah Games in Israel. He was drafted out of Harvard-Westlake High School in Los Angeles and signed a contract without going to college.[22]

Zack Gelof grew up in Rehoboth Beach, Delaware, where he attended Hebrew school at the Seaside Jewish Community but did not have a bar mitzvah. His parents are both attorneys. He attended

Cape Henlopen High School (where he was class president for four years), then played for the University of Virginia.

Dalton Guthrie's father Mark, who pitched in the majors from 1989 to 2003, is Christian. His mother, Andrea Balash Guthrie, is Jewish, the daughter of immigrants who fled Hungary in the 1950s. He grew up in Sarasota, Florida, and attended the Goldie Feldman Academy at Temple Beth Sholom before transferring to public school. He graduated from Venice High School, then played for the University of Florida. Team Israel recruited Guthrie, but he decided to spend the time in spring training in hopes of making the Phillies roster. But he'd like to play for Team Israel in the future. "My grandparents would be excited if I played for Team Israel," he explained. "I guess I've always considered myself half-Jewish, but I'm going to have to find out more about my Jewish background."[23]

Spencer Horwitz had a Jewish father and non-Jewish mother. "I've been around the Jewish culture my whole life and I've grown to love it and just appreciate it and respect it," he told an interviewer.[24] He attended St. Paul's School for Boys in Brooklandville, Maryland, and played baseball at Radford University. He played for Team Israel in 2023.

Dean Kremer was born and raised in Stockton, California. His parents are Israelis who moved to the US after they completed military service in Israel. His grandparents and extended family still live in Israel, where he had his bar mitzvah. Kremer grew up speaking Hebrew at home. He pitched for San Joaquin Delta College and the University of Nevada. Discussing the decision by Sandy Koufax not to pitch for the first game of the 1965 World Series because the game fell on Yom Kippur, Kremer said: "I would do the same." He won a gold medal pitching for Team USA in the 2013 Maccabiah Games in Israel and won the MVP award while pitching for Team Israel in the European Championship in both 2014 and 2015. He pitched for Team Israel in the 2017 and 2023 World Baseball Classic.[25]

Matt Mervis, son of two Jewish parents, grew up in Potomac, Maryland, attended Georgetown Preparatory School, and played baseball for four years at Duke University, where he majored in political science.[26] His grandmother lived in Israel before immigrating to the United States. He played for Team Israel in 2013.

Eli Morgan was born in Rancho Palos Verdes, California, to Diana and Dave Morgan, former deputy sports editor for the *Los Angeles Times*. He went to Peninsula High School and joined the baseball team at Gonzaga University as a walk-on.

Joc Pederson was born to a Jewish mother and non-Jewish father. On his mother's side, the family tree extends back to membership in a San Francisco synagogue in the mid-1800s. Pederson's mother, Shelly, trekked to her late father's old synagogue to find proof of Joc's Jewish heritage so he could play for Team Israel in 2013.[27] He played for Team Israel again in the 2023 WBC. He went directly from Palo Alto High School to the minor leagues.

Kevin Pillar was born to a Jewish mother and non-Jewish father, grew up in West Hills (a suburban part of Los Angeles) and went to Chaminade College Prep. He played for California State University at Dominguez Hills, graduating with a degree in mathematics.[28]

Kenny Rosenberg was born in Mill Valley, California, a suburb of San Francisco, to a Jewish father and non-Jewish mother.[29] He attended Tamalpais High School before playing for California State University, Northridge. He explained: "I grew up in a largely non-religious household. However, I had a bunch of Jewish friends and attended my fair share of bar and bat mitzvahs. I also have been to two Jewish weddings and they were both an absolute blast! The energy on the dance floor is unparalleled."[30]

Bubby Rossman was born in La Habra, California, to a Jewish mother and non-Jewish father. "I don't remember ever going to a synagogue. I didn't go to Hebrew school. I didn't have a bar mitzvah. My high school was 60–70% Latin. I was the only Jew only on my baseball team. I didn't know any Jews in my high school. My mom tried to incorporate it [Jewish identity] into my life." He went to La Habra High School and pitched for California State University at

Dominguez Hills. To play for the Israel team in the European baseball league, he visited Israel and got dual citizenship. "When I was in Israel I went to synagogue and became more familiar with my heritage. I wanted to know what my grandparents and great-grandparents went through. If I get married, I'd like my kids to get to go to understand their Jewish identity."[31] He played for Team Israel in 2023.

Ryan Sherriff was born in Culver City, a Los Angeles suburb, attended Culver City High School, then played for West Los Angeles College and Glendale Community College. His parents are Jewish and his maternal grandparents were Holocaust survivors who spent time in concentration camps. He pitched for Team Israel in 2017.

Jared Shuster grew up in New Bedford, Massachusetts, the son of two Jewish parents, Bennett and Lori Shuster.[32] He attended New Bedford High School before transferring to Tabor Academy in Marion, Massachusetts. He played college baseball at Wake Forest University.

Garrett Stubbs was born in San Diego to a Jewish mother and a Catholic father. He was raised Jewish, attended Hebrew school every Wednesday from age eight to 13, and celebrated his bar mitzvah at Temple Solel in Cardiff-by-the-Sea, a San Diego suburb. He played for the University of Southern California Trojans from 2012 to 2015 and won the 2015 Johnny Bench Award as the nation's best collegiate catcher. He played on Team Israel in 2023.

Rowdy Tellez was born in Sacramento, California, to a Jewish mother and non-Jewish father. His grandfather played in the Mexican Baseball League. He jumped directly from Elk Grove High School in California to the minor leagues.

Zack Weiss began blowing the Rosh Hashana shofar at age 8 at Congregation B'nai Israel in Tustin, California. He played for UCLA. He became a dual US-Israeli citizen in 2018 and played for Team Israel in the 2021 Olympics in Tokyo and in the 2023 World Baseball Classic.[33]

These 22 players' connection to their Jewish identity ranges from those who were raised with Jewish beliefs and practices to those who only began to explore their Jewish heritage as adults. In this way, they mirror the experiences of twenty-first century Jewish Americans and the spectrum of identification found among those in their age group. ∎

Notes

1. See http://www.jewishbaseballnews.com/players/ and https://jewishbaseballmuseum.com/. I have also drawn on Peter S. Horvitz and Joachim Horvitz, *The Big Book of Jewish Baseball*, New York: S.P.I. Books, 2001; Josh Perlstein, ed., *Chasing Dreams: Baseball and Becoming American*, Philadelphia: National Museum of American Jewish History, 2014; Burton A. Boxerman and Benita W. Boxerman, *Jews and Baseball, Volume 1: Entering the American Mainstream, 1871–1948*, Jefferson, NC: McFarland & Company, 2005; Burton A. Boxerman and Benita W. Boxerman, *Jews and Baseball, Volume 2: The Post-Greenberg Years, 1949–2008*, 2009: Larry Ruttman, *American Jews & America's Game*, Lincoln: University of Nebraska Press, 2013; Peter Ephross with Martin Abramowitz, *Jewish Major Leaguers in Their Own Words*, Jefferson, NC: McFarland Publishers, 2012; Peter Levine, *Ellis Island to Ebbets Field: Sport and the American Jewish Experience*, New York: Oxford University Press, 1992; Erwin Lynn, *The Jewish Baseball Hall of Fame*, New York: Shapolsky Publishers, 1987; Dave Cohen, *Matzoh Balls and Baseballs*, Havenhurst Books, 2010; Robert Stephen Silverman, *The 100 Greatest Jews in Sports*, Lanham, Maryland, Scarecrow Press, 2003; and Howard Megdal, *The Baseball Talmud*, Triumph Books, 2022.
2. See Rebecca Alpert, "Who Is a Jewish Baseball Player?" in William Simons, ed., *The Cooperstown Symposium on Baseball and American Culture*, Jefferson, NC: McFarland Publishers, 2005.
3. Steven Riess, "Race and Ethnicity in American Baseball: 1900–1919," *Journal of Ethnic Studies*, 4, No. 4, Winter 1977, 39–55; Rob Ruck, *Raceball: How the Major Leagues Colonized the Black and Latin Game*, Boston: Beacon Press, 2011.
4. Hasia Diner, *The Jews of the United States*, Berkeley, California: University of California Press, 2004.
5. In 1866, several Brooklyn teams and the Philadelphia Athletics paid a few ballplayers between $20 and $25 a week. A Philadelphia newspaper discovered this and caused a controversy. The National Association of Base Ball Players, fervently against professionalism, held a fact-finding hearing to determine if Pike and two other Athletics teammates, Patsy Dockney and Dick McBride, had accepted $20 a week for their services. The matter was dropped when nobody showed up for the hearing. Source: Richard Hershberger, "Baseball's Financial Revolution of 1866 and the Rise of Professionalism," in Don Jensen, editor, *Base Ball 10: New Research on the Early Game*, Jefferson, NC: McFarland and Company, 2018, 84–98.
6. Steve Riess, *Touching Base: Professional Baseball and American Culture in the Progressive Era*, Urbana: University of Illinois Press, 1999, 189.
7. Leonard J. Greenspoon, ed, *Jews in the Gym: Judaism, Sports, and Athletics*, West Lafayette, Indiana: Purdue University Press, 2012; Levine, Ellis Island.
8. "Bob Berman" in Ephross, *Jewish Major Leaguers*.
9. Peter Dreier, "Odessa Has a Rich Jewish History," *Forward*, April 27, 2022 https://forward.com/opinion/500968/odessa-ukraine-has-a-rich-jewish-baseball-history/.
10. Mark Armour and Daniel Levitt, "Baseball Demographics, 1947–2016," SABR https://sabr.org/bioproj/topic/baseball-demographics-1947-2016/.
11. Sidney Goldstein, "American Jewry, 1970: A Demographic Profile, *American Jewish Yearbook, 1971*, https://www.jewishdatabank.org/content/upload/bjdb/304/NJPS1971-AJYB_Article.pdf.
12. Ira Sheskin and Arnold Dashefsky, "United States Jewish Population, 2022," in Arnold Dashefsky and Ira Sheskin, eds., *American Jewish Yearbook 2023*.
13. US Census Bureau https://www.census.gov/data/tables/time-series/demo/educational-attainment/cps-historical-time-series.html.
14. US Census Bureau.

15. Roster for 2023 Team Israel: https://www.sportingnews.com/us/mlb/news/israel-world-baseball-classic-roster-joc-pederson-dean-kremer-2023-wbc/vlduabxuzlvjblqas9gyzf1i.

16. Louis Bader interview with Peter Dreier, March 7, 2023.

17. Richard Bleier interview with Peter Dreier, March 1, 2023.

18. Jeff Seidel, "Orioles Have High Hopes for Jewish Pitcher," Jmore: Baltimore Jewish Living, June 5, 2017. https://jmoreliving.com/2017/06/05/orioles-have-high-hopes-for-jewish-pitcher/?related_post_from=8867.

19. David Ostrowsky, "Pitcher Scott Effress Goes to Bat for Players Association," Atlanta Jewish Times, June 16, 2022, https://www.atlantajewishtimes.com/pitcher-scott-effross-goes-to-bat-for-players-association/; Scott Effross, bar mitzvah notice, *Cleveland Jewish News*, January 18, 2007, https://www.clevelandjewishnews.com/archives/scott-effross/article_24e3bbd6-e4dc-532e-9e27-470852b1f57b.html.

20. Obituary for Charlotte Layton, Cindy's Layton's mother, indicates that she was not raised Jewish. *Boston Globe*, October 3, 2011.

21. Howard Blas, "Team Israel to Major League Baseball: Jake Fishman's Debut with the Miami Marlins," Jewish News Syndicate, August 16, 2022, https://www.jns.org/team-israel-to-major-league-baseball-jake-fishmans-debut-with-the-miami-marlins/.

22. David R. Cohen, "Fried is Working to Fill Koufax's Shoes," *Atlanta Jewish Times*, August 25, 2017, https://www.atlantajewishtimes.com/fried-is-working-to-fill-koufaxs-shoes/.

23. Dalton Guthrie interview with Peter Dreier, February 6, 2023.

24. "Get to Know Spencer Horwitz, Blue Jays Prospect and Team Israel Sparkplug," The Canadian Jewish News, Menschwarmers podcast, March 12, 2023, https://thecjn.ca/podcasts/get-to-know-spencer-horwitz-blue-jays-prospect-and-team-israel-sparkplug/.

25. "Dean Kremer," page in the Jews in Major League Baseball category at the Jewish Virtual Library, https://www.jewishvirtuallibrary.org/dean-kremer.

26. Josh Frydman, tweet dated February 17, 2023, including the text, "Doing the important reporting at Cubs Camp, like asking Matt Mervis about his Jewish lineage: 'All four of my grandparents are Jewish.' Did you identify as Jewish growing up? 'Yes. Not super religious though. No Bar Mitzvah. We prioritized sports over Hebrew school.'" https://twitter.com/Josh_Frydman/status/1625897864147931138.

27. Hillel Kuttler, "Meet Joc Pederson, The Jewish Rookie Powering the LA Dodgers Run to the Playoffs," September 10, 2015, Jewish Telegraphic Agency, https://www.jta.org/2015/09/10/sports/meet-joc-pederson-the-jewish-rookie-powering-l-a-dodgers-run-to-playoffs.

28. Gabe Stutman, "Kevin Pillar Settles Into a New Team and the Jewish Baseball Spotlight," August 16, 2019, Jewish Telegraphic Agency, https://www.jta.org/2019/08/16/sports/kevin-pillar-settles-into-a-new-team-and-the-jewish-baseball-spotlight.

29. Rosenberg's mother, Deborah Dilley, is the daughter of two non-Jewish parents. Mary Ann Thielen Dilley, obituary, https://www.danielfuneralhome.com/obit/rose-mary-ann-thielen-dilley; Walter Dilley, obituary, https://www.legacy.com/us/obituaries/sctimes/name/walter-dilley-obituary?id=6985274.

30. "Interview: Small Town Boy, Big League Aspirations–Kenny Rosenberg," The Great Rabbino: Jewish Sports Everything, https://thegreatrabbino.com/2020/02/12/interview-small-town-boy-big-league-aspirations-kenny-rosenberg/.

31. Bubby Rossman interview with Peter Dreier, March 2, 2023.

32. Milton Gershon, Obituary, https://www.legacy.com/us/obituaries/legacyremembers/milton-gershon-obituary?id=24126520.

33. Alexandra Goldberg, "Meet the American Pitcher Who Brought new Turf to Israel," April 6, 2022, Hillel.org, https://www.hillel.org/meet-the-american-pitcher-who-brought-new-turf-to-israel/.

The Henry Chadwick Award was established by SABR to honor baseball's great researchers—historians, statisticians, analysts, and archivists—for their invaluable contributions to making baseball the game that links America's present with its past.

Apart from honoring individuals for the length and breadth of their contributions to the study and enjoyment of baseball, the Chadwick Award will educate the baseball community about sometimes little known but vastly important contributions from the game's past and thus encourage the next generation of researchers.

The contributions of nominees must have had public impact. This may be demonstrated by publication of research in any of a variety of formats: books, magazine articles, and websites. The compilation of a significant database or archive that has facilitated the published research of others will also be considered in the realm of public impact.

SARAH LANGS by Karl Ravech

It was the night of November 2, 2016. In the city of Chicago and across the country, fans were glued to their television sets and radios. It was Game Seven of the World Series, in Cleveland, where nine innings had been played when it started to rain. The tarp was put on the field, delaying the outcome and giving Cubs fans every reason in the world to think, "It's happening all over again." The Cubs and Indians players trudged off the field.

The Cubs players were summoned to a small weight room off their clubhouse at Progressive Field. They had just blown a three-run lead in the eighth inning and outfielder Jason Heyward wanted a word with the team. Pessimism was everywhere, except in that weight room.

Meanwhile, just feet beyond the right-field grass, standing in an auxiliary bullpen, unfazed by the weather conditions, was a wide-eyed female baseball researcher working for ESPN. There was nowhere on the planet Sarah Langs would rather have been. Born and bred to be involved with baseball, she was intimately familiar with Chicago baseball, having attended the prestigious University of Chicago. Sarah had a front-row seat for the history that was about to unfold, and she was not there just to watch but to chronicle the event. At the age of 23, Langs was madly in love with the game and her heart was racing, waiting like the millions of baseball fans to see what would unfold when the raindrops subsided.

Sarah was born on May 2, 1993, to Charles and Liise-anne. Both her parents are doctors and had baseball in their DNA. Charles is a lifelong New York Mets fan, while Liise-anne grew up on the West Coast and rooted religiously for the San Francisco Giants. While growing up in New York City, Sarah had no choice but to be exposed to baseball. It was her choice to fall in love with the game and make a career in it.

Sarah could have been a scout. On her first day of sixth grade, she gave her new teacher, Josh Bacharach, a detailed breakdown of every child in the class, from their homework habits to their attentiveness. But Sarah wanted to write—about baseball. Bacharach encouraged her to follow that dream, and she did so through high school and college where she covered sports for the *Chicago Maroon*. Bacharach is responsible for launching her into orbit like the many home runs she has written about over the last decade.

Langs is synonymous with her trademark saying—"Baseball is the best"—an all-encompassing maxim highlighting every single aspect of the game while emphasizing the joy Sarah derives from each. With her more than 120,000 followers on X (formerly Twitter), Sarah will share pictures of dogs at the park, players doing great things and players doing silly things, kids with their parents in the stands, women and their ever-increasing roles in baseball—all of them preceded by "Baseball is the best!" Sarah's love is genuine and infectious. Her followers feel her passion and they are in awe of her eternal optimism. Sarah has ALS, and if you only followed her on social media you would never know it.

Diagnosed in the summer of 2021, ALS has robbed Sarah of her ability to run and walk, but not fly. Her speech is not as clear as it once was, yet she proudly continues to appear on the MLB Network as a baseball analyst. Her social media following is loyal and growing. Sarah is an educator, a historian, and a true fan of the game. Her job is to put into context any current achievement. Very few in the industry have established themselves so quickly. Sarah has done it publically and gracefully, while fighting a disease with no cure.

During the 2023 World Series, I texted Sarah and asked her if any other player as young as the Texas Rangers' Evan Carter had started a Game Seven and hit third in the order. She responded within minutes: "at 21 years & 55 days old, Evan Carter is the 2nd-youngest player to start batting third in a Game 7, older than only: 1952 WS G7 Mickey Mantle: 20 y, 353 d. Love a casual 'one other guy' and it's Mantle!!!" For

Sarah, every single nugget she uncovers is like striking gold. You can feel her smile when she hits send.

The rain eventually subsided that night in Cleveland. Jason Heyward's words of wisdom had their desired effect. The Cubs scored two runs in the 10th inning and won the World Series. Sarah was there to see it and has been at every World Series since. Curses be damned. Hopefully soon we will say the same for ALS. Baseball has brought us many miracles and thankfully it has brought us Sarah Langs. ∎

LARRY GERLACH by Steve Gietschier

Growing up in Lincoln, Nebraska, Larry Gerlach remembers watching *The Pride of the Yankees* when he was seven years old or so. Lou Gehrig's speech got to him—no surprise there—and he became a baseball fan and a Yankees fan simultaneously. Lincoln was home to a team in the Class A Western League, and Larry's relatives, including his father, a hard-working laborer, took him to a few games in the late 1940s. He remembers watching one game with two players who looked awfully small and young. It turns out they were Philadelphia A's prospects Bobby Shantz and Nellie Fox. Another solid memory was anticipating and then listening to the 1950 World Series on the radio. He rooted for the Yankees, but the local newspapers heralded the Whiz Kids, particularly Richie Ashburn, the Phillies center fielder from Tilden, Nebraska. "I still remember the Phillies' starting lineup," he said, "but not the Yankees," who swept Philadelphia.

Within a few years, Larry and his pal Kenny Fox were attending every Lincoln Chiefs home game except on Sundays when his family visited his maternal grandparents, where the adults spoke German and Larry followed the games on the radio. The 1956 season ratcheted up Larry's interest in baseball even further. That was the season when first baseman Dick Stuart hit 66 home runs for the Chiefs and drove around town in a yellow Cadillac convertible with California license plates. Larry and Kenny were at the ballpark all the time. The players let them in through the players' gate, adjacent to which was the umpires' dressing room. One night they ran into Max Stone, a local umpire who handled Chiefs' games regularly. He had ejected a hot-headed young left-handed pitcher the night before for throwing a ball over the grandstand. Stone was friendly. He told stories, answered

questions, and signed a ball for Larry, giving him his first autograph. "After that," Larry remembered, "I began watching umpires, how they positioned themselves, how they made calls, how they handled various situations."

Larry graduated from high school and enrolled at the University of Nebraska. As a freshman, he received encouragement from an English professor, and then in his sophomore year he took a course in American history that changed his life. "It was," he said, "history as I had never heard it taught."

He graduated from Nebraska and received his master's degree there, too. Rutgers beckoned, and he moved to New Jersey to get his doctorate in history. But not baseball history. Larry's specialty was the era of the American Revolution, and on the strength of his early work in that field, he received and accepted an offer to teach at the University of Utah. He rose from assistant professor to associate professor to full professor, served as chair of the history department, associate dean of the College of Humanities, and founding director of the Utah Humanities Center. Plus, he put in nearly a decade as Utah's NCAA Faculty Athletic Representative. When he retired in 2013, the university granted him emeritus status.

Having been promoted to full professor in 1977, and having published 10 books and seven scholarly articles in his chosen field, Larry decided on a change of pace. Ever the historian, he started interviewing "old-time" umpires in person, work that resulted in his seminal book, *Men in Blue: Conversations with Umpires*, published by Viking in 1980. Instead of the usual blurbs, the back of the dust jacket of the first edition is filled with quotations from the subjects themselves, including this gem from John "Beans" Reardon: "If the Pope was an umpire, he'd still have trouble with the Catholics."

In 2021, SABR named the book one of its top 50 books of the past half-century. It remains a classic, demanding shelf space in every baseball library.

Along the research trail, Larry discovered SABR. He joined in 1978, published an article in *The Baseball Research Journal* in 1979, and attended the St. Louis convention that summer. SABR president Cliff Kachline welcomed Larry, his wife, Gail, and T.J., their son. A second son, Jonathan, would be born later. In 1989, Larry paid his first visit to the Hall of Fame and attended SABR's Albany convention. Sitting in on several research committee meetings, he was struck by the lack of any concern for umpires. He approached then-president Gene Sunnen, who authorized a new committee on the spot. Larry recruited Dennis Bingham, a Chicago umpire, as his co-chair, and Dennis suggested "Umpires and Rules" as the committee's formal name.

The Umpires and Rules Committee did most of its substantial work through a monthly newsletter that Larry edited. Like many SABR projects, the committee newsletter became a tool of empowerment. He urged committee members, most of whom had never published anything, to research and write articles on various aspects of the history and practice of umpiring, as well as the rule book in all its complexity. Moreover, with Larry at the helm, committee members began the arduous task of compiling various lists: annual rosters, games worked, ejections.

Larry took several roles in SABR governance, too, serving on the Publications Committee (1990–91) and the Seymour Book Award Committee (1995–96, 2000–06). He was elected to the Executive Board in 1991 and was SABR's president from 1997 to 1999. For his work on SABR's behalf, he won the Bob Davids Award, SABR's highest honor, in 2001.

In 2017, SABR published *The SABR Book of Umpires and Umpiring*. Larry co-edited the book with Bill Nowlin and contributed the introduction and nine articles. He remains an active scholar. The University of Nebraska Press will soon publish his *Lion of the League: Bob Emslie and the Evolution of the Baseball Umpire*.

"Umpires' memoirs are not enough," Larry says. "We need full biographies of major league and minor league umpires. They are important figures in baseball history, and their stories need to be told." In addition, Larry would like to see work on college umpires, especially those who have handled the College World Series. "And," he added, "we need a solid history of the umpires' strike of 1979."

Most importantly, Larry would like the National Baseball Hall of Fame in Cooperstown to acquire enough artifacts to mount a permanent exhibit on umpires. "After all," he is quick to note, "umpires are the third team on the field. There has never been a major league game played without them." ∎

LESLIE A. HEAPHY by Roberta Newman

Around 1988, University of Toledo graduate student Leslie A. Heaphy was stuck. Unable to come up with a research topic for a required class in labor history, she wandered the stacks of the library, looking for inspiration. Running into a fellow graduate student from the history department, she asked his advice. "What do you want to do?" he asked, and she answered: "Something with baseball." Not knowing whether it was even a viable option, she brought the idea to her advisor. "Why not?" he responded. Why not, indeed. And so began Leslie's deep dive into baseball history, researching and writing about the Negro Leagues for her 1995 PhD thesis. This is a dive from which she has yet to emerge.

Upon completing her doctorate, Leslie joined the faculty of Kent State University at Stark in North Canton, Ohio, as an assistant professor, and she was promoted to associate professor in 2004. She teaches a broad range of topics from across the history curriculum. These include courses on women's history, sports history, baseball and literature, and, most recently, a summer class on the Negro Leagues.

Neither Leslie's love of baseball nor her love of history began at the University of Toledo, Kent State Stark, or even Siena College, from which she received her BA. She has been an inveterate New York Mets fan for as long as she can remember. And her fascination with history goes back almost as far. Growing up in Livingston Manor, New York, Leslie was surrounded by books. She caught the reading bug from her parents, so much so that her first non-babysitting job was at a library. But what really piqued her curiosity were the people, places, and things she encountered during the year she spent in Scotland while in second grade. Her fascination with the country's history was encouraged by her mother, a native

Scot. "Getting to see so much that early," she says, sent her down the path to becoming a historian.

Leslie's involvement with SABR began in 1989, when she was looking for help with her research. She found it in the organization's Negro Leagues Committee. She has been a dedicated SABR member, and a major force in Black baseball research, ever since. Indeed, she produced one of the first books on Negro League baseball since the original publication of Robert Peterson's *Only the Ball Was White* in 1970. *The Negro Leagues: 1869–1960* (McFarland, 2002), quickly became an essential source on the topic and remains so. So, too, is *Black Ball: A Negro Leagues Journal*, which she helped found in 2008, and has edited ever since. Of course, these are not Leslie's only contributions to Black baseball research. She is responsible for a great many book chapters, articles, and encyclopedia entries. To help foreground Black baseball research, Leslie has been one of the organizers of the Jerry Malloy Negro League conference since 1998.

Leslie's impact on Negro League research reaches beyond SABR. A voting member of the landmark 2006 Baseball Hall of Fame Negro League committee, she had a hand in electing seventeen players and executives for inclusion in the Hall. In 2020, Leslie served as a member of a SABR task force responsible for investigating whether the Negro Leagues should be considered major leagues. The task force determined that seven Negro Leagues that operated between 1920 and 1948 should be considered "major," and Major League Baseball extended that recognition to them shortly after. Negro League statistics have been included in the Baseball Reference database since late 2020, and plans are in place to add them to MLB.com, as well.

Her contributions as a historian would be enough even if limited to the Negro Leagues, but Leslie is also a scholar and something of an activist when it comes to the various roles of women in baseball. Chairing SABR's Women in Baseball committee since 1993, her publications on the topic, both for SABR and outside the organization, are as essential to knowledge about women and the game as her work on Black baseball.

Leslie edited the *Encyclopedia of Women in Baseball* (McFarland, 2006), along with Mel May. The book is an invaluable resource. Perhaps unsurprisingly, her current research centers on women's participation in the Negro Leagues, and the wider contributions of Black women to baseball, all in historical context.

Leslie has also been instrumental in another baseball institution. For more than three decades, Penny Marshall's film, *A League of their Own* (1992) has inspired little girls to dream of playing baseball for the Rockford Peaches. And since 2014, the International Women's Baseball Center—now located in Rockford, Illinois—has worked to bring the contributions of women to the sport, both currently and historically, to the fore. To this end, the IWBC has hosted both tournaments and conferences. Collaboration between SABR and the IWBC, while Leslie sat on both boards of directors, created the annual Women in Baseball conference. Leslie has been central to the IWBC's development, and is currently serving as the organization's president. Her aim is to tell the story of women's baseball beyond *A League of their Own*, and to inspire and enable others to do so.

First elected to SABR's board of directors in 2010, Leslie currently serves as vice president. Then, she was the only woman on the board, adding an essential voice that might otherwise not have been heard. Now, with the inclusion of more women in the organization's leadership, Leslie's impact cannot be understated. Her 2014 Bob Davids award, SABR's highest honor, bears this out.

But above all else, Leslie A. Heaphy is a historian and a teacher, one who loves to share her passion for her subject matter with her students and with researchers and scholars, alike. To Leslie, history is storytelling in context. Of the constant evolution of baseball history—in fact, of all historical inquiry—she says, "You can only make the story the best it can be, based on what you have at the moment." Her ongoing contributions to the field, building upon current knowledge, make the story more inclusive, make the story more thorough, make the story better. ∎

Contributors

ALAN COHEN chairs the BioProject fact-checking committee, and is a datacaster (MiLB stringer) with the Eastern League Hartford Yard Goats. He also works with the Retrosheet Negro Leagues project and serves on SABR's Negro Leagues Committee. His biographies, game stories, and essays have appeared in more than 70 baseball-related publications. He has four children, nine grandchildren, and one great-grandchild, and resides in Connecticut with wife Frances, their cats Zoe and Ava, and their dog Buddy.

LARRY DEFILLIPO is a retired aerospace engineer who lives in Kennewick, Washington with his wife Kelly. A SABR member since the late 1990s, his work has been published in *The National Pastime* and *Yankee Stadium 1923-2008: America's First Modern Ballpark*, and presented at the 2023 Fred Ivor-Campbell 19th Century Baseball Conference. He's also authored biographies of several prominent baseball figures and stories about a variety of important nineteenth-century games, for SABR's Biography and Games Projects, respectively.

ED DENTA is a retired professional engineer and lifelong baseball fanatic. Ed umpired Florida high school baseball for 18 years. Ed combines an analytical background and fervor for history/statistics to research and author sports-related artifacts. Ed is an active member of the Roush-Lopez Chapter of SABR in the Tampa Bay area.

PETER DREIER teaches politics at Occidental College. His most recent books are *Baseball Rebels: The Players, People, and Social Movements That Shook Up the Game and Changed America* and *Major League Rebels: Baseball Battles Over Workers Rights and American Empire*, both published in 2022.

DR. WOODY ECKARD is a retired economics professor living in Evergreen, Colorado, with his wife, Jacky, and their two dogs, Petey and Violet. Among his academic publications are 13 papers on sports economics, five of which relate to MLB. More recently he has published in SABR's *Baseball Research Journal*, *The National Pastime*, and *Nineteenth Century Notes*. He is a Rockies fan and a SABR member for over 20 years.

TOM FERRARO got a Joe DiMaggio bat at age 5, making him a lifelong Yankee and baseball fan. Another passion, dating back to childhood, was being a reporter, at his high school and college newspapers and then *The Hagerstown* (MD) *Morning Herald*, United Press International, *New York Post*, Bloomberg News, and Reuters. He spent most of his half-century career covering a subject that doesn't come close to the beauty of the national pastime: national politics.

RICHARD HERSHBERGER is a paralegal in Maryland and the author of the book *Strike Four: The Evolution of Baseball*. He has written numerous articles on early baseball, concentrating on its origins and its organizational history. He is a member of the SABR Nineteenth Century and Origins committees. Reach him at rrhersh@yahoo.com.

MATTHEW JACOB is a member of SABR's Bob Davids chapter and a Detroit Tigers fan. He is coauthor of *Globetrotter: How Abe Saperstein Shook Up the World of Sports*. The biography explores Saperstein's formation of the basketball team as well as the many roles he played in Black baseball. *Globetrotter* will be published by Rowman & Littlefield in October 2024. He lives in Arlington, Virginia.

HERM KRABBENHOFT is a lifetime Detroit Tigers fan, retired organic chemist, and longtime SABR member (since 1981). Among the various baseball research topics he has pioneered are: Ultimate Grand Slam Homers, Consecutive Games On Base Safely (CGOBS) Streaks, Quasi-Cycles, Imperfect Perfectos, Minor League Day-In/Day-Out Double-Duty Diamondeers, Downtown Golden Sombreros. Herm is the author of *Leadoff Batters of Major League Baseball* (McFarland, 2001). He has received three SABR Baseball Research Awards (1992, 1996, 2013).

DAVID KRELL is the chair of SABR's Elysian Fields Chapter. He has written four books: *Our Bums: The Brooklyn Dodgers in History, Memory and Popular Culture*, *1962: Baseball and America in the Time of JFK*, *Do You Believe in Magic? Baseball and America in the Groundbreaking Year of 1966*, and *The Fenway Effect: A Cultural History of the Boston Red Sox*.

CHARLIE PAVITT has been a SABR member since 1983. His Statistical Baseball Research Bibliography is now integrated into SABR's Baseball Index; his Sabermetric Research Literature Review (https://charliepavitt.home.blog/) is intended to be a complete survey of the literature and consistently gets updated. He is currently compiling sabermetric terms for a fourth edition of *The Dickson Baseball Dictionary* (https://www.baseball-almanac.com/dictionary.php).

JOHN SHOREY is a history professor emeritus from Iowa Western Community College, where he taught an elective course on Baseball and American Culture for 20 years. He has written articles and chapters on a variety of baseball topics for various publications and is a regular contributor to *Baseball Digest*. He has presented his research at the Cooperstown Symposium on Baseball and American Culture along with other baseball conferences.

DONALD SLAVIK is employed on an MLB grounds crew, where he brooms infield dirt, rakes/chalks baselines, prepares bullpens, and fluffs up the grass. He is happy he got past a rocky first practice tarp pull that rolled up his iPhone. Don grew up in Chicago and now lives in Cincinnati. He is an avid fan of the Chicago White Sox and Cincinnati Reds.

KEVIN WARNEKE, who earned his doctoral degree from the University of Nebraska-Lincoln, is a fundraiser based in Omaha, Nebraska. He co-wrote *The Call to the Hall*, which tells the story of when baseball's highest honor came to 31 legends of the game.